BLACK POWER ON CAMPUS

JOY ANN WILLIAMSON

Black Power
on Campus

THE UNIVERSITY OF ILLINOIS,

1965–75

UNIVERSITY OF ILLINOIS PRESS

URBANA AND CHICAGO

© 2003 by the Board of Trustees
of the University of Illinois
All rights reserved
Manufactured in the United States of America
C 5 4 3 2 1
∞ This book is printed on acid-free paper.

Library of Congress Cataloging-in-Publication Data
Williamson, Joy Ann.
Black power on campus : the University of Illinois, 1965–75 /
Joy Ann Williamson.
p. cm.
Includes bibliographical references and index.
ISBN 0-252-02829-5 (cloth : alk. paper)
1. University of Illinois at Urbana-Champaign—History—
20th century. 2. African American college students—Illinois—Political activity. 3. Discrimination in higher education—Illinois. 4. African Americans—Civil rights. I. Title.
LD2380.W55   2003
378.773'66—dc21   2002015832

To my ever-loving family

and

to Black Illinois students

before me who paved the way

What is happening in the United States is one facet of the world-wide "revolution of rising expectations." Colonialism is dead. White supremacy is dying. Governmentally imposed segregation will be abolished in the United States eventually. There is no stopping place between the granting of a few rights and full citizenship. Once the first Negro was educated, once slavery was abolished, America made her choice. Negroes will demand and secure the same rights as other citizens. No other Americans have asked for more than this, or settled long for less.

—Jack Peltason, University of Illinois faculty member and future chancellor, 1961

Contents

Acknowledgments

This book has not been an individual endeavor. Several colleagues and friends contributed to it and sustained me through the writing process. James Anderson, Anthony Antonio, Ronald Butchart, Larry Cuban, and David Tyack read various chapters at different stages. They were very generous with their time, and their expertise greatly improved the manuscript. James Anderson, in particular, has always made room in his busy schedule to read various drafts and offer advice on any and every part of the manuscript. I cannot express how grateful I am to him. Also, the archivists at the University of Illinois, including Bill Maher, Chris Prom, Ellen Swain, and Bob Chapel, made the arduous task of combing through materials a much easier process than it could have been. Their knowledge of archival holdings at the university was invaluable. Jane Mohraz's editing substantially improved this book. In every writing venture my family has provided support, emotional and otherwise. My parents, Willard and Donna Williamson, and my sister, Julie, continually check in to make sure I am on track and offer support regardless. Rod Sias has been a close confidant and constant source of strength.

A postdoctoral fellowship from the National Academy of Education and the Spencer Foundation allowed me the time to concentrate on the work and finish it in a timely fashion. Generous support from Stanford University also helped bring this book to fruition.

Parts of the introduction and chapter 1 are substantially revised and expanded versions of an article entitled "In Defense of Themselves: The Black Student Struggle for Success and Recognition at Predominantly

White Colleges and Universities," which appeared in the *Journal of Negro Education* 68, no. 1 (Winter 1999): 92–105.

This project would not have become a reality were it not for my interviewees, who showed an interest in the project, graciously opened their homes and memories, and continue to support my career. I believe I am part of their legacy and consider this book an attempt to give back to those who helped make Illinois a more diverse, hospitable, and academically rewarding campus.

In particular, I am indebted to Clarence Shelley, the first director of the Special Educational Opportunities Program and now associate vice chancellor emeritus. I am only one of many students who has benefited from his presence at Illinois. His retirement from Illinois ended over thirty years of service to Black students in particular and the university in general. He will be missed.

Abbreviations

BSA	Black Students Association
CORE	Congress of Racial Equality
EOG	Equal Opportunity Grant
ISR	Illinois Street Residence Hall
NAACP	National Association for the Advancement of Colored People
SEOP	Special Educational Opportunities Program
SNCC	Student Nonviolent Coordinating Committee

Introduction

The history of Black students at predominantly white colleges and universities is a complicated one of discrimination, racism, protest, and resilience. Their experience, mode of resistance, and focal point for protest shifted over time and closely mirrored the ebb and flow of the Black freedom struggle in the United States. An unwavering belief in the importance of education made schools, including postsecondary institutions, an important battleground for Black liberation efforts. Black students became the battering rams and in many ways the vanguard of the struggle for equal education. From the late 1960s through the early 1970s, in particular, Black college students not only participated in societal reform but also determined the path of it. During the Black Power era, Black youths became the ideological leaders of the Black struggle. They helped redefine the goals and tactics of the struggle and demanded change in American institutions, including their college campuses.

This book examines the role of Black students at one institution, the University of Illinois at Urbana-Champaign. Its purpose is twofold. First, it is a comment on how social movements influence institutions of higher education. Black students, bolstered by Black Power, demanded fundamental changes to campus curricula, policies, and structure. They took Black Power principles and molded them to fit their specific context: Black students attending a predominantly white university. Second, it is a comment on the nature of higher educational reform during the late 1960s and early 1970s. It analyzes the interaction between students and administrators and how their relationship shaped higher education. The text provides an examination of institutional responsiveness to particu-

lar clientele, an understanding of how agents within an institution precipitate reform, and an analysis of one of the benchmarks in American
educational history.

Some scholarship on the educational reforms of the 1960s employs
a top-down perspective.[1] University response to federal initiatives and an
increasing sense of social responsibility are identified as the primary catalysts for change. Scholars also credit administrators and faculty for initiating changes on their campuses.[2] This top-down perspective not only
identifies legislative mandates and administrator-initiated policy shifts
as the most important historical markers but also assumes a national
consensus on the worth of ethnic studies programs, cultural centers, and
other race-based campus initiatives. The complexity of the historical
process is lost with this type of analysis. Top-down interpretations min-
imize the alienation Black students experienced at predominantly white
institutions, ignore the daily struggles of Black students to maintain psychological and academic well-being, and disregard the fact that Black
students chose to participate in the Black student movement despite
pressure to the contrary from parents, administrators, and other sources.
Of course federal initiatives and liberal administrators and faculty played
a role in institutional change, but the role of Black students and their
belief in Black Power principles should not be minimized. Even though
most campuses had only a few Black activists, these students fought institutionalized racism on campus with Black Power ideology, carved a
niche for themselves in the Black liberation struggle, and were at the
center of higher education reform.

As Sheila Slaughter, a scholar of higher education, pointed out, the
curricular changes of the 1960s and 1970s must be understood as the result of pressure from social movements occurring outside the universities. Faculty and administrators did not automatically create curricula in
response to the demographic shift in the student population. Rather, according to Slaughter, they made "little effort to accommodate the curricular interests of these groups [including Black students] until student and
community activists forced new knowledge created by them into the curricula."[3] Social movements, including the Black Power movement, were
the catalysts in curricular change. The same can be said about the influence of social movement constituents on institutional reform beyond
curricula. For instance, Black students, following Black Power principles,
demanded and obtained Black studies programs, cultural centers, increased
Black student enrollment, more Black faculty, and other concessions.
Faculty and administrators were not necessarily antagonistic to Black
students and their demands, but it was Black students who initiated de-

mands for reform and created conditions under which their universities were forced to respond. Institutional reform did not come easily, and Black students had to keep university administrators' feet to the fire.

The University of Illinois experienced a Black student movement similar to that at other campuses across the country, but a confluence of factors made Illinois unique. First, by all accounts, Champaign-Urbana was southern in its attitudes toward race. Until the middle 1960s, restaurants, barbershops, and theaters were segregated. The campus did not even open residence hall housing to Black students until 1945. Black students of the Black Power era entered an environment that was at best benign and at worst overtly hostile. Second, the Black student population was relatively homogeneous. Most Black students came from Chicago's South Side and West Side. At the time, Chicago was considered the most segregated city in the United States. Black Illinois students lived and attended school in a de facto segregated environment soaked in racism that did little to prepare them for competition at Illinois. Third, their experiences in Chicago provided a unique backdrop for and influence on their activism. Chicago became a flash point of Black community anger in the late 1960s. The city experienced riots in 1966, had a popular chapter of the Black Panther Party headquartered on the West Side, experienced more riots after the assassination of Dr. Martin Luther King Jr., and hosted the now famous Democratic National Convention in 1968. Black students at the University of Illinois witnessed these events and were influenced directly by their experiences in their hometown. Fourth, Black students had an unusual amount of influence on the nature of reform at Illinois and were invited to participate in university recruitment efforts and sit on university committees. Never had students been given such status and input on such important decision-making bodies.

Black students did not come to the university simply to bring Black Power to central Illinois. They attended Illinois because it offered a first-rate education. The Black freedom struggle, paired with their experiences on campus, catapulted them into the center of reform. Building a campus movement took time, and a number of divisive issues within the Black student body hindered its development. But, by late 1968, Black students at Illinois had a cohesive structure through which to present their grievances, experienced leaders, and the will to protest. Through the Black Students Association, Black students issued a list of demands, all of which were grounded in Black Power principles. They presented their list to the administration in an attempt to improve their quality of life on campus as well as to force the university to insert itself in societal reform.

Illinois administrators had been interested in diversifying the student population and providing support networks for Black students before the Black student demands, but their efforts were distinctly different from the reform initiatives Black students demanded. Administrators had proposed changes based on a cultural deprivation understanding of Black student underachievement and had focused on improving the individual instead of changing the institutional structure of the university. Black students emphasized more fundamental issues and demanded institutional reform rather than cosmetic changes. Black students identified the problem as originating within the university rather than within themselves and their community. The shape of reform proposed by the university sometimes conflicted with Black student ideas on the subject. Together, university administrators and Black students negotiated the form and structure the changes would take.

University administrators were receptive to some of the demands, but the negotiation process often was difficult. Administrators were caught between an increasingly vocal and aggressive Black student community (paired with an already aggressive white student community) and pressure from Illinois legislators and citizens to maintain control of the campus. As a public institution, the university was vulnerable to public and financial pressure. It struggled to maintain a semblance of order while protecting the right of dissent and academic freedom. Administrators' support of university autonomy regarding its operations brought the institution into conflict with angry and dismayed state residents and representatives. The university had to walk a fine line between supporting First Amendment rights and alienating its financial support base. Its public image suffered at different times, but university officials did continue to work with Black students on the demands the university considered legitimate.

The most reliable sources in reconstructing the Black student movement and the institutional reform process are the participants themselves. Memos, course syllabi, student newspapers, official campus reports, position papers, and other materials written during the late 1960s and early 1970s and interviews with participants thirty years later reveal the complexity of the time. Materials produced by the university and interviews with former administrators expose how the university attempted to diffuse particular situations and redirect student efforts but at the same time defended itself and Black students against attacks from Illinois legislators, citizens, and university alumni. Black student materials and interviews reveal how they deliberately baited the university and employed rhetoric to sway people to their side but were terrified of being sent home for protest activities and were far from uniform in their opinions on how to proceed. Former administrators and students alike agree that the 1960s and 1970s were a difficult but very important and influential time in higher education reform. Despite their differences and the stressful environment in which they existed, all the participants believe their efforts were worthwhile.

The story of a Black student movement and higher educational reform is reconstructed by examining the in-between layers, the layers between the national level and the local level, between reform initiatives and the actual reforms. Identifying Black student demands and tactics as an outgrowth of Black Power is not surprising, but how did popular Black Power rhetoric filter its way to the University of Illinois? How did Black students appropriate Black Power ideology and mold it to fit their purposes? How did Black students then transform their understanding of Black Power theory into practice? Some of the Black student–initiated reforms were co-opted by the university, some were squashed, and others were implemented as students envisioned. Some of the administrator-initiated reforms were influenced by Black students. So how did a reform initiative become campus policy? How did this forced negotiation between two groups with different kinds of power color the outcome of certain campus reforms? This examination of these layers reveals how institutional change came to pass and demonstrates the important place of Black Power in the history of higher education.

1   Black Youth Forcing Change

African Americans at white universities in the first half of the twentieth century, though few in number, protested the treatment they received on their campuses. Their grievances often were individual and arose in response to particular acts, but various African American students did not idly accept the abuse they received. As the Black freedom struggle gained momentum in the 1930s, 1940s, and 1950s, so, too, did Black student struggles at white higher educational institutions. African Americans more aggressively attacked racism and segregation with co-ordinated protest. African Americans students, like African Americans in general, manifested the spectrum of opinion on how best to achieve their goals. Some activists chose the courts as their battleground. Others employed more immediate methods of protest, such as direct-action tactics, to further the cause of liberation and educational equality. Still others did not participate at all. In this way, African American students varied in the manner in which they reconciled being *Black* at a *white* institution.

The 1950s and 1960s became a defining moment in Black liberation efforts. The birth and growth of the nationwide civil rights movement invigorated African Americans. Backed by legal victories and federal legislation, the civil rights movement barreled forward and created lasting reforms in society in general and education in particular. Its power lay in its being a mass movement with coordinated protest, media attention, sustained momentum, and unwavering adherents. Black students were an important part of the movement. Black and white college students worked to rid their campus towns of segregation and discrimination (seldom did they look at their institutions at this time). When the tide of the Black freedom struggle shifted from integration to Black autonomy, Black students again played a large role. Many Black students became the ideological leaders of the Black Power movement. As the civil rights movement and Black Power movement became watershed moments in societal reform, so, too, did the 1960s Black student movement precipitate widespread reform in higher education. Black students learned from the movements of which they were a part and brought the protest strategies, ideologies, and goals to their immediate context: the university. Their participation enlarged the role of youth in the fight for racial advancement, societal reform, and equal education.

The History of African American Students at Predominantly White Institutions

African American attendance at white institutions can be traced to the early nineteenth century, though their enrollment remained extremely sparse. The first African American to receive a degree from such an institution was John Russwurm, who received a bachelor's degree from Bowdoin College, Maine, in 1826. For the next several decades, white institutions in the North remained, for all intents and purposes, closed to African Americans. In a few cases, African Americans enrolled in white northern institutions with little fanfare. In others, college administrators, faculty, and students actively discouraged African American attendance. In still others, town residents, however welcoming the local college, forced institutions to close their doors or refuse enrollment.[1] These northern white attitudes revealed the tensions surrounding race relations before and after the Civil War. Accepting African American applicants terrified many northerners. Nat Turner's 1831 insurrection, increasingly aggressive abolitionists, the end of the Civil War, and fear of newly emancipated African Americans swarming to northern cities completely unnerved many northern whites.[2] Such hostility, compounded with the fact that most Black secondary schools in the North remained inferior, meant that very few African Americans attended white postsecondary institutions. From 1826 to 1890, only thirty African Americans graduated from these institutions. By 1910, the number remained under seven hundred. Enrollment nationwide was approximately fifteen hundred by the late 1920s.[3] The 1930s and 1940s exhibited a continuing pattern of almost complete segregation of the races in higher education.

African American students met intense resistance and hostility when they attempted to enroll in all-white southern institutions until the late

1960s. Historically Black colleges and universities were founded later in the nineteenth century through the mandates of the Morrill Acts of 1862 and 1890 and remained under white administrative and philanthropic control for decades. On the heels of the Civil War and African American emancipation, the federal acts provided each state with land and funds for establishing public universities to serve the state's residents. Southern states used the land and funds to set up a dual system of college education to preserve racial segregation, as state laws and customs demanded. In the 1920s, African Americans returned from World War I with a renewed fervor for egalitarian education. The New Negro was born. The New Negro of the 1920s more aggressively agitated for equal rights, exalted African American culture, and demanded self-determination.[4] Such sentiment evidenced itself in both attitude and organization through Marcus Garvey's United Negro Improvement Association, the Harlem Renaissance, the growth of the National Association for the Advancement of Colored People (NAACP), Carter G. Woodson's Association for the Study of Negro Life and History, and the waves of rebellion on Black campuses. The New Negro continued to place a high value on education, including college, and the number of students enrolled in Black colleges increased sixfold, from 2,132 in 1917 to 13,580 in 1927.[5] At such Black institutions as Fisk, Howard, Tuskegee, Hampton, and Wilberforce, African Americans resolved to determine the path of African American education for themselves.

Fisk University provides a good example of the ways students took the reigns of the struggle for equal rights and a proper education, though at most Black institutions students were not so aggressive. Located in Nashville, Tennessee, and established after the Civil War, Fisk was considered the premier liberal arts institution for African Americans. Like most Black institutions, Fisk depended largely on white philanthropy, most of which determined that the proper form of African American education was vocational training rather than the classical liberal curriculum. According to the historian Raymond Wolters, to solicit funds, Fisk's white president endeavored to prove that Fisk had not strayed too far from the vocational model of education and that its students "were not radical egalitarians but young men and women who had learned to make peace with the reality of the caste system."[6] This infuriated students and alumni, including W. E. B. Du Bois. In protest, Du Bois collected depositions from alumni regarding how the shifted mission of the institution sought to undermine initiative and self-respect and persuade elite Black youth to forget egalitarian principles and adjust to the system. In 1924, students staged a demonstration against the president and issued a list of demands, including reinstatement of the newspaper, track, football, and the student council; these demands were not irrational because most schools (especially white schools) had everything Fisk students demanded. In February 1925, the conflict came to a head. Approximately one hundred Black male students defied the lights-out curfew and instead yelled, sang, smashed windows, and chanted "Du Bois! Du Bois!" The president called in the local (white) police to arrest the students. Protesting the arrests, the student body went on strike for ten weeks. In April, the president submitted his resignation, and later that year many of the student demands were met.[7] Such actions would have been considered unthinkable twenty years earlier, but the pervasive New Negro sentiment meant that African Americans more aggressively confronted power-holders and forced change. For their part, Black students fought against paternalism and industrial education and demanded more control over their own institutions. They left a mark on undergraduate education and paved a way for future generations of Black college students.

World War II veterans, like their World War I predecessors, returned from the war with reinvigorated hopes for equality of opportunity, including access to a quality education. This time, however, veterans had a powerful tool to enable them to take advantage of higher education: the Servicemen's Readjustment Act, otherwise known as the GI Bill, a federal incentive enabling veterans to go to college. According to David Sansing, "To blacks in postwar Mississippi higher education was the avenue of upward mobility, the 'yellow brick road' to the American dream."[8] The same can be said of African Americans in other states as well. African American veterans, in particular, attempted to take advantage of the possibility of increased access to higher education. They found closed doors. White institutions denied Black veterans attendance because of segregationist practices; Black institutions had to turn many away because they could not accommodate such an influx of students. Such realities frustrated veterans who had fought for their country in the name of democracy and freedom only to return to segregation, racism, and Jim Crow. Many joined local NAACP chapters to fight for equal opportunity and became indispensable to the civil rights movement in the South.[9]

African Americans interested in graduate or professional programs beyond the bachelor's degree were limited in their options because most Black institutions did not have graduate programs and because they were not allowed to attend white institutions. African Americans seeking advanced study had to leave the South. This continued throughout the first half of the twentieth century but came under heavy attack beginning in the 1930s. By the 1930s, the NAACP, the most visible African

American rights group, had gained power, financial backing, and dedicated recruits from the few law schools that admitted African Americans. Desegregating graduate and professional programs became a major initiative for the organization's Legal Defense Fund. The fund helped many African Americans, qualified in every capacity except race to attend predominantly white southern institutions, file lawsuits against segregated institutions.

In the late 1930s, an African American student in Missouri who received a bachelor's degree from Lincoln University (a Black institution in Missouri) attempted to enroll at the University of Missouri School of Law; a law school for African Americans did not exist in the state. Rather than accept his application, the state of Missouri offered to pay his tuition and fees at a law school in one of the surrounding states that admitted African Americans, a policy similar to that of many southern white institutions. He declined, filed suit, and took the case to the U.S. Supreme Court. In 1938, the Court found in *Missouri ex. rel. Gaines v. Canada* that the university violated the equal protection clause of the Fourteenth Amendment because the state had not provided a "separate but equal" law school for Negroes as mandated by the 1896 *Plessy v. Ferguson* decision. Hence, the Court ordered the African American student admitted to the University of Missouri School of Law.[10]

Other suits soon followed. The Supreme Court heard three more important cases that began to open the door to African Americans interested in advanced degrees in the South. In 1948, the Court affirmed its *Gaines v. Canada* decision by finding similarly in *Sipuel v. Board of Regents.* The University of Oklahoma School of Law had barred an African American student's attendance even though the state did not provide a separate law school for educating African Americans. Again, the Court based its decision on the Fourteenth Amendment. Two years later, African Americans brought two other cases to the Supreme Court. Both exhibited the South's rabid resistance to desegregation. Oklahoma State University, following the mandates of the *Sipuel* decision, admitted an African American student pursuing a doctorate in education in 1950; however, the university kept the African American student separate from the other white students, as the laws of the state required. He had his own desk in a row reserved for African American students—he was the only African American student at the time—and was assigned a specific table in the library and cafeteria. Providing more fodder for the dissolution of segregationist education policies, the Court found in *McLaurin v. Oklahoma State Regents* that the "restrictions imposed upon appellant impair and inhibit his ability to study, to engage in discussions and exchange views with other students, and, in general, to learn his profession."[11] That white students might refuse to associate with him was irrelevant. His admission to the university and subsequent segregation flew in the face of the Fourteenth Amendment and previous Court decisions because the university effectively denied him an equal education.

Watching segregation in graduate and professional schools erode with each Supreme Court decision, Texas created a law school for African Americans to discourage their application to the University of Texas Law School. The Negro law school was separate but far from equal. It had inferior facilities; it had fewer professors, students, and library volumes; and it generally lacked the ability to provide African American students the networks and contacts with other members of the Bar necessary to ensure a successful career. During the same year as the *McLaurin* decision, the Supreme Court again found in favor of the appellant in *Sweatt v. Painter.* Though Texas had attempted to provide African Americans with a separate law school, the education they received was not substantially equal to that of the students at the University of Texas Law School. As in previous decisions, the Court ruled that the Fourteenth Amendment required he be admitted to the University of Texas.

The Black freedom struggle's momentum continued to build during the first half of the twentieth century as new organizations, such as the Congress of Racial Equality, fought for racial justice, Black enrollment in higher education continued to increase, and African American protest became more organized and collective. African Americans continued to chip away at legalized discrimination. A defining moment came in 1954, when the sweeping *Brown v. Board of Education* of *Topeka, Kansas* Supreme Court decision struck down the notion of separate but equal education and affirmed that the Fourteenth Amendment applied to all American citizens. The Court's decision spoke specifically to the unconstitutionality of educational discrimination and segregation, but it also had a wide impact on African American life in general: it rejuvenated Black hopes and invigorated their struggles to gain broader liberation. Though directed at primary and secondary schools, *Brown* also lent credence and legal support to the attempts of African Americans seeking to enter historically white postsecondary institutions. As a whole, northern white institutions had enrolled few African American students until the 1940s. In the 1950s, white institutions in the border states rescinded many of their exclusionary policies, but not until the 1960s would historically white southern institutions of higher education admit African American students, and then only one by one and after intense resistance. Regardless of region, only four thousand African American college freshmen had entered white institutions nationwide by 1954.[12] African Americans continued to identify education as pivotal in the struggle for equal rights and freedom and considered access to white institutions vital.

African American students at white institutions in the North during the first half of the twentieth century were not quiet accommodationists. However, the tenor of the time and legalized discrimination necessarily restricted the available options for recourse. Also, their low numbers at any given campus would not allow for the types of protest occurring at Black institutions. But many, whether as individuals or groups, did resist racist behavior and policies. Their protests were sparse and often isolated events; nonetheless, the 1960s generation was not the first to resist racist treatment and demand change at white institutions. Their complaints and struggles resembled those of Black students attending white institutions in the early 1960s: numerical isolation and a complete exclusion from the official social life of the campus. During the early part of the century, Black men and women could not attend school dances, were segregated at other campus events, and were excluded from sports teams, literary societies, fraternities and sororities, and other extracurricular activities. Suffering under the same sorts of treatment, Black students in the 1960s devised a parallel and permanent social life for themselves when their numbers would allow.

Again like students of the 1960s, some students in the earlier generation of African Americans at white institutions believed they should match every injustice with resistance. In essence, the spirit of the New Negro came to white college campuses in the 1920s. As a freshman at New York University in 1927 stated, "If New York University knows that for every offense there is a strong organization ready to 'strike back' she will not be so inconsiderate in her actions. She is fully capable of paying the price each time, it is true, but she will not be willing to pay if she knows that it will be exacted every time."[13] Acts of resistance included University of Chicago students' defying the voluntary cafeteria segregation policy and, as one of the participants described it, intentionally "plaguing [white students] by deliberately seating ourselves at a table where some white person had fled to escape eating with Negroes."[14] As a foreshadowing of events at the University of Illinois in the late 1960s, African American women at Oberlin College refused to vacate the rooms assigned to them but coveted by white students in 1919. With the help of the NAACP, the most influential rights group at the time, their campaign was successful.[15] Black students at white campuses also focused on segregation in their campus-town communities. One example of many is the University of Michigan's Negro-Caucasian Club's sit-in protest of segregated restaurants in Ann Arbor.[16] Throughout the 1950s, many African American students (as well as white students) followed this path and concentrated their protest efforts on the surrounding communities rather than on the university itself.

Demonstrating the persistent and varied attitudes of African American students throughout the century, many subjugated their racial group concerns to their individual survival while on campus rather than participate in protest. Reconciling the tension between working toward racial advancement and getting along on campus by assimilating to white mores could prove difficult. This is not to say that these earlier college students were not interested in racial advancement and liberation. Many interpreted their individual success as a cog in the wheel of collective racial uplift and actively worked for African American rights and liberation after graduation. However, African American college students attending white institutions prior to the 1960s often *had* to be concerned primarily with their individual survival either because they were the only African American student on campus or one of a few or because the intensely hostile campus climate necessitated an emphasis on individual survival. Allen Ballard, remembering his own experience as one of two African American students at Kenyon College in the early 1960s, articulated the experience of many Black students: "We were, in fact, forced to suppress our natural inner selves so as to conform to the mores of a campus dominated by upper-middle-class Americans. For eighteen hours a day, our manners, speech, style of walking were on trial before white America."[17] While some Black students chose to protest, many other Black students did not decry the racism inherent in their treatment on white campuses, nor did they dispute the racist assumptions of white university institutional structures and curricula. Rather, they tended to see themselves as students first and African Americans second.

Southern higher educational institutions remained intransigent about desegregating their campuses even after the series of Supreme Court decisions dismantling segregation in education. Bolstered by the building momentum of the civil rights movement's ideology, goals, and successes, African Americans continued to test the Court decisions and the executive branch's resolve in enforcing the law. In 1956, Autherine Lucy attempted to integrate the University of Alabama School of Library Science with the backing of a court order restraining the university from rejecting her on the basis of her race. One day after her enrollment, a riot erupted on campus and the surrounding city that lasted three days. Less than a week later, the university asked Lucy to leave the campus for her own safety. The board of trustees then barred her from the campus

Pg 14

relates to Oo 64

·niversity acted in contempt of court
Lucy should be readmitted, but
' regarding the university's
ᵔlabama was integrated
.ates Vivian Malone and
.der, National Guard protec-
tion, .   ..aiiace's now infamous speech while standing in the   .ɔoɪhouse door.[18]

James Meredith was the first African American to graduate from a
southern white institution. Meredith was attending Jackson State College, a historically Black college in Mississippi, when he attempted to
transfer to the University of Mississippi. After two false starts in 1961,
Meredith's case worked its way through the judicial system to the Fifth
Judicial Circuit Court in 1962, where the court found the state of Mississippi in violation of previous court rulings regarding desegregation in
education. Since violence was expected, federal marshals accompanied
Meredith as he attempted to register. Governor Ross Barnett, local police, and other state officials barred his entrance to the registrar's office.
Federal pressure subsequently ensured Meredith's enrollment. Riots en-
sued in which over one hundred marshals were wounded and two persons were killed. Meredith remained on campus despite harassment, discrimination, and attempts on his life. Federal troops remained on campus
until he graduated in 1963.

African American student protest during the first half of the twentieth century closely mirrored African American protest nationwide.
Both on campus and in the larger society, African American liberation
efforts often existed in isolation from one another prior to the late 1940s
and early 1950s. African Americans and whites began the rumblings of
coordinated protest through such organizations as the Niagara Movement, NAACP, and United Negro Improvement Association in the early
part of the twentieth century. When momentum built as World War II
ended, international pressures increased, and African Americans entertained more aggressive and coordinated tactics, the civil rights movement emerged. Meaningful desegregation remained a primary goal of the
movement into the 1960s, and African Americans in general and African American students in particular employed legal remedies and such
direct-action tactics as boycotts and sit-ins to attack discriminatory
practices. Of course segregation continued in the larger society, but African Americans and sympathetic whites eroded its legal basis through
consistent pressure and eventual federal, state, and local support.

Black college-aged youths played a significant role in eroding discrimination and racism both on their own campuses and in the larger society. Students at Black colleges in the South forced their institutions to offer a curriculum that would prepare them to uplift the race rather than groom them for manual labor. Outside their campuses, Black students played an equally critical role. In fact, it would be students who touched off a nationwide sit-in movement in Greensboro, North Carolina, in 1961 and organized one of the most important rights groups in the twentieth century, the Student Nonviolent Coordinating Committee.[19] The extremely small number of African American students on white campuses in the North precluded collective and organized protest of the kind occurring on Black campuses. Some, however, openly and aggressively protested university policies and practices when the situation merited. By the 1940s, the few African Americans at white institutions joined with white students to combat segregation and discrimination in their local communities. White institutions and campus communities differed in their receptivity to African American student concerns, but students continued to combat racism and segregation at their campuses and communities, including the University of Illinois.

The History of Black Students at the University of Illinois

Champaign County, approximately one and a half hours south of Chicago and located in central Illinois, remained a predominantly rural area surrounded by smaller towns and dominated by independent farming until the mid-twentieth century. Though located above the Mason-Dixon line, the county resembled southern states in its attitude toward and treatment of African American residents. As the Black population in the county grew during the late nineteenth and early twentieth century, the white population became concerned. Emancipation, the new railroad, and the defense industry attracted African Americans to the area, with the largest increases occurring after the Civil War, World War I, and World War II.[20] Not all white residents opposed such migration, but racist sentiment was far from latent. For instance, large Ku Klux Klan meetings took place throughout the county and included a mass rally at a park in Urbana in 1924.[21] County residents did not wholly endorse Klan sentiment and hostility, but the twin cities of Champaign and Urbana established firm patterns of educational and residential segregation early in the twentieth century. In the 1930s, a combination of federal housing programs, restrictive covenants, and banks' lending policies led to the creation of all-Black areas and a dual housing market in Champaign and Urbana.[22] Residential segregation patterns created educational segregation patterns, and most Black students in Champaign attended all-Black or predominantly Black elementary schools throughout much of the twentieth century.[23] By the late 1960s, Blacks still had higher rates of deteriorated housing, unemployment, and infant mortality and had a median family income almost half that of whites.[24]

The University of Illinois was established and evolved in this context. Chartered in 1867 and made possible by the Morrill Acts, Illinois Industrial University, as it was then called, began developing a curriculum emphasizing agricultural training, mechanical arts, and military tactics. The student body included fifty white males who were taught by a faculty of three. Three years later, the university's board of trustees voted to admit women. The draft bill for the university in 1863 explicitly provided for the enrollment of any *white* Illinois resident, though the final charter did not include such language because it would have been inconsistent with the recent Emancipation Proclamation and Thirteenth Amendment.[25] However, an African American student did not enroll in the university until twenty years later. In 1887, the institution, now calling itself the University of Illinois, admitted its first African American student, Jonathan Rogan. He remained only one year, and it was not until 1894 that another African American student, another man, enrolled. The first African American man would not graduate from the university until 1900; the first African American woman graduated in 1906. African American undergraduate enrollment slowly climbed throughout the first part of the twentieth century. Their numbers rose from 2 in 1900, to 68 in 1925, 138 in 1929, and 148 in 1944. Though their numbers multiplied, never did they amount to more than 1 percent of the student population.[26]

African American students at Illinois experienced discrimination on and off campus. Perhaps emboldened by legal victories in the South and the more aggressive mood of Black liberation efforts, some Black students involved themselves in protest. In 1946, the university's board of trustees reaffirmed it policy to "favor and strengthen those attitudes and social philosophies which are necessary to create a community atmosphere in which race prejudice can not thrive."[27] But discrimination continued. On campus, housing became a flash point. In the first half of the twentieth century, only two women's dormitories existed. Not until 1945 did African American women receive space in the dormitories and only after a very public campaign by concerned African Americans in Chicago, home for most African American students. Charles J. Jenkins, an African American state representative, mounted a personal campaign to open the residence halls to African American women by petitioning the university, meeting with the university president Arthur Cutts Willard, and soliciting possible candidates for application to the dormitories. The Illinois Association of Colored Women's Clubs also became very active in the desegregation campaign. In the tradition of the Black press, the *Daily Defender*, the African American Chicago newspaper, held university administrators' feet to the fire by publicizing the dormitory situation and chastising the university. The newspaper deliberately used buzzwords for racism and discrimination in an article entitled "Just Like Dixie: No U of I Dorms for Negroes," pointing out that "Jim Crow has crowded Negro girl students completely off the University of Illinois campus."[28] President Willard, mildly receptive to the pressure, promised Representative Jenkins and the Colored Women's Clubs he would ask the director of the Division of Student Housing "to hold space for two girls for the time being, because I want the group which is interested in the situation to feel that the University is being absolutely fair."[29] In August 1945, the acting director of housing alerted the president that two African American women, Quintella King and Ruthe Cashe, had accepted their dormitory contracts for the 1945–46 academic year. Other African American women would follow, but all were assigned rooms together—the university desegregated the dormitories by allowing African American women to reside there, but African American and white women were not allowed to room together. The Housing Division averted accidents by soliciting race and national origin information on the dormitory applications.[30]

Discriminatory practices by local landlords and restrictive covenants in real estate further limited housing options. Many African American students lived in African American fraternity or sorority houses; of the five African American Greek organizations on campus in the 1940s, three maintained houses, and one maintained a suite of rooms. Other African American students lived with local African American families. This took a toll on students. African American community residents lived in a segregated part of Champaign, called the North End, quite a distance from campus. Traveling to and from campus by foot meant lost time for study and recreation, while white students could take advantage of both. The university itself recognized the housing problems African American students faced. In a 1935 report, the university lamented the fact that African American students not living in fraternity or sorority houses had to walk a long distance to attend classes and participate in campus life. However, the report was quick to explain that living conditions had improved since the early part of the century—a claim disputed by African American students and Champaign residents.[31]

In addition to the discriminatory housing situation, African American students faced overt and covert discrimination on campus. In the early part of the twentieth century, white students sponsored a Hobo Parade during Homecoming, where students would dress as indigent people. Students made picture postcards of the hobos in blackface and imitated other minority groups, such as Jews and the Irish.[32] In the mid-1930s, rumors flew that certain professors refused to give African American students a grade higher than *C*. The university kept African American men off the basketball team out of courtesy to "a Big Ten understanding," while the football coaches and team created a hostile enough environment to deter African American males. Similarly, the university refused African American male enrollment in advanced military courses.[33] Documents suggest white women's organizations—except sororities—were slightly more open to African American female participation. For instance, the Women's League, a social and service club, invited African American women to its teas.[34] However, many white student groups excluded African American men and women either through clauses in their constitutions or by more subtle tactics.

Regardless, African American students made themselves a part of the campus and took advantage of university life to the best of their ability. A few participated in established university organizations, including Glee Club, literary societies, and the student newspaper, the *Daily Illini*. Others created organizations parallel to those established by the university or white student groups. Reflective of the Black cultural renaissance sweeping the nation in the early twentieth century, several African American–sponsored organizations used the African American cultural heritage as a basis for their existence and mission. Like their contemporaries, W. E. B. Du Bois and Carter G. Woodson, they brought increasing race sentiment to the college campus.[35] African American fraternities and sororities and local churches provided most of their social activities. In the early 1930s, African American students formed Cenacle, an honorary society for African American students that sponsored plays with African American student actors and a book exhibit in the university library featuring African American authors.[36] In 1938, Black students published the *Scribbler*, "the official voice of the Negro students enrolled in the University of Illinois," and discussed segregation in Champaign, the debate over voluntary segregation, as well as lighter subjects.[37] In the early 1950s, students celebrated Negro History Week, founded by Carter G. Woodson in 1926, with invited speakers, movies, and plays.[38] In this way, African American students created social and extracurricular outlets for their artistic interests, social welfare, and racial consciousness. Like African Americans in general, African American students at the University of Illinois demanded to be seen *and* heard.

Off campus, African Americans encountered discriminatory treatment in barbershops, theaters, and restaurants. Since most local eating
establishments practiced segregation, African American students had to
return to their host family's home or their fraternity or sorority houses
for meals. Other arrangements—though questionable in what they meant
for relations between African American students and white students—
existed. For instance, Lucy Gray, an African American house manager at
a white fraternity, Alpha Chi, hired an exclusively African American male
staff to alleviate their meal problems. They were allowed to eat the fraternity's leftovers as part of the payment for their services. Hence, they
would not have to make the long walk to the North End for the evening
meal and could remain on campus to study in the evening.[39]

In 1945, a small number of concerned African American and white
students, faculty, and community members formed the Student Community Interracial Committee. Very much like the NAACP and employing
techniques borrowed from the growing civil rights movement, it combated discrimination and segregation in the local community by threatening lawsuits against segregated establishments, picketing, and holding
workshops in public relations, human relations techniques, and Negro
history. It had only moderate success but began to lay the groundwork
for future victories. The committee changed and evolved during the early 1950s, but the group remained committed to the desegregationist
cause, as evidenced in the organization's 1951 preamble to its constitution: "We, students and faculty members of the University of Illinois, and
residents of Champaign County, recognize the danger to our community of discrimination among racial, religious, ethnic, or other culturally
defined groups, and of the human tensions arising out of such differences." The organization pledged to investigate every reported case of discrimination, combat all totalitarian influence in the area of intergroup
relations, and provide a program of education to promote understanding
between diverse groups.[40] Students at the University of Illinois organized
and entered the civil rights fray by attacking segregation and discrimination in their local community.

The Student Community Interracial Committee began a letter-writ-
ing campaign to the state's attorney regarding segregation in local restaurants in 1946. Each letter itemized the discriminatory treatment, names
of people and witnesses involved, date of the treatment, and the address
of the restaurant to pressure restaurants into following the law that prohibited segregation. Students also conducted tests of establishments where
African Americans experienced discriminatory treatment. White student
committee members replicated African American students' failed at-

tempts to receive service in order to determine whether the establishment treated whites differently. While the committee found widespread discrimination, few restaurants changed their policies through the late 1950s and early 1960s. Until then, proprietors continued to require African Americans to leave the restaurant, sit at the back, or eat in the kitchen.[41]

Local theaters and barbershops maintained similar policies. Local theaters asked African American patrons to sit in a reserved section. Theaters went so far to keep the races separate that they asked white patrons sitting in the reserved section to relinquish their seats. One theater manager explained that it was not fair for whites to take seats reserved for colored people. If whites did, Negroes would have nowhere else to sit in the theater since most whites refused to be seated next to Negroes (hence the reserved section).[42] White barbers in campus town refused to cut Negroes' hair, citing (wrongly) an Ohio law where those providing a personal service—including haircuts—could use discretion in offering their services. When found in noncompliance with Illinois law, barbers resorted to other tactics. Some reported they did not have the equipment necessary to cut Negroes' hair or that it was against union rules, others declared they would embarrass Negro customers to the point they would not wish to return, and a few even threatened physical harm. Evidencing the odd nature of discrimination and the relationship between African Americans and whites in America, barbershops proudly displayed pictures of J. C. Caroline, an African American student and All-American football player, in their windows but refused him service.[43]

Off-campus housing continued to be an issue in the early 1960s. In 1960, the university revised its Code of Fair Educational Practice to include a clause reaffirming the university's position on discrimination in housing: "The University will approve no new privately operated student rooming house unless the owner agrees to make its facilities available to all students without discrimination with respect to race or religion."[44] By 1962, 51 percent of the rooming houses continued to operate on a discriminatory basis. Not until the mid-1960s were university efforts successful. Discrimination in seating African American patrons in restaurants and theaters abated in the late 1950s, but discrimination in hiring African Americans in local establishments continued into the 1960s. The campus chapter of the NAACP made the Champaign hiring issue a priority and had the logistical aid of the national and Illinois NAACP branches and local community organizations. Urged on by national leadership and demonstrating sympathy for the civil rights movement in the South, the campus branch conducted a "freedom rally" in the early 1960s and picketed national chain stores discriminating in the South.[45]

Attacking on-campus issues proved just as complex as attacking national issues. The university maintained policies of nondiscrimination, but the policies were not always translated into practice. For instance, the white Greek system at the university remained impenetrable for African Americans seeking to join fraternities and sororities. As of October 1959, no new student organization restricting membership on the basis of race or religion received university recognition,[46] but existing fraternities and sororities proved another matter. Several white fraternities and sororities had restrictive clauses in their national constitutions. The university encouraged voluntary complicity with university nondiscriminatory policies and urged the Greek organizations to sign nondiscriminatory statements. Some did. Others refused on the basis of free association. The issue remained so pressing in the early 1960s that Harry Tiebout, a white faculty member who was the adviser for the campus NAACP chapter, informed the national leadership in 1961, "Our major on-campus project will be cracking the segregation pattern in fraternities and sororities. We have made extensive plans and expect to wage a vigorous struggle."[47] Some in the university, including the Urbana chapter of the American Association of University Professors, fully supported the NAACP's efforts. Others, including President David Dodds Henry, qualified their support, citing the thorny issues involved.[48]

The university closely monitored and controlled NAACP protests regarding fraternity and sorority exclusionary policies and other issues while the protesters were on university property. In 1961, amidst growing numbers of civil rights protests, the university issued regulations to all student groups regarding proper conduct. Protesters could not impede pedestrian, bicycle, or motor traffic, block entrances to buildings, harass passers-by, disturb classes by noise or picketing, or picket at the same time and place that an opposing group was picketing. If university functions were the target, students had to submit written notification twenty-four hours in advance.[49] When worried about noncompliance, the university reminded the NAACP of proper conduct and even denied its petitions to protest. The university's in loco parentis ethos and attempts to keep politics out of higher education would be shattered before the end of the decade.

Despite university efforts to control protests, its often lukewarm commitment to racial equality, and intransigent local proprietors, desegregation efforts eventually were successful. Like Black student initiatives on other white campuses in the North during the first half of the twentieth century, protests began as sporadic, individual events. By the late 1950s and early 1960s, students began forming organizations for the explicit purpose of dismantling segregation. Student demands and tactics mirrored those of other increasingly aggressive and empowered African Americans in the wake of World War II, the *Brown* decision, and the burgeoning civil rights movement nationwide. Champaign-Urbana restaurants, theaters, and barbershops desegregated their facilities. African American women and men moved into campus dormitories. The university refused to advertise off-campus housing of those landlords known to practice discrimination or acknowledge any student organization known to discriminate. Campus life began to open for African Americans interested in participation. Accordingly, African American students slowly increased their involvement with established student organizations, though they continued to participate in and initiate their own organizations.

It is important to note, however, that Black student thought regarding protest activity in the 1940s and 1950s was far from monolithic. A few students chose to agitate for change during their time on campus, while others refused to participate in the protests. Many avoided situations where they would encounter discrimination, could not comprehend why African American students would put themselves in a position to encounter it, or reported being oblivious to discrimination on campus.[50] Many focused their energies on academics rather than social issues. Overall, they were successful in their academic pursuit, particularly considering the tangible and psychological effects of discrimination, humiliation, and segregation they suffered on and off campus. Throughout the first half of the twentieth century, African American students at the University of Illinois maintained grade point averages and graduation rates comparable to those of whites.[51] Their low numbers and intense pressure to conform to white mores precluded much organized protest in the first half of the century. But as their numbers grew and pressures to assimilate abated or were ignored, many Black students began to view academic success and protest activity as inextricably linked on the path to Black liberation. The targets and strategies of protest changed, but the mission remained the same—creating a campus environment in which they would thrive and feel comfortable while at the same time using their talents to change the world around them.

The Black Power Movement Comes to Campus

The civil rights movement's ideology of nonviolence and the goal of integration lost favor with a large segment of the African American community during the middle to late 1960s. After decades of attempting to force their way into the existing social order only to meet intense white resistance and repression, many African Americans, including the youth, became disillusioned with integration to the point of disdain. Instead of seeing integration as the answer to Black America's problems, some re-defined it as a philosophy that ignored questions of power and worked to usurp the Black community of the skills and energies of its most pro-ductive members. Further undermining faith in the goals and tactics of the civil rights movement were the murders of Black youths, such as Sammy Younge, James Chaney, the four girls killed in a church bomb-ing in Birmingham, Alabama, and many unnamed others. Doubts about the federal government's dedication to improving the conditions of Af-rican Americans, suspicions regarding the extent to which white liber-als could be considered true allies, and the large discrepancy between expected results and actual achievements produced a shift in ideas on the proper tactics and means to gain Black liberation. Many African Ameri-can youths grew frustrated with the slow pace of change and demanded more power, real power, Black Power.

The Black Power movement was inaugurated 16 June 1966. Earlier in the month, James Meredith, the African American who successfully integrated the University of Mississippi, began the "March against Fear" to prove an African American could walk from Memphis, Tennessee, to Jackson, Mississippi, without being harmed. He was shot on the second day. Various rights groups, including the NAACP, the Southern Christian Leadership Conference, Congress of Racial Equality, and the Student Non-violent Coordinating Committee (SNCC), vowed to continue his journey, renamed the "Meredith March." While in Greenwood, Mississippi, the police arrested several marchers, including Stokely Carmichael, a mem-ber of SNCC. Frustrated and infuriated, Carmichael addressed a rally of six hundred people: "We been saying freedom for six years and we ain't got nothin'. What we gonna start saying now is 'Black Power!'"[52] It was not the first time in history the phrase had been used, but it was the first time it reached such a large audience and became a national flash point.

Attempting to define Black Power more fully, Carmichael and Charles V. Hamilton, a political scientist, authored *Black Power: The Politics of Liberation in America.* They described Black Power as "pride rather than shame in blackness, and an attitude of brotherly, communal responsibil-ity among all black people for one another." It became a call for African Americans to recognize and be proud of their heritage, build a sense of community, define their own goals, and control their own organizations. To accomplish these tasks, Blacks were called to unite: "Before a group can enter the open society, it must first close ranks. By this we mean that group solidarity is necessary before a group can operate effectively from

a bargaining position of strength in a pluralistic society." Under the ban-
ner of Blackness, they would be able to address their grievances and demand their share of the American Dream.[53]

While criticized for being too vague or ill-defined, Black Power became a widely popular ideology. Blacks used it as they deemed necessary
and fit. Regardless of the definition, Black Power usually included political, economic, cultural, and psychological components. Black political
power meant Black police officers, tax assessors, mayors, and legislators.
Black economic power meant equality of the standard of living of African Americans and the development of community institutions. Black
cultural power meant cultural autonomy. Black psychological power
meant self-determination and self-definition. Along with Carmichael,
such young ideologues as H. Rap Brown, Imamu Amiri Baraka, Ron
Karenga, and Julius Lester helped define the nature of Black Power and
popularize its concepts and principles.

The 4 April 1968 assassination of Dr. Martin Luther King Jr. seemed
to validate the call for Black Power and the closing of ranks. Warning what
King's murder would mean for the Black rights struggle, Carmichael, at a
news conference soon after King's death, announced, "I think white America made its biggest mistake because she killed the one man of our race
that this country's older generations, the militants and the revolutionar-
ies and the masses of black people would still listen to."[54] Carmichael
suggested that the mediating force between increasingly frustrated African Americans and the white power structure died with King. Which way
would the struggle turn now? As a young Black man yelled in the streets
after hearing of King's death, "Now that Dr. King's dead, we ain't got no
way but Stokely's!"[55] Black students at predominantly white institutions
were a part of this growing movement and sought to make Black Power
real at institutions of higher education across the nation.

Black students attending Black institutions in the South had continued their history of activism in the early part of the 1960s. Most nota-
bly, Black students from North Carolina A&T touched off a nationwide
sit-in movement to protest segregationist policies in public facilities. Like
African American students at white institutions, most of the students
directed their efforts at societal ills—namely segregation—outside their
institutions until the late 1960s. However, with the onset of Black Power, the urban uprisings in such cities as Detroit and Los Angeles, and the
increasing enrollment of Black students at white institutions, Black students on white campuses became the vanguard of the student protest
movement. Black student activism turned toward their own institutions,
and Black student activism grew. Students on various campuses talked

to one another about strategy, published their demands in one another's newspapers, and even traveled to one another's campuses for support.[56] Linked by a common acceptance of Black Power ideology and similar campus concerns, the Black student movement was born.

Two pieces of federal legislation had a tangential influence on the rise of Black Power on college campuses by expanding educational opportunity and access for African Americans in the 1960s. Both illustrated the large influence of civil rights movement demands on federal policy. The Civil Rights Act of 1964 ordered a census of all U.S. postsecondary institutions identifying students by race or ethnicity, thereby dramatizing the low number of Black students at white institutions. That legislation also warned administrators at these institutions that federal monies would be withheld from any institution found to be in noncompliance with the act's equal opportunity mandates. The Higher Education Act of 1965 (HEA) expanded the amount and types of financial assistance available to those pursuing higher education. Although the financial aid provided by the HEA was not limited to African American students, Blacks benefited most from the grants, low-interest loans, and work-study opportunities it created. Campus-based affirmative action initiatives also contributed to an increase in African American enrollment at white institutions. As a result, African American college student enrollment doubled between 1964 and 1970, with the greatest proportion of the increase noted at historically white institutions.[57] By the early 1970s, approximately two-thirds of all African American college students attended predominantly white institutions.[58] This increase coincided with the burgeoning Black Power movement of the late 1960s and early 1970s. Black students, now reaching a critical mass on some predominantly white campuses, formed a coherent community and began coordinated protest.

Though their numbers remained small on individual campuses, Black students became more involved and more aggressive in their protest activity. Some were spurred to action by the assassination of Dr. Martin Luther King Jr.; some by the police murders of students at South Carolina State University at Orangeburg in 1967 or Jackson State College (Mississippi) and Kent State (Ohio) in 1970; still others for more personal reasons. Regardless, during the 1968–69 academic year, Black students were involved in 57 percent of all campus protests at predominantly white institutions.[59] In the first half of 1969, Black students were involved in 51 percent of all campus protests, though they were less than 6 percent of the total college population.[60] Even though their numbers were small and many campuses had an even smaller number of *active* Black students, many began demonstrating against racist school policies and sought to make Black Power real on their campuses. Many interpreted their role as the mouthpiece for Blacks who lacked the skills necessary to articulate their grievances effectively. As one-time SNCC chairman H. Rap Brown suggested, "One thing which the Black college student can do, at this time, is to begin to legitimatize the brother's actions—begin to articulate his position, because the college student has the skills that the [average Black American] doesn't have."[61]

Some critics asked why Black students attended predominantly white institutions, why they pursued a degree at an institution that was de facto racist and segregated. Various reasons existed. The prestige of the University of Illinois, its close proximity to Chicago (home for most Black Illinois students), and the availability of financial aid packages kept many Black students enrolled at the university. Black students at other predominantly white campuses expressed similar reasons for their attendance. Also, an emerging definition of Black student "success" helped Black students resolve the perceived dissonance between practicing Black Power ideology and attending a predominantly white institution. On one hand, most Black students recognized the prestige and academic reputation of white institutions would be beneficial for their future career pursuits. On the other, they believed it their duty to force those institutions to reflect Black understandings of a proper education and create an environment where Black students could thrive. Further, these students sought to share the benefits of the excellent education white institutions had to offer with the Black communities from which they came and to which they would return as leaders in racial uplift. Thus, like many of their predecessors, Black students of the 1960s and 1970s believed their individual achievement enabled group advancement.

Many Black students experienced a sense of alienation when they arrived at predominantly white campuses in the early to middle 1960s. The small number of Black students on any given campus contributed to this sense of isolation. Many did not feel welcome to participate in student life and organizations, such as fraternities and sororities, student government, or academic associations. Instead of feeling they were members of an inclusive institutional body, many Black students felt more like appendages that were to be tolerated but not integrated into the whole. Overt hostility from various members of the majority student body, faculty, staff, and administration exacerbated this sense of alienation and sometimes led to Black students' heightened emotional distress and isolation. Although the increased enrollments of Black students at predominantly white institutions during the late 1960s alleviated some of this alienation, the lack of a sense of belonging and persistent racial hostility on majority-white campuses continued. Black students often sought to protect and promote their psychological health and well-being by developing various support services and programs.

Black student alienation at predominantly white institutions, coupled with a growing racial consciousness among Blacks nationwide as a result of the spread of the Black Power movement, influenced the rise of Black student unions. Black students began organizing these groups on white campuses during the late 1960s. They went by many names—Black Students Association, African American Students Society, and United Afro-American Students, among them—but all worked toward providing Black students with a structured and legitimate power base from which to force change at their institutions. Regardless of the university setting, Black student unions shared common characteristics, goals, and benefits for Black students. Generally, they were, as William Exum succinctly put it, "exclusively Black in membership, monolithic in appearance, highly self-conscious, and motivated by sociopolitical concerns."[62] Furthermore, Black students formed the organizations for the purpose of instilling solidarity and unity among Black students and other people of African ancestry, expressing the positive aspects of Black culture, and providing a training ground for political organization and leadership. The benefits of the unions were that they met social and psychological needs, offered a safe environment in which students could explore identity issues, and facilitated the development of collective values and ideological beliefs.[63]

Richard McCormick described how Black students at Rutgers University's Newark, New Jersey, campus recognized the need to create an organization to promote their issues in September 1967. That year, Black Rutgers students interested in forcing change at the institution and promoting the welfare of the surrounding African American community joined the campus chapter of the NAACP. However, several of the students decided that the NAACP did not sufficiently reflect their values and goals. A month later, they formed the Black Organization of Students (BOS) at Rutgers. As a Black former student active on the campus during the 1960s explained, "We as idealistic young people felt that the NAACP had served a useful purpose . . . but now it was time to move forward." The BOS became a buffer between Rutgers's Black students and their institution, which, according to an article in the *Rutgers Observer,* Black students perceived as a "ridiculous, sorrowful, pitiful, and arrogant urban [university]."[64]

Despite their honorable intentions, many Black student unions reported limited membership in the early stages of their existence. Black students at various campuses attributed increased union membership and politicization to the April 1968 assassination of the civil rights movement leader Dr. Martin Luther King Jr. With their enlarged memberships and the adoption of the Black Power ideology and political spirit, these organizations began pursuing their mission—changing their institutions to fit their notions of a proper education and campus environment—in earnest. Black students' demands echoed from universities across the nation. At San Francisco State College, New York University's University College, Cornell University, the University of California at Los Angeles, Northwestern University, Ohio State, Wayne State, the University of Wisconsin at Madison, and many other predominantly white institutions, these demands often included calls for the recruitment and retention of more Black students and faculty, the creation of Black studies departments, and the designation of separate campus facilities for Black students. Many demands spoke directly to the need to alleviate the alienation experienced by Black students at white institutions, provide them with alternative social outlets, and make their postsecondary education more relevant to their situation as Blacks in the United States.

In fall 1966, the members of the Black Student Union at San Francisco State College (SFSC), for example, demanded the creation of a department of Black studies at that institution. In 1969, their vision became a reality. Black students at SFSC endeavored to make the Black studies department a manifestation of Black Power ideology and the new concept of Blackness. Just as this emerging concept grew beyond pigment—persons of African descent had to be Black on the inside, or identify with their race intellectually and emotionally, as well as the outside—the designers of the new department insisted that it, too, have a Black ideological and intellectual center. As Nathan Hare, the department's first director, maintained, "If all a black-studies program needs is a professor with a black skin to prattle about Negro subject matter, then our Negro schools would never have failed so painfully as they have."[65] The demand for Black studies spread to other predominantly white campuses across the nation in the later 1960s. Wary of student protests, succumbing to political pressure, and mindful of the changing definition of the purpose of education, many university administrations hastily began creating Black studies programs of their own. By 1971, over five hundred such departments and programs existed at predominantly white institutions across the nation.[66]

Black students, faculty, and administrators worked to infuse Black studies with the Black Power ideology. Generally, Black studies departments assumed no neutrality in their role in this struggle. They were, in Vincent Harding's words, "proudly, openly pro-Black and recognized pre-

dominantly white universities as part of the American political structure."[67] Many who were involved in the establishment and operation of
Black studies programs did not view a college education as an instrument
by which to socialize young adults into the dominant culture. Instead,
they saw the postsecondary experience as serving an openly political
purpose and as an instrument with which oppressed peoples could learn
to change society. The purpose of Black studies was threefold: corrective,
to counter distortions, misperceptions, and fallacies surrounding Black
people; descriptive, to accurately depict the past and present events con-
stituting the Black experience; and prescriptive, to educate Black students
who would eventually uplift the race. More broadly, Black studies functioned as a self-help tool that enabled Black students to go back to their
communities and assume leadership roles and as an expression of Black
autonomy that enabled them to determine the direction and nature of
education for themselves, though within a white campus context.[68]

Black students also demanded separate facilities on campus. One
student at San Francisco State College explained the need for separate
housing and dining facilities by declaring, "It is not only desirable that
we have separate living and eating facilities, it is imperative if we are to
survive in this society. We must have the chance to appreciate our own
kind and our own culture."[69] Many Black students at white campuses
across the country echoed this statement and demanded separate residence halls, classrooms, and cafeterias for Blacks only. A few institutions
complied. At Rutgers University's New Brunswick campus, Black students demanded and received a "Black section" in one of the residence
halls on campus.[70] With university sanction, Black male students at
Cornell University established an all-Black male residence hall, Elmwood
House, in 1966. The next year, Black Cornell women established Wari,
an all-Black female residence hall.[71] Most institutions refused to establish separate residences or cafeterias, claiming that the provision of separate services and benefits based on race or ethnicity violated Title 6 of
the Civil Rights Act of 1964.

Nonetheless, many white institutions supported the creation of Black
cultural centers on their campuses. Typically, these centers, or "Black
houses" as many were called, were designated for use by Black students
of the institutions and often by Black nonstudent residents of the surrounding university communities. The centers primarily promoted the
exaltation and exploration of Black culture and the Black aesthetic and
provided Black students and other Black campus personnel with a safe
haven—a place where they could escape the pressures of university life
and interact with other Blacks in mutually supportive peer groups. Black

cultural centers at white campuses became places where workshops, lectures, musical and dramatic performances, literary events, and dances were held and where Black student organizations were headquartered.

Black cultural centers at white institutions often housed Black student newspapers. Many Black students at majority-white institutions considered mainstream campus newspapers a biased and often racist source of information and controlled by white students. To provide their own outlet for voicing their concerns and issues, Black students at Rutgers initiated the *Black Voice* newspaper. Black students at New York University's University College established *Black News*. Black students at Washington University in St. Louis published *Black Talk*, while Black students at Cornell published the literary magazine *Watu*.[72] Such publications were important vehicles for the dissemination of Black Power ideology and rhetoric on white campuses across the nation. These publications also facilitated both organizational and personal aims. Black student unions used the publications as forums to discuss organizational business, advertise upcoming social events, make demands of the administration, and offer alternative interpretations of campus unrest. Individual Black students used the newspapers as a means of self-expression by contributing opinion pieces, prose, poetry, and book/media reviews. The creation of Black student publications provided Black students a forum and offered further psychological and tangible validation of their thoughts and opinions.

During the late 1960s, Black students increasingly paired school with protest; the struggle could not wait until graduation. This new combination emerged parallel to the burgeoning Black Power ideology, one that included preservation of Black identity, preference for an ethnically centered curriculum, and an orientation toward collective racial advancement. Consequently, their attitudes resonated in the redefinition of the successful Black student as one who excelled in academics and had clear career goals but who also fully participated in the Black student movement and the Black Power movement. These new successful Black students committed themselves to the welfare of all Black students. Black student unions, Black studies departments, and Black cultural centers embodied this by encouraging and supporting academic success as well as reaffirming racial identity and providing students with the tools they needed to attack and reform racist systems of domination. Beyond the campus, successful Black students had to work for the collective good of the Black community. They also evidenced their dedication to Black community uplift by increasing outreach to Black communities, demanding more occupational opportunities on campus for Black community residents, and creating greater access to the institution by Black community residents—all of which came to pass in the 1960s and 1970s. When the university refused to provide outreach services, Black students often initiated their own programs, including tutorial services for primary and secondary school children, mentoring services for younger children and teens, and such cultural activities as poetry workshops, dance workshops, and various heritage-affirming courses.

Patricia Gurin and Edgar Epps noted this shift in their pioneering study of Black students at Black colleges and universities in the United States. Their study demonstrated that Black college students' commitment to collective identity and political action, on one hand, and their commitment to individual achievement and career success, on the other, were not necessarily mutually exclusive or at opposite poles. Instead, these goals were merely "independent of each other."[73] In other words, Black students could be committed to individual concerns as well as to social change. Indeed, the Black student who most effectively combined the two was viewed as most successful. This conclusion appears to be equally true for Black students attending predominantly white institutions in the late 1960s and early 1970s.[74]

At least one additional concept of a successful Black college student emerged during this era and coincided with the Black Power movement ethos. One definition held that the successful Black student was the opposite of a "sell-out": a Black person who befriended or dated whites, subscribed to a philosophy of integration and assimilation, and did not participate in Black student-sponsored events. By contrast, the successful Black student was well-rounded, respected by other Black students on campus, socially aware, and academically fit. He or she conformed to the physical, psychological, and behavioral conceptions of Blackness and then translated those concepts into activism on campus. As a Black former University of Illinois student recalled, "Your academic success wasn't what you were measured by, it was your participation in relevant things."[75] Black students at Illinois valued academics enough to print the names of all the Black students who received at least a *B* average in their newspaper, the *Black Rap,* and congratulate them on their success.[76] Black students at New York University's University College also linked academics and social responsibility. In a September 1968 issue of the campus newspaper, *Heights Daily News,* a University College Black Student Union officer described the purpose of the organization: "Our main job will be to keep [the new freshmen] here for four years, have them graduate and go back into the Black Community and help build it up."[77]

The 1960s Black student protests at individual campuses should be considered part of a larger Black student movement. Black students actively participated in the Black Power movement and translated its goals and tactics into actions appropriate for a college campus. An umbrella organization coordinating protest on several individual campuses did not exist, and students at different campuses rarely chose appointed days for protest activities. But Black students did talk to one another, learn from one another's struggles, and subscribe to a similar understanding of Black Power. Very much like activists in the civil rights movement and the Black Power movement, local communities responded to their particular situations in different ways. However, activists worked toward common goals and used similar tactics to persuade or force their adversaries to effect social change. The same can be said of Black students at various white campuses across the nation. No matter where they were located, Black students demanded similar concessions from administrators and used a common ideology to understand their role in the Black liberation struggle and to agitate for reform.

A close link between the U.S. sociohistorical context and African American educational efforts has existed throughout history.[78] African Americans in the late nineteenth century and early twentieth often had little recourse for their grievances. By the 1920s, the confluence of various Black rights organizations and New Negro sentiment meant that African Americans demanded equality and respect in a much more coordinated and aggressive fashion. Mechanisms for justice were not always receptive, and frequently their complaints fell on deaf ears. However, the 1920s and 1930s generation began to attack the legal foundation of racism and segregation that enabled the 1950s and early 1960s civil rights movement to make enormous gains. By the mid-1960s, the legal basis for segregation had disappeared, and civil rights activists, both African American and white, tested America's resolve in implementing the court decisions and federal policies.

On the heels of the civil rights movement, many African Americans became disillusioned with the pace of change. Toward the late 1960s, African Americans employed more aggressive means and tactics in the struggle for liberation. Concurrently, they redefined Black identity as political and adopted the ideology of Black Power. Such sentiments filtered into and were in part defined by Black students on predominantly white campuses, including the University of Illinois. They, too, had remained relatively quiet on campus until the 1940s and 1950s. Forming coalitions with whites, African American students began to attack racism and discrimination in the surrounding community. By the late 1960s, they had organized coherent race-exclusive associations, Black student unions, through which to air their grievances. Across the nation, Black student struggles resembled one another in nature, scope, demands, and tactics. Unlike their predecessors, Black students attending white campuses in the late 1960s and early 1970s were enough of a critical mass to force change at their institutions. Their aggressive nature, common experiences, coordinated protest, and national media attention made the late 1960s a unique moment in Black student reform efforts.

2 From Negro to Black:
The Black Students Association

Be proud . . . not ashamed.
Be real . . . not phony.
Be Black.
There is strength in that alone.

—*Drums*, November 1967

The mid-1960s continued to be difficult for African American students at the University of Illinois in terms of numerical isolation and alienation from campus social activities. By 1967, only 223 African American undergraduates attended Illinois, a modest increase from the middle of the century and still only 1 percent of the student population.[1] However, the civil rights movement's successes and ever-increasing African American demands for equality and respect influenced Illinois students, and some involved themselves in protests around campus. As the prevailing ideology of the African American freedom struggle shifted, so too did African American Illinois student attitudes on appropriate protest activity and understandings of liberation. Demonstrating the dramatic shift in ideology was the shift in racial self-referents. As in the broader society, African American students at Illinois during the 1950s overwhelmingly identified themselves as Negro.[2] By the late 1960s, *Negro* had become a pejorative term and had been eclipsed by *Black*—a racial self-referent as well as a particular ideology embodying political, cultural, aesthetic, and organizational components. Black students at Illinois heralded the new Blackness and began to formulate their own particular understanding of it. They then took that understanding and used it to create a supportive environment for themselves—an environment that would foster different and more militant forms of protest.

Creating an organization that appealed to Black students and encouraged protest proved difficult, and building a campus movement would not be an easy or immediate process. While some Black students involved themselves in the movement, others simply wanted to get along on campus, make friends with other ethnic groups, and enjoy college life. Still others remained silent, fearing that their only chance at a first-rate education might be sacrificed on the alter of direct social action. Rather than engage in protest, they interpreted their individual college attendance and success as the most readily available mode of racial uplift. Their attitudes did not mean that these Black students decided to forfeit their Black identity or that they were not interested in Black liberation. Nor should pre-1968 Black students be juxtaposed against post-1968 Black students to understand one group as apathetic and the other activist. However, pre-1968 Black students experienced a different campus ethos. Many arrived before the Black Power movement and subscribed to a civil rights, integration model of racial relationships. Not until later in the decade would their numbers and shifting ideology precipitate a more militant form of grassroots protest based on an ethic of Black self-determination.

The Campus Climate in Black and White

Beginning in the mid-1960s, the University of Illinois campus became increasingly volatile and marked by student protests. However, Black students and white students often focused on completely different issues. Campus protest groups, with the exception of the NAACP and the Student Nonviolent Coordinating Committee, were de facto segregated.[3] Black students were not ostracized from white protest organizations through organizational mandates, but they did not see their futures inextricably linked to the issues white students protested. Racial issues were paramount to Black students, but rarely did race become a defining issue in white student protest.[4] White activists set their sights on broad and international issues, such as free speech and ending the war in Vietnam, while Black students focused on domestic and immediate concerns, such as adjusting to an overwhelmingly white university and eradicating racism and discrimination. Black students viewed white student protest issues as ephemeral and abstract and instead focused on creating healthier conditions for themselves in their immediate environment—the University of Illinois campus.

BLACK STUDENT PROTESTS

In the early to middle 1960s, many Black students focused simply on adjusting to the drastically different environment that the University of Illinois offered. When recounting their initial impressions of the campus in 1965 and 1966, many former students remembered being struck by the sheer number of white students, who outnumbered Black students 99 to 1. Though a few of the Black students had attended high school with white students or had been in academic tracks with white students, many, especially those from Chicago, had lived in predominantly Black communities and had attended predominantly Black schools. Many felt overwhelmed when they arrived on campus. Describing how the small number of Black students affected daily interaction, Dan Dixon commented, "My first semester I saw one Black person on campus Monday, Wednesday, and Friday between my 2:00 class and my 3:00 class. That was the only Black person I ever saw. . . . When I found a Black milieu, I ran for it."[5]

Black students of the early 1960s often felt isolated from one another. The small number of Black students did not necessarily result in a tightly knit Black student community.[6] Instead, many former students noted the different cliques of Black students. Friendships often crossed group boundaries, and the boundaries often were fluid. However, many still felt disconnected and longed for some kind of unity. As Christine Cheatom Holtz stated, "I don't want you to have the impression that from 1964 to 1967 that the undergraduate Black students were a real cohesive community. It felt different than that. There were so few of us, and we lived so far apart. It felt fractured."[7] Their low numbers meant daily contact with other Black students was sparse. Often they were the only Black student in class or the only Black person on the residence hall floor.

Reflecting the national sentiment on Black liberation in the early 1960s, many Black students felt as Edna Lee Long-Green did about getting along on campus: "My whole focus was blending in. I didn't want to stand out."[8] She engaged in social activities with both Black and white friends and related well to her white residence hall floormates. She described the interaction between Black and white students as natural, not hostile. Many Black students were very optimistic about attending Illinois and looked forward to getting to know non-Black students. Some had heard rumors of racism and discrimination, but they chose to attend Illinois regardless and to make the most of the experience.[9] In some cases they were successful.

However, racial tension on campus was not nonexistent. According to various former Black students, including those who noted primarily friendly relationships with whites, overt hostility to them existed. The university itself gathered evidence in the middle 1960s that substantiated former students' remembrances. University staff interviewed Black and white students about discrimination and racism on and off campus as part of an investigation of pervasive rumors spreading across campus. Several Black students remembered feeling alienated, lonely, and ignored. Others remembered harassment from dormitory staff, campus police, and faculty. White students recounted being intimidated by white classmates when socializing with Black friends. The university never made the tapes public but did use them as fodder to encourage different campus units to adhere to university nondiscrimination policies.[10] The university and Black students remained optimistic that such treatment was isolated in nature yet agreed that steps should be taken to improve the campus racial climate. Successful friendships between races existed, but Black and white students often functioned in separate worlds on campus, particularly in social situations. Into the late 1960s, Black students remained isolated from one another and alienated from the larger campus community.

Many Black students joined Black fraternities and sororities to alleviate their sense of isolation. The organizations became very popular on many predominantly white campuses during the twentieth century, including Illinois. They enabled students who felt isolated from one another and alienated from the larger campus community to come together. They acted as a buffer between Black students and the hostile campus and provided social outlets for Black students to unwind and relax. The organizations were created in the spirit of leadership development, academic achievement, and individual improvement. They continued to play an important role in Black student adjustment to the university into the 1960s. But, by the middle to late 1960s, some Black students began to criticize Black Greek organizations. Some questioned the organizations' dedication to racial uplift. The fraternities and sororities were powerful and were part of a national network but did not use their resources to mobilize the Black community for societal reform. In the opinion of some students, the Black Greek desire to emulate white Greek organizations led them to provide parties and other social events instead of leadership for the Black liberation struggle.[11]

Other Black students sought to involve themselves in protest-minded groups and brought with them a background in civil rights concerns. Many former students later recounted their history of involvement with civil rights protest. Boyd Jarrell remembered his involvement in protests against the use of Willis Wagons in Chicago. He and others accused the city of using the mobile classrooms, nicknamed Willis Wagons for the superintendent of schools, Benjamin Willis, as a way to maintain segregation in Chicago schools.[12] Yolanda Smith Stanback-Williams, a transfer student from the University of Illinois at Chicago (UIC), remembered being involved in protest while at UIC: "Did I take my experience with that kind of organizing kids to buck the system to [Illinois]? I guess I must have."[13] David Addison was a member of SNCC and participated in voter registration efforts and sit-ins in the South.[14] Terry Cullers had a background of activism in his family that influenced him to pursue civil rights concerns.[15] Other former students also indicated they were involved with Black attempts at liberation before coming to campus, including participation in Dr. Martin Luther King Jr.'s open-housing drive in Chicago, a flirting affiliation with the Illinois chapter of the Black Panther Party, and sit-ins and marches in Chicago.

Black and white students interested in civil rights joined the campus chapter of the NAACP. However, Black students became increasingly frustrated with campus and community discrimination and entertained alternative ideas on how to improve their situation. During the mid-1960s, many found the NAACP tactics and mission out of sync with the times. Their sentiment on the NAACP reflected the attitudes of Black youth nationwide, which were aptly expressed by Cleveland Sellers, a SNCC worker: "Our parents had the NAACP. Its practice of pursuing 'test cases' through the courts, using laws and the Constitution to fight racial discrimination was suited to their temperaments. We needed something more. As far as we were concerned, the NAACP's approach was too slow, too courteous, too deferential and too ineffectual."[16] Black students began to entertain more aggressive methods and looked to the national Black liberation struggle for ideological and organizational guidance.

One attractive model was the Congress of Racial Equality (CORE), an interracial national organization formed by students in Chicago in 1942. Originally, the organization located itself in the pacifist tradition of nonviolence and committed itself to ridding American society of prejudice and racism.[17] The University of Illinois CORE chapter was organized in December 1966, absorbed the NAACP, and NAACP members became CORE members.[18] Both the national CORE and the campus chapter resembled the national platform of the NAACP in goals but differed in tactics. According to the campus chapter's constitution, the organization would work to "abolish discrimination based upon skin color, race, religion or national origin, stressing nonviolent, direct action methods."[19]

Black student militancy at Illinois got a boost from events occurring in Chicago in 1966. The city exploded in a three-day riot, the groundwork of which had been laid two decades earlier. Many Black students were born during the migration of southern Blacks to northern cities in the 1940s. The influx of Blacks forced Chicago to act quickly to build more housing and schools in Black neighborhoods. The city wanted to make sure Blacks would not move into white neighborhoods or attend predominantly white schools. Segregation was not legally mandated, but it was legally sanctioned. In the early 1960s, Black Chicagoans tried to force the city to allow Black students to attend predominantly white schools. Instead, the city assured Black parents that there were no vacancies in the white schools, gerrymandered school district boundaries, and created mobile classrooms (the Willis Wagons one former student protested). The Black community responded with sit-ins and mass student walkouts in the high schools. Neither was successful, and schools remained segregated.[20] Residential segregation, facilitated by restrictive covenants, exacerbated school segregation. The covenants proved so effective that by 1950, approximately two-thirds of Chicago's Black residents lived in neighborhoods at least 90 percent Black, making Chicago the most segregated city in the United States.[21] As with school segregation, the city decided to provide more housing where Blacks lived rather than attack the segregationist patterns themselves. The policy led to overcrowding and deteriorating housing conditions that steadily worsened by the 1960s.

Civil rights activists, including the parents of some Black students at Illinois, attempted to engage city officials in discussions of possible remedies to the city's racial problems, but their efforts were ignored or pushed aside repeatedly. The worsening conditions in Chicago brought Dr. Martin Luther King Jr. and the Southern Christian Leadership Conference to the city in 1966. King and his allies believed their Chicago campaign could become an example of what was possible in a northern urban setting, but even King could not persuade city officials to budge on segregationist policies. King commented on the inflexibility of Chicago's Mayor Richard J. Daley: "[H]e fails to understand that if gains are not made, and made in a hurry through responsible civil rights organizations, it will open the door to militant groups to gain a foothold."[22] The persistent intransigence of white city officials and increasingly angry Black Chicago residents brought King's prophesy to life shortly after his arrival. The frequent civil rights movement defeats, paired with the shifting mood of Black Americans regarding civil rights and Black Power, became the kindling that would ignite the Black Power movement in Chicago.

During a July 1966 heat wave, Black children trying to stay cool turned on city fire hydrants. A city ordinance prohibited use of the hydrants, but the ordinance was not strictly enforced, especially during the summer. Worried that the heat wave would lower water pressure, police closed the hydrants. In one West Side community, the police repeatedly tried to close a hydrant that the Black community was determined to keep open. The police called for help as the crowd grew larger and angrier. Eventually, the police used their clubs to quell the crowd and in the process beat, pushed, and bloodied bystanders. Word of the incident spread. Chicago civil rights leaders and Dr. King, who was still living in Chicago, tried to calm the crowd. However, by the end of the evening, ten people were injured, twenty-four were arrested, and nine stores were looted. The next night eleven people, including six police, were wounded, thirty-five were arrested, and several stores were vandalized and looted before hundreds of police restored order. Neither civil rights activists nor city officials were able to stop the nightly disturbances, and the rioting continued the next day. Two people were killed, thirty were wounded, two hundred were arrested, and more stores were firebombed and looted. Unable to handle the growing unrest, Mayor Daley called in the National Guard, which was finally successful in ending the riot. The grand total of arrested persons rose to 533, with 61 police wounded.[23]

Black students attending the university were home for summer vacation during the riot. Though none of the former students reported participating, their participation was not necessary to foster increasing Black Power sentiment. They were aware of the conditions igniting the riot. They had experienced Chicago's educational and residential segregationist policies. It was the educational system they indicted for inadequately preparing them for college; it was the residential policy that denied them the interaction with whites that would have alleviated the culture shock they experienced at Illinois. Black Chicago, including Illinois students, examined alternative strategies for dismantling segregation. Some reexamined the goals of integration. Rather than fight to integrate Chicago's white schools and communities, many sought to strengthen the Black community from within. They sought to make the ghetto a self-reliant and self-supporting community using the principles of Black Power.

In the same year, the national CORE adopted Black Power and the right of armed self-defense.[24] Influenced by the national organization, events in Chicago, and the shifting ideology of Black liberation, the campus CORE chapter altered its focus. Whereas it had included white students during its early existence, it soon became an exclusively Black organization working for Black community concerns.[25] The campus CORE chapter now worked toward unity among Black students and between Black students and Champaign residents, demanded an increase in Black student recruitment, and initiated the call for a Black history course to improve Black self-image, to insert African Americans in American history, and to educate the naive "to remove stereotypes."[26] Their service to the Black student community included providing academic assistance for incoming Black students, bringing prominent speakers and entertainers to campus, and acting as the organization through which Black students could bring grievances against the university.[27]

The organization also attempted to clarify the definition of Black Power, an expression that had only recently been inaugurated and that African Americans across the country were attempting to understand. The campus chapter of CORE understood Black Power to encompass principles of pride, autonomy, self-defense, mobilization of the Black community to confront power-holders, and unity. Demonstrating their increasing hostility to whites and the philosophy of integration, Black students at Illinois also included hostility: "[Black] Power creates a conduit through which the Negro can concentrate his candid reply to white condescension and cockiness. That candid reply is simply, 'Eat shit.'"[28]

Students brought their civil rights and Black Power concerns to campus but often focused on more immediate concerns—graduating from the university. The demanding nature of academics often tempered Black student involvement in protest activities. Black students used the university symbol, Chief Illiniwek, to describe the pressure and stress of academic demands. They portrayed the Chief as a malicious force attempting to kill their aspirations through intense competition and a high dropout rate. In their minds, it became Black students versus the Chief. They explained the academic failure of their peers: "The Chief got him. He won't be coming back." And they warned, "Watch out, or the Chief will scalp you." This pressure unnerved many Black students. Some indicated that a hostile racial climate in the classroom negatively affected their academic success, a claim substantiated in part by the university's own audiotapes regarding discrimination and racism on campus.[29] Many were also distressed at having been at or near the top of their graduating high school class but finding themselves unable to compete in college. The Chicago public schools did not adequately prepare them for college academics. James Eggleston explained, "It was the first time that everybody really dealt with failure. . . . There were no support programs in place because they probably didn't understand that we were in an environment that we weren't used to."[30] Accordingly, many Black students focused their energies on getting good grades so that the Chief would not get them.

Compounding the threat of academic failure were the attitudes of many parents. While some parents supported their child's involvement in social justice concerns on campus, many others dissuaded them from protest activity. Sandra Norris Phillips explained certain parental attitudes: "Our parents had been the get along type. They made it into middle-class America. When they sent us away to school we had a sense that we were supposed to act right, do right, get good grades, and graduate."[31] Other former students recounted how their parents warned them not to go away to school and cause trouble. Parents wanted their children to take advantage of the opportunity to attend a prestigious school and leave the protest to others. Understandably, many Black students chose to focus on academic success as a primary concern. However, in the late 1960s, many students increasingly viewed the struggle for social justice as consistent with their overall aspirations for success and a better life.[32] Their attitudes, skills, beliefs, and actions regarding Black liberation surfaced and formed the basis for the emerging Black student movement.

WHITE STUDENT PROTESTS

Meanwhile, white students aggressively attacked the university on a variety of fronts beginning in 1967. The foundation for one of the protest issues was set in place two decades earlier. In 1947, the Illinois legislature passed House Bill Number 711, "An Act to Prohibit the University of Illinois from Extending the Use of Its Facilities to Subversive, Seditious, and Un-American Organizations," also known as the Clabaugh Act. Charles Clabaugh, a Republican senator from Champaign, sponsored the bill, which clearly reflected the anticommunist sentiment sweeping the nation in the middle of the twentieth century. The bill came under heavy attack from members of the university, including the president, George Stoddard, but it was not seriously challenged until 1967. In late 1966, the W. E. B. Du Bois Club, a coalition of liberal and socialist white students, sought university recognition. Debate on its status reached the board of trustees because its recognition could have legal consequences. In February 1967, the board voted to return the matter to regular administrative channels because it did not find concrete proof that the club was subversive or dedicated to the violent overthrow of the United States. Campus administrators promised to formally recognize the group immediately following the board's decision. Some regarded the decision as a victory for free speech and academic freedom. Others, including conservative student groups and Representative Clabaugh, now chairman of the House Committee on Education, declared war.[33]

A month later, the board of trustees reversed its decision, citing new information affirming that the campus chapter of the Du Bois Club maintained informal connections with the national organization, which was under investigation by the U.S. attorney general for being a communist front. Faculty and student groups angrily responded to the shift in position and fired salvos at the board of trustees. The Liberal Arts and Sciences faculty passed a resolution condemning the trustees for their action: "This faculty deeply deplores that action and views its consequences with great concern for the future of the University of Illinois, its faculty, and its students. This denial of recognition and especially the precedent set thereby threatens the fundamental right of the faculty and students to have free discussion, controversy and intellectual exchange. . . . This faculty is profoundly angered to see its vital principles and procedures so severely impaired."[34] Further aggravating the situation, the Student Senate and Students for Free Speech sponsored a talk by Louis Diskin, a member of the U.S. Communist Party, in March 1967. The Committee on Visiting Speakers—made up of faculty representatives—cleared Diskin's appearance since there was no evidence that Diskin would advocate the violent overthrow of the U.S. government, and campus administrators did not dissuade him from speaking. A crowd of over two thousand students, faculty, and others arrived to support the lecture or to protest Diskin's speech.[35]

Students at the Chicago branch of the university, inspired by similar events on their campus, filed a class-action suit against the board of trustees on behalf of all University of Illinois students, including those in Urbana. The students claimed the Clabaugh Act violated the First and Fourteenth amendments and asked "that the defendants be permanently enjoined from enforcing the Clabaugh Act in so far as it relates to the rights of the plaintiffs." The U.S. district court concurred and struck down the act and all related statutes, declaring them illegal and void in July 1968.[36] The victory highlighted the waning power of the board of trustees to control the campus and restrict the free speech activities of campus constituents. Liberal students and faculty applauded the decision as an affirmation of academic and intellectual freedom. Campus administrators generally agreed with the ruling, but the case brought much unwanted attention and criticism and created a public relations nightmare. To some outsiders, it appeared the inmates ran the asylum, a perception that could be extremely damaging for a state-supported institution.

A second set of white student demonstrations mirrored protests on other campuses against university complicity in the Vietnam War. Targets included buildings housing military research and recruitment activities by companies involved in the war effort. On 25 October 1967, approximately 150 to 200 students and faculty conducted a sit-in, demonstration, and teach-in against the Dow Chemical Company, which was recruiting potential employees on campus. Students inside the building were ejected for imprisoning and confining a faculty member, invading university premises, littering, and threatening the safety of persons and property. Twelve students faced university sanction for their involvement. However, no police were involved, and no student faced criminal charges—a situation quite unlike the one Black students would face one year later.[37] Various faculty members wrote the newly appointed chancellor, Jack Peltason, defending the students and acknowledging their own participation. They asked the new chancellor to be mindful of discrepancies between sensational media coverage of the demonstration and their own observations, the peaceful nature of the protest, and the lofty goals of student demonstrators. As one professor put it, "What the students did was an act of social responsibility."[38] Eventually, the university dropped all charges against the students, but anti–Vietnam War protests continued, eventually prompting the appearance of the National Guard in 1970.[39] The increasingly aggressive actions regarding Vietnam increased tensions between the campus administration, campus constituents, and the public. Administrators had to strike a delicate balance between protecting free speech and ensuring that the activities of those who disagreed with the protesters were not hindered—all while attempting not to appear too lenient on protesting students and faculty.[40]

In early 1968, white students expanded their protest focus by insisting on educational reform and a place in it. Demands included increased opportunities for independent study, an expansion of honors programs to include more students, extension of library hours, and academic credit for certain extracurricular activities that contributed to intellectual and moral growth. More radical goals included the dissolution of the grading system and required courses and a complete overhaul of curricula.[41] Various white students displayed their displeasure at the centennial convocation events at Illinois in March 1968. One student, Paul Schroeder, addressed the group of faculty, administrators, students, interested others, and the Illinois governor, Otto Kerner: "Our University is simply not listening to the critical questions of our age. Our educators were schooled before Hiroshima, before Watts and Detroit, before automation and anonymity." He maintained that students were not encouraged to develop critical thinking skills necessary for the late twentieth century but were instead taught in an archaic classroom environment where professors lectured and students regurgitated. The university's educational mission, methods, and goals had to change, he declared, and the students demanded a role: "Without our participation the faculty, the administration, and the government will continue to be unable to provide for our needs."[42]

After his speech, the students walked out of the auditorium, further illustrating the increasingly tense campus climate where students (and often faculty) continually confronted the administration aggressively and in public. The issues were far different from those Black students would raise only one month after the convocation, but meanwhile, such protests and demonstrations dominated the local newspaper headlines and minds of the Illinois legislators. The university administration, under pressure from the board of trustees, Illinois legislature, and horrified Illinois citizens, refined its protest management efforts and sought to regain control of the campus.

Black students remained completely removed from such protests. They were interested in Vietnam draft issues but protested the war for different reasons. White students protested American imperialism in a foreign country, while Black students contended they should not fight in a war to liberate foreigners while remaining oppressed at home. Cecil Cheatom, a Black student at Illinois, refused to report to active duty when drafted in March 1968, citing racial injustice as the primary reason. In his letter to the draft board, he stated, "I find it completely incomprehensible that the United States Government would really expect me, a black man, whose human rights and rights of citizenship are not recognized in this country to go to war in the service of that same country! . . . I am interested in obtaining my freedom and the freedom of my people *here,* in this country, and *now.* If I have a fight, that fight is here."[43] White students did participate in the NAACP, and some of their other protest organizations did support civil rights movement aims.[44] But Black and white students did not protest together.

In the late 1960s, interracial groups were sparse, and issues of race continued to split the student body. The NAACP and other integration-oriented organizations still existed on campus but faced competition for Black members from newly formed Black Power–oriented organizations, including CORE. Like African Americans in the larger community, Black students were not a monolithic group in any sense, including their ideas on the proper tactics and goals of Black liberation. However, Black Power–oriented organizations gained momentum with a significant part of the Black student population. The shift contributed to the already tense campus climate. White student protests against university policies and complicity in the Vietnam War already were in full swing. Black student activists entered this mix advocating Black autonomy and expressing increasingly hostile attitudes toward whites at the expense of civil rights movement goals and tactics.

The Formation of the Black Students Association

In 1966, Black students at Illinois began discussing the need for a Black student organization to work for Black student concerns. In January 1967, Rodney Hammond proposed the formation of "a sort of ad hoc committee of Negro students. It's not a civil rights group, not a social group either, but a sort of superordinate organization which would represent all Negroes on campus, sort of like a funnel to represent all the variant opinions of Negroes on campus, and a vehicle to which the white power structure can address itself."[45] Other Black students shared his ideas, and at first CORE fulfilled this purpose. But some students remained wary of participating in a campus chapter of a national organization and wanted an organization whose sole purpose was to address Black student concerns at Illinois. In an effort to create a forum for discussion, a political pressure group, and an agitating body, Black undergraduate and graduate students formed the Black Students Association (BSA) in October 1967. CORE members soon became BSA members and leaders, and the campus CORE chapter was dissolved by the end of 1967. The new organization adopted the motto "We hope for nothing; we demand everything," linked itself to the emerging Black Power movement, and declared itself the organization through which Black students would force the university to recognize and act on Black issues.

The organization assumed a hierarchical structure, with a president, vice president, secretary, treasurer, and sergeant at arms, and inaugurated various committees representing its diverse interests and mission: newspaper, public relations, Black liaison, cultural and special events, discrimination, and direct action. It declared itself "open to all students who are interested in the promotion of Knowledge of the Black American's Cultural Heritage."[46] All Black students could become members of BSA by virtue of their ethnicity, but just because BSA declared that *all* Black students automatically could become members did not mean that all Black students participated in BSA, followed its policies, or accepted its leadership. BSA had only seventeen members, including the executive council, as of 1 November 1967.[47]

Black Power sentiment provided a powerful organizing tool, but tensions among Black students threatened the emerging organization. The conflict between Black Greek members and independents plagued Black students at Illinois throughout the 1960s and contributed to their wariness of the new organization.[48] The debate surfaced in the BSA executive committee election: could a Black student be dedicated to aggressive social protest and societal reform and be Greek at the same time? Historically, Black Greek organizations were the most powerful Black organizations on campus, were well entrenched in the student and university community, and served social and supportive purposes for Black students attending a predominantly white institution. Would they transform themselves from social organizations to political organizations? Consistent with their constitutional mandates, Black Greek organizations did not throw their weight behind BSA or aggressive social protest. They chose to remain focused on providing social outlets, aims that militant Black students found bourgeois and antithetical to the cause of Black liberation. Participating in Greekdom did not, however, preclude relationships between Greeks and non-Greeks. Greeks and non-Greeks dated, roomed together, and formed lifelong friendships. Neither was Greek life inherently counter to protest activities. However, individual Greeks interested in racial justice concerns had to look outside the Greek system.

Initially, the campus CORE chapter received such interested Greek and non-Greek individuals, but participation was limited. Subtly connecting this to the Greeks, Paul Brady, a Black student from Chicago, explained the small numbers as a reflection of complacency, middle-class attitudes, and a focus on campus social life.[49] Dan Dixon, a member of Kappa Alpha Psi, a Black fraternity, directly attributed the small numbers to Greek participation: "CORE had started, but it was dying a slow death on campus. Nobody was going because most of the folks were Greeks." The Greek attitude toward the formation of BSA often was hostile. Some viewed it as an attempt to usurp power from Black Greek organizations, while others saw it as an attempt by Black students rejected by Black Greek organizations to create their own group. As Dixon remembered, "Some said, 'Leave them alone. They failed at everything else. That will be their Greek group, CORE, SNCC, whatever.'"[50]

Adding to the hostility between Black Greeks and BSA non-Greek organizers was the issue of the leadership and direction of the organization. Black Greeks often were offended by the perceived attitude of BSA organizers. As Dixon put it, "It was like, 'You can come, but we know Black thought. You aren't Black. You need to come to the meetings and find out how to be Black.'"[51] Conversely, Black independents worried that Black Greeks would taint the purpose of the organization. At the electoral meeting, Black Greeks arrived en masse to gain control of the emerging organization. Dan Dixon was elected president, but all other Greek candidates lost. Though Black independents outnumbered Greeks on the executive council, they worried their worst fears had been realized and cautioned:

The results of the Black Students Association elections will hopefully not reflect the future of the BSA as an organization whose aim is to work on behalf of BLACK interests. . . . What people want to know is: where was this mass participation by the Greeks before—in CORE and/or the provisional BSA? Those few Greeks who did participate in the provisional BSA participated as individual black students and not as members of a socially oriented organization. The Black Students Association does not need a division among its members, however it must be acknowledged that one does exist between Greeks and non-Greeks. With more Greek participation in BSA, these differences will hopefully be ironed out.[52]

BSA had to contend with not only hostility from Greeks but also continuing Black student apathy. In a 1967 interview in the *Daily Illini*, Paul Brady recounted how difficult it was to recruit members and get Black students interested in concerted protest because they misunderstood Black Power. Rodney Hammond, in the same article, attributed the apathy to a lack of solidarity.[53] Thirty years later, Sandra Norris Phillips remembered, "Many of the students . . . came from a middle-class, get along, wait-and-see existence. Others were very much afraid of getting involved in that kind of movement."[54] Neither Black Power nor the new organization did much to convince some Black students to get involved.

However, other Black students credited their growing Black consciousness to the BSA. They described their awakening in psychological terms. Blackness was no longer a matter of color. It was, above all else, a question of consciousness. Many former students discussed their previously unconscious state and encounters that contributed to a growing awareness of Black identity. Edna Lee Long-Green stated, "I don't know if I was Black when I came in 1965."[55] A variety of incidents, including the BSA formation, jolted her out of her Negro-ness and into a search for Black identity. By the time she graduated, she had initiated a Black-centered dance troupe and had helped host a cultural showcase of Black artistic talent. Likewise, Sandra Norris Phillips described the formation of BSA as the encounter that pushed her toward Blackness: "I know going through the growing pain phase I became more aware of a conscious identity as a Black student. When I came there, I was . . . a student who happened to be Black. When I left, I was a Black who happened to be a student."[56] This conversion experience was more relevant for some students than for others. Some never experienced the conversion described by other students. Instead, they brought their Black consciousness with them to campus. Regardless, during the 1967–68 academic year, BSA did not develop a large following, and attendance at meetings remained limited.[57]

A further challenge to the emerging organization was the tension between Black students and the Black community surrounding the campus. Students in the 1960s remembered that their predecessors were not permitted to live on campus and had to live with Black Champaign residents on the north side of town. They noted that, historically, the relationship between the "town" and "gown" was necessary, supportive, and positive. However, as students moved into the residence halls, they removed themselves from the Black Champaign community. They still visited the community for services, such as haircuts and food, but they did not live there. They became occasional visitors who returned to campus after receiving services from the Black community. Adding to the increasing strain between Black students and Black Champaign residents were male competition for women, Black student elitist attitudes toward Champaign residents, and campus parties closed to non-Greeks, which meant that non-Greek students and community residents could not attend.[58] In an effort to reunite town and gown, BSA endeavored to include community concerns in its agenda. In the first edition of its first newspaper, *Drums*, BSA pledged itself to opening campus parties and facilities to Champaign-Urbana residents, but the tension remained.[59]

Despite tensions, BSA plugged along and developed an agenda. In late 1967, BSA built on CORE's efforts to increase the number of Black students on campus. According to BSA, increasing their numbers benefited the university as well as Black students: it made the campus more representative of the state's population and helped assuage psychological stress. The small number of Black students deeply affected their emotional well-being and friendships. "Being there, it was so lonely. When people flunked out, it was devastating. Every year you had to make new friends. If you made three friends, two of them would leave," James Eggleston remembered years later.[60] According to William Savage in an article in *Drums*, BSA took up the effort "due to lack of initiative of the University" and because "the black students here would be able to relate much better to other blacks, thus making our efforts more successful."[61] With the university's sanction, BSA representatives visited eleven predominantly Black Chicago high schools during winter break. They spoke about BSA and the University of Illinois, encouraged those interested to apply, and distributed applications. The BSA recruitment initiative indicated an active merging of academic and social justice concerns in ways different from previous students' efforts. As Rodney Hammond stated, "We were all going through a set of stages from being focused, as students traditionally were at the University of Illinois, on ordinary concerns and self-interest to who we were as Black people."[62] Recruiters informed students that traditional models of individual achievement—

where Black rights concerns were subjugated to self-interest and advancement—were no longer sufficient. Black students could have both academic success and be involved with social justice concerns on campus and in the larger Black community.

Though still a small organization, BSA held fairly regular meetings to discuss organizational business and published a campus newspaper, *Drums,* beginning in November 1967. BSA used the newspaper to air its grievances and advertise the role of the Black student in the Black Power movement. Its constant calls for unity reflected the fact that many Black students refused to be swayed by Black Power rhetoric and BSA's mission. BSA fought on and began to entertain direct confrontation "with any institution within or outside the University" and the use of "any tool necessary" in fighting against Black apathy and for liberation.[63] BSA members explicitly stated their connection to the larger Black Power movement and their role in it: "It is our responsibility to interpret to each student the changing attitude of the Black Movement nationally and locally and to reflect Black Consciousness."[64] The organization took it upon itself to ensure that all African Americans on the campus and in the surrounding community were aware of and participants in the Black Power movement.

Accepting the new definition of Blackness, Black Illinois students threw off the term *Negro* in favor of *Black.* While still being used in the main student newspaper, the *Daily Illini,* the word *Negro* was never used as a descriptive racial term in any of BSA's newspapers. As in the national movement, it was assigned a derogatory meaning. John Lee Johnson, a Black Champaign community activist closely affiliated with BSA, stated, "I resent the word 'Negro'; it means second class fool and one who does not want to be free. I am black and black means just the opposite."[65] Johnson's statement not only addressed the *Negro-Black* dichotomy but also revealed the tone of the Black Power–minded Champaign-Urbana community and Black Illinois students. While some used *Negro* and *Black* interchangeably to describe people of African descent based on pigment, Black students used the terms to denote particular ideologies of liberation. By late 1967, Black students referred to themselves and other African Americans as "Brothers" and "Sisters" and denounced those ascribing to a civil rights philosophy as "Negroes" and "Uncle Toms."

In its newspaper, BSA's appeal to unity could take the form of aggressive harassment, and often unity could be conflated with conformity.[66] In 1967 editions, BSA members berated Black students they felt were not participating in the Black Power movement. Many BSA-authored articles and publications attempted to convince the dissenters that Black Power was the proper road toward Black liberation. For instance, in an article entitled "Accept What You Are," a BSA executive committee member, Christine Cheatom, berated Black women who used hair straighteners. Trying to convince African Americans to become serious about Black liberation, including psychological liberation, the article stated, "*No one with straightened hair is an enlightened Black. You may be militant, you may be intelligent but if you can not see any beauty in the average black woman's unstraightened hair, then you are still brainwashed.*"[67] The use of hair straighteners, processes, and skin-bleaching creams became a sign of weakness, desire to assimilate, denigration of the African heritage, and internalization of a white standard of beauty. Conversely, the acceptance of physical expressions of Blackness bolstered the self-esteem and self-worth of Black women. Jacqueline Triche Atkins stated, "I remember the first time I got my Afro. . . . It was an outward expression of pride. That was the seed that let that pride grow and grow."[68] Other students described a similar experience. But having unstraightened hair did not necessarily mean true Blackness; one had to fully appreciate one's Afro. The hair issue grew so intense that during the November 1967 BSA-sponsored Black Heritage Weekend, Black students felt compelled to sponsor a discussion of it: "Resolved: That Blacks must go Natural."[69]

By March 1968, BSA's organizational structure functioned well enough for it to be productive. In its short existence, the organization had managed to publish four issues of its newspaper, sponsor the Black Heritage Weekend, participate in the recruitment of future Black students, and prompt the university to discuss seriously the initiation of a Black history course. BSA began to broaden its focus by examining larger issues and contemplated demanding more Black professors, a Black student center, and equal rights and good wages for university auxiliary staff. In the spirit of the era, each BSA initiative was infused with the ideology of Black Power. With their raised level of consciousness of Black America's problems, BSA students used the emerging definition of Blackness to appeal to a sense of Black unity on campus. By April, BSA members still wondered how to encourage more of their peers to join the movement.

National Influences and Local Consequences

The 4 April 1968 assassination of Dr. Martin Luther King Jr. provided one of the catalysts in increasing Black Power sentiment at Illinois. His murder stunned the campus, Champaign-Urbana, and the entire nation. After his death, Black students examined the roadblocks in the path of Black liberation. They mourned the assassinations of Medgar

Evers, John Kennedy, and Malcolm X. They discussed and were affected deeply by the conditions igniting riots in Chicago, Watts, and Newark, the Vietnam War, and civil rights defeats in the South. They protested the police who murdered students at Black colleges in Mississippi and South Carolina.[70] Dr. King's assassination was the last insult they could endure. As Terry Cullers stated, "It slowly started in 1963, with the assassination of Kennedy, and then it just accelerated. The most power-packed time was between 1967 and 1970. . . . 1968, in the middle of all this stuff happening on this campus, King is assassinated. Two months later, Robert Kennedy is assassinated. . . . There was a feeling in 1968 of, 'What in the world is happening? Is this country really going to hell in a handbasket?'"[71] King's murder bolstered their resolve and confirmed their belief that nonviolence for the sake of a moral statement was not only inappropriate but also useless. For some, it acted as the encounter that pushed them toward Blackness. They turned away from civil rights movement tactics toward a more aggressive, self-defensive strategy.

After reeling in disbelief and anger, many activists commented on the impact of King's assassination. In an article published the day after the murder, John Lee Johnson called King's death an awakening and stated he was sorry about the death but "believed it would be a tool for the Black man to break out of the shell he's fallen into under King's leadership." Black students echoed Johnson's statement in the same article. Rodney Hammond voiced his outrage: "There is no doubt in my mind now that violence is the only way to get anything." He further declared, "I speak for all young black militants when I say that our attitudes emphasized that now the white man was more than ever a 'monster' to be distrusted and feared. The white man has lost the only black friend he had. From now on he will have to deal with us black militants."[72]

Many cities exploded after King's death, including Chicago. According to Chicago's Black newspaper, the *Daily Defender,* looting, sniper-fire, and arson consumed much of the Black community for days after news of the assassination. As they did in 1966, city officials called in National Guard troops to restore order. By 8 April 1968, 270 juveniles had been arrested, and at least 6 under the age of twenty-four were dead. Students attending predominately Black high schools vented anger on white classmates, voted to petition school boards to rename their high schools in honor of Dr. King, held memorial services, and initiated a mass student walkout.[73] Many Black students attending Illinois had graduated from the same high schools in which the disturbances occurred and had already begun recruitment efforts at some of them, including Hyde Park, Marshall, Tilden Technical, and Englewood. Further fueling frustrations,

Mayor Daley ordered police to shoot any arsonists and looters. The order drew heavy fire from Black Chicago civil rights activists. Alderman A. A. Rayner, an Illinois alumnus, led the charge: "I have heard both Stokely Carmichael and H. Rap Brown and neither have ever said anything nearly as inflammatory as the remarks made by Daley." He continued, "What Daley has said will without a doubt make even the best non-violent person mad as hell." Similarly, Anna Langford, a civil rights attorney, stated, "Since I left [for] Atlanta to attend Dr. King's funeral, I don't feel non-violent anymore."[74]

Another catalyst in the growing Black Power sentiment on campus was the link between Black Illinois students and the Illinois chapter of the Oakland, California, Black Panther Party. Panthers fervently advocated autonomy in the Black community and a more confrontational method of achieving liberation—armed self-defense. Panther chapters organized across the United States in the late 1960s; the Illinois chapter was chartered in November 1968. In January of 1969, BSA and Students for a Democratic Society invited Illinois Black Panther Party's Deputy Chairman Fred Hampton, Deputy Minister of Defense Bobby Rush, and member Diane Dunne to speak to students at the university about the approaching revolution and the need for the Black community to arm itself. Approximately one month later, on 7 February 1969, two Illinois Black Panthers were arrested at the Illini Union. William Brooks, minister of education, and William Dunne, a lieutenant, were charged with disorderly conduct and resisting arrest. BSA vigorously defended those arrested and claimed that the Panthers were targeted because they dressed in full Panther uniform. Both Panthers were released early the next morning.[75]

The next day, eleven African Americans were arrested approximately thirty miles from the campus in the town of Rantoul. Nine of the eleven were suspected members of the Black Panther Party. Arrested on charges of defrauding an innkeeper, theft of services, and conspiracy to defraud an innkeeper were Jeldean Eldridge, a member of the BSA newspaper staff; Ronald Satchel, a former student at Illinois who at the time of the arrest was a Black Panther; and Illinois Panthers Bobby Rush, Fred Hampton, Ted Boston, and William Dunne.[76] Several months later, at 4:45 A.M. on 4 December 1969, the Chicago police stormed the Illinois Black Panther Party headquarters at 2337 West Monroe Street in Chicago. After approximately ten minutes of gunfire, Fred Hampton and Mark Clark, a Panther visiting from Peoria, Illinois, were dead. Both had been visitors on the Illinois campus. Ronald Satchel and Brenda Harris, another former University of Illinois student, were injured in the raid.[77]

Black students at Illinois never created a chapter of the Black Panther Party, yet they were clearly aware of and influenced by the Panthers. Black students often hosted Black Panther visits and attended Panther political orientation classes, they defended both the Panthers and their ideology of Black Power, and several former students recounted years later the influence of Panther ideology and tactics on them as individuals and on the Black student movement in general. Rodney Hammond remembered, "Fred Hampton and what they were doing on the West side of Chicago was very important to me. How that translated on the campus is hard to say other than as contributing more and more to this idea that we can do for ourselves and we can defend ourselves. It was very important even if it meant relinquishing the principle of passivity and non-violence. . . . I felt attached to what Fred [and the Panthers] were doing for the community in Chicago."[78] Fred Hampton's death, in particular, further radicalized Black students. Many had known him as a friend, confidant, and comrade-in-arms in the Black freedom struggle.[79] His murder at the hands of police validated the belief that Black freedom fighters were being gunned down systematically and that the Black community had to consider more aggressive self-defense.

By mid-1968, the confluence of Dr. King's assassination, increasing frustration with power-holders, and events in Chicago pushed Black students at Illinois toward Black Power and resolved some of the tension between protest and academics and between involvement and apathy. More Black students began to come together and work collectively for Black student concerns.

———————

It was in this context that an affirmative action initiative brought more than five hundred Black students to campus in the fall of 1968. The new students not only had to contend with the pressures of attending college and being away from home for the first time but also entered an environment in which continuing Black students encouraged them to place themselves in opposition to the university and question its commitment to Black students. Black activist students found building a campus movement a difficult struggle, but by 1968 they had a well-developed organization, semi-experienced leaders, and a communication network through their campus newspaper. With the arrival of five hundred new Black students, they would have a critical mass for protest possibilities.

3 The Special Educational Opportunities Program

The federal government initiated various policies amid the growing urgency of racial reconciliation in the 1960s. The 1964 Civil Rights Act and the 1965 Higher Education Act were enacted against the backdrop of the Black liberation struggle. Higher education institutions were affected by these federal policies, and many, including the University of Illinois, genuinely believed that universities had an important role to play in alleviating racial injustice and took steps to use their campuses as tools for societal reform. In 1965, President Lyndon Johnson's Executive Order Number 11246 further challenged American institutions to play a role. The executive order provided that government contractors "will take affirmative action to ensure that applicants are employed, and that employees are treated without regard to their race, color, religion, sex, or national origin."[1] Though the order focused on employment, many higher education institutions understood the charge and established similar policies.

With federal financial support and pressure to adopt affirmative action plans and timetables, universities began to develop affirmative action programs. The programs often conflated the groups they sought to recruit, shifting between using such labels as minority students, disadvantaged students, and African American students. The confusion and the fact that African American students usually received the most attention racialized affirmative action programs, which would cause societal consternation in the 1960s as well as forty years later.[2] Universities defended their programs as a two-pronged policy to rectify past racial injustice and to correct present discriminatory practices and conditions. The 4 April 1968 assassination of Dr. King intensified the need for quick action and meaningful progress in race relations. The country, in the throes of an increasingly aggressive Black liberation struggle and the growing unpopularity of the war in Vietnam, worried it would be torn apart at the seams. Immediate steps were necessary to maintain the nation's integrity and public confidence. Administrators at institutions of higher education responded to the sense of urgency and federal government pressure by hurriedly devising affirmative action programs for their campuses.[3]

Illinois administrators had discussed increasing equal educational opportunity and the role of a university in alleviating racial injustice in a report made as early as 1963. Between 1963 and 1968, such program development occupied a large part of the university's time, and administrators employed the two-pronged rationale of past and present wrongs to bolster the programs. Certain campus initiatives never reached fruition, while others were only mildly successful; however, each program marked a gradual move toward affirmative action in admissions. Blacks were the major targets of university initiatives, but never did Illinois restrict affirmative action to Black students. Rather, the university designed programs for disadvantaged students—those from economically and culturally depressed areas and from racially isolated urban high schools.[4] Dr. King's assassination prompted the university to accelerate its efforts. In early May 1968, Illinois announced the creation of the Special Educational Opportunities Program (SEOP), a program to recruit more disadvantaged students, especially Blacks, to the campus. With the aid of BSA and admissions staff, Illinois sought to identify and recruit five hundred students for the program, which came to be known as Project 500.

The SEOP was unique for at least two reasons. One, it was an incredibly ambitious program, and few other universities sought to recruit and enroll such a large number of students so quickly, much less in one year. Two, Black students had an unusual amount of influence on the program. In the early to middle 1960s, students were unimpressed with administrator proposals and programs and often chastised the university for half-hearted efforts regarding equal opportunity. The initiation of SEOP boosted Black student confidence in the administration, though the students remained wary of procedures for recruitment and program development. To calm tensions on campus and because Black students had demonstrated a willingness to recruit Black high school seniors in previous years, Illinois administrators sought the assistance of BSA. Black student volunteers were intimately involved with recruitment and, according to the university administration, deserved kudos for their efforts. Students were not directly involved in other aspects of the SEOP development. For instance, they did not help devise admission requirements or restructure classes. But they did influence other SEOP support programs devised by administrators and faculty, including tutoring and advising services and other support structures. SEOP marked the beginning of a very unique time in student-administrator relations—rarely would students have such an influence on the shape, nature, and direction of a university program.

The Beginnings of SEOP

In late 1963, against the backdrop of the civil rights movement, Illinois administrators and faculty began discussing how to increase the number of Black students. President David Dodds Henry created the University Committee on Human Relations and Equal Opportunity and charged it with preparing an inventory of relevant research, suggesting ways to investigate problems of equal opportunity, and advising university personnel regarding the status of human relations on campus.[5] The committee debated whether its charge included only African American students or the disadvantaged defined more broadly, including those—regardless of race—from economically depressed areas. A focus on African Americans emerged, but the committee steered clear of race-exclusive proposals and remedies.[6] Through the committee's suggestion, a conscious effort to increase substantially the enrollment of Black students became a basic goal for Illinois. In its November 1964 report, the committee cited the monumental underrepresentation of African Americans in "almost all of the status roles and favorable conditions of our relatively affluent and largely white dominated society." In an effort to compensate for "the grievous record of the past and present," both nationally and on the campus, the committee suggested the university reexamine its role in perpetrating oppression. The committee highlighted the low number of African American students, faculty, and employees and pointed to the fact that "the 'public service' to the state to which we are dedicated [has not] been at all focused on the racial problems of the state and its citizens." The committee also suggested Illinois remember and reclaim the historical role of the university as the birthplace for social, cultural, and economic revolutions. The recruitment and retention of more African American students was one means to this end.[7]

The imbalance of minority student enrollment because of discrimination had to be remedied, and the committee urged the university to take an active role: "It is not sufficient simply to affirm the principle of nondiscrimination in all aspects of the university's undertakings. Instead it is urgent to develop an affirmative action program to help overcome handicaps stemming from past inequality so that all shall have equal opportunity to develop their talents to their fullest capacity."[8] The committee suggested expanding the enrollment of "innately able but educationally, socially and economically disadvantaged" students, encouraging those already enrolled to complete their education, and assisting those with the potential to go on to graduate school.[9] Illinois did not propose special admission categories at this time. Instead, the programs would assist those disadvantaged students qualified to enroll and help those already enrolled to graduate at a higher rate.

The faculty generally supported such proposed efforts and pressured the administration to act.[10] The Illinois committee of the American Association of University Professors Committee on the University and Race Relations issued a report regarding its concerns in 1964: "the university cannot escape involvement in this racial crisis, even if it desired such an escape. Our choice then, is not between involvement and non-involvement, but rather between the various kinds of participation that are open to us." The committee expressed concern about the small number of African American students and faculty and pledged to involve itself in university remedies to the situation.[11] One particularly outspoken member of the faculty, W. Ellison Chalmers, agreed with the committee's assessment and challenged the university to be more aggressive in its role to end racial discrimination. Chalmers recognized various university policies as nondiscriminatory; however, he believed the restrictive housing policies of landlords and Greek houses and the Black student perception of extensive discrimination because of formal and informal practices lead to continued racial isolation. Chalmers also lamented the fact that the university had yet to announce a concrete plan to recruit a large number of African American freshmen. In his estimation, "Despite this relatively good record of nondiscrimination, the University's contribution to the adjustment of the racial crisis must be judged to be minimal. . . . For the total problem, as thus stated, we of the University have responded with only an infinitesimal amount of 'affirmative action.'"[12]

When contemplating possible initiatives and answering the critiques by faculty, the university administration was cautious about describing its efforts so it would not alarm Illinois citizens and alumni wary of newly constituted programs for disadvantaged students. President Henry carefully iterated such sentiment in a State of the University address in January 1964: "I am in no way suggesting that we should alter our standards for any student or for any employee. . . . But, as we build ramps for our

physically disabled students, without violating our standards, I believe
that we must offset some of the disabilities arising from racial and social inequality by building psychological and special assistance 'ramps'
for young people who need them."[13]

Increased competition to enroll at Illinois compounded the university's desire to assuage concerns. The baby-boom generation came of age
during the mid-1960s and increasingly sought higher education. The 1964–
65 academic year marked the first time the university had to deny enrollment to several thousand qualified students.[14] Racialization of affirmative
action—Black students perceived as unqualified versus white qualified
students—made the issue even more complicated. The university was very
aware that affirmative action policies could alienate white constituents
who believed their children could not enroll at Illinois because a Black
student received special consideration. Public discontent could damage
a state-supported institution, and the university aggressively sought to explain itself and maintain positive public relations. The university made
it plain that it would not relax admission standards for any student but
would more aggressively seek those who met qualifications.

To monitor university progress toward equal educational opportunity,
the Committee on Human Relations and Equal Opportunity proposed
collecting racial data for all students, a suggestion that coincided with
the 1964 Civil Rights Act mandate to collect such figures. Illinois had
not collected racial data before but began to request such information on
registration forms in 1966. That year, the university counted ninety-three
African American freshmen. The next academic year, it counted fifty-
nine.[15] Beyond satisfying the federal requirement, the committee considered such knowledge necessary to advance the university's interest in
providing opportunities to diverse students. It made clear that the information would be collected after admission and would be used for research
and statistical purposes, not to discriminate against individuals or groups.[16]
The figures—never did Black students amount to more than 1 percent of
the student population—dramatized the small number of Black students
at Illinois and the need for affirmative action in addition to nondiscrimination policies.

In an effort to recruit more students and play its part in solving the
racial problem in the state as well as the nation, Illinois began devising
programs and policies to increase diversity on campus between 1964 and
1966. At first, campus initiatives occurred in isolation. No overarching
university-wide program existed. The College of Education initiated an
undergraduate exchange program with a historically Black college. The
College of Engineering proposed a program to recruit Black graduate stu-

dents. The College of Law created its own equal opportunity fellowship because federal funds were restricted to undergraduates. College deans and directors modified probation and drop rules because "some students whose initial performance was quite low, suddenly began to demonstrate a solid academic capacity—but they were eliminated by the rules."[17] Since many disadvantaged students could not attend college because of financial constraints, the University Foundation sought and provided additional financial resources. Separate campus units initiated a support program for freshmen from disadvantaged areas, including extra counseling, tutoring, and other supportive activity. The Office of Admissions monitored applications of students attending particular inner-city Chicago schools.[18] Despite these efforts, the number of Black students during the mid-1960s remained low. Although Black enrollment was average or above average compared with Black enrollment at other predominantly white universities in the North, Illinois began to examine ways in which to attract Black students more successfully.

Pressure on administrators came not only from faculty but also from white students. In 1964, a group of white students in the Ad Hoc Committee of Students for Human Dignity and Social Peace urged the Committee on Human Relations and Equal Opportunity forward and chastised the university for lip service to educational reform. Black students were not unconcerned about conditions on campus, but they were small in number and had yet to form an organization to act as a conduit for Black student concerns. White students in the ad hoc committee took up the issue and produced a report regarding their doubts about university commitment to defeating racism and discrimination on campus. The report enumerated complaints about the Illini Union's programming policies, the athletic program's treatment of Black athletes, Black students' isolation from the official social life of the campus, and harassment by campus police—grievances corroborated by university audiotaped interviews with students, individual faculty observations, and university-sanctioned research.[19] The ad hoc committee demonstrated a particular interest in the relationship between the campus social atmosphere and academic performance and even cited the 1954 *Brown* decision to support its claim that social inhibitions adversely influenced academic achievement. The students demanded that the university more aggressively attack racism and discrimination on campus and implored it to "end any practice that is considered inconsistent with these policies and tends to produce the resultant hostility that can only fractionalize and separate a community of students."[20] The report, however, did not ask that more Black students be admitted.

Administrators at Illinois were responsive to campus pressure, federal mandates, and the demands of the broader civil rights movement and were sincerely interested in diversifying the campus, improving the campus racial climate, and playing a role in societal reform. In the summer of 1965, Illinois inaugurated an experimental program both to promote equal educational opportunity and to investigate the academic needs of students, particularly Black students, from disadvantaged high schools.[21] Illinois recognized that such students often encountered academic difficulties even though they met university admission requirements—a combination of the student's high school percentile rank, admission test score, and completion of academic subjects prescribed for the curriculum the student wished to enter. Such a record normally predicted satisfactory college achievement, but disadvantaged students regularly received lower grade point averages in college and evidenced more academic difficulties than did other students.[22] Under the auspices of the College of Liberal Arts and Sciences, seventeen Black students and three white students already admitted to Illinois for the 1965–66 academic year attended an eight-week verbal communication course on campus. The summer program provided participants with "intensive guidance, counseling and testing, intended to reveal, and training and teaching, intended to correct or alleviate such deficiencies as might interfere with the successful prosecution of college work."[23] Such deficiencies included physical ailments (hearing loss or astigmatism), lack of basic skills (slow reading pace), and inadequate academic preparation (remedial use of oral or written English). The participants completed questionnaires and interviews during the summer program, and the university charted their progress through their first year at Illinois. Most of the students were enthusiastic about attending Illinois and believed they could succeed academically, and most were described by their teachers and tutors as at least "fair" in their motivation to succeed. Attempting to gauge Black student attitudes toward the university, program organizers asked, "Negro students sometimes will express mixed feelings about the way they're received on a large, predominantly white campus. How do you feel about this university as a place for Negro students?" Most were optimistic or neutral in their attitudes.[24] Unfortunately, these same students encountered a sometimes harsh social and academic reality, one that lead to alienation and academic troubles for many of them.[25]

By mid-December, the end of the summer participants' first semester, the group studying the students came to no definite conclusions about the effects of the summer program "since so much of the students' academic record is still in the future." Their improvement on most measures was unimpressive; however, the students did demonstrate a slight gain in mid-semester academic achievement. The primary benefit of the program was that the university got the opportunity to understand better the academic problems and attitudes of Black students. The university realized that eight weeks was not enough to improve significantly the academic performance of students from disadvantaged high schools. Instead, it suggested recruiting prospective Illinois freshmen during their junior year of high school. It also suggested that future summer programs continue to enroll those students with low-level verbal ability but expand to include those who were highly able but would not attend Illinois without special encouragement and help.[26]

To build on the momentum of the 1965 summer program, the university hurriedly devised programs in subsequent years. In May 1966, President Henry and the Committee on Human Relations and Equal Opportunity solicited assistance in creating a new summer program to begin only two months later, in July. During the 1966–67 academic year, the university offered, under the direction of the dean of women, Miriam Shelden, academic, counseling, and advisory assistance to Black and white freshmen defined as disadvantaged. All Black students were invited to participate. Enrollment for other students was restricted to those with an American College Test (ACT) score under 23 and attendance at a high school at least 80 percent Black. Like the previous summer program, the 1966 program was not an admissions program but a supplemental program for students already admitted to the university under regular admission procedures. It had ninety-one African Americans and thirty-seven whites.[27] The ambitious program encountered various obstacles because of the lack of lead time and the newness of special programs. However, at the end of their first year, 50 percent of program students were in good academic standing, a marked improvement over the 70 percent of disadvantaged freshmen on academic probation in 1963 and 1964.[28]

Shelden and other program organizers recommended the program be continued though in altered form—it should be limited to Black students rather than disadvantaged students and the director of the program should be Black. The restriction of enrollment to Black students in 1967–68 was the university's first foray into race-specific programs. The program organizers justified the move by locating it in other enrollment restrictive programs, "since we have special programs for foreign students and for physically handicapped students, there is justification for a program for Negroes."[29] They also proposed a two-year undergraduate Division of Special Services for those students who met admission criteria but would need additional academic assistance to succeed at Illinois. After two years in the program, students would transfer to regular programs and majors throughout the university. Additional allowances for students included special sections of existing courses, reduced course loads, and extra academic advisement.[30] But the proposal was tabled to allow the new chancellor, Jack Peltason, time to determine the direction of the program.[31]

The appointment of a new chancellor and the upcoming 1967 summer vacation prompted the university to delay making concrete decisions on the future and direction of disadvantaged student recruitment and support services. However, the university took seriously the call to increase the number of Black students enrolled and its own commitment to increase educational opportunities for disadvantaged students. By early 1968, the university was in the process of implementing a program to allow approximately two hundred Black high school seniors to enroll for the 1968–69 academic year, more than doubling the average number of Black freshmen in recent classes. But administrators worried about the culture shock many would experience and the effect it would have on academic performance. A report on the 1966–67 experience had stated, "For most of them, it has been a first exposure to the predominantly white world, and the first encounter with major failure. Because of the times in which we live, these two factors become inextricable entwined, with sobering results."[32] By 1968, administrators understood that aggressive recruitment needed to be paired with support services to promote academic success and adjustment.

The university issued a separate report in March 1968 (known as the Spencer Report for its author, Professor Richard Spencer, head of the Ad Hoc Committee on Special Education) regarding the increase of African American student enrollment and retention. Though both Black and white students admitted to Illinois met admission requirements, the report highlighted the fact that white students regularly outperformed Black students, particularly those Black students from segregated Chicago high schools. Consistent with much of the social science literature at the time, the report followed a cultural deprivation model of African American student problems at Illinois. The report contented that a conflict between "university values and attributes" and "ghetto values" contributed to Blacks' limited academic success and that the Black student would need to "get through a period of unlearning *prior* to his learning a subject matter field untenable to his own culture or language system."[33] To facilitate the academic achievement of disadvantaged students, the report suggested the university alter criteria for academic probation, reduce the freshman course load, and establish counseling and tutorial services. Black students, particularly those from Chicago, would benefit from academic support systems. However, the cultural deprivation model missed the mark on the extent of university reform necessary to make Illinois a much more hospitable and academically rewarding campus. The report located the problems of achievement in Black students, thereby absolving the university from initiating aggressive internal reforms and precipitating only cosmetic changes to the campus.

The Spencer Report, however, did produce target enrollment numbers. The university planned to reserve a specific number of slots for "Negro and culturally deprived students" over the next several years—again, non-Blacks were included in the formula, but Black students would make up the bulk of the program. Enrollment figures would peak at five to six hundred, or 10 percent, of the entering freshman class by 1973. The university reserved half of the slots for regularly admitted culturally deprived students and the other half for students based on "new variables found to be indicative of potential success," including competitiveness, creativity, and letters of recommendation. Four years after the students were enrolled, the university aimed to graduate at least 30 percent of them, equal to the graduation rate of all students. The report acknowledged that the university "at present is not fully capable of meeting these objectives"; hence, the increase would happen in phases from 1969 to 1973. The recruitment effort would not begin in the 1968 academic year.[34]

The university would not be allowed the luxury of time to plan and gradually phase in the program. The 4 April 1968 assassination of Dr. Martin Luther King Jr. made the need for equal educational opportunity immediate and forced the university's hand. As a result of King's death, segments of the campus and community—especially BSA, which by this time had become more visible and vocal—demanded that more African Americans be admitted in the fall of 1968. In 1960, Blacks constituted 10.3 percent of the Illinois population and 5.1 percent of the Champaign County population; by 1970, Blacks constituted 12.8 percent of the state population and 15.2 percent of the county.[35] On the Illinois campus in 1967, they were only 1.1 percent of the student population (223 undergraduates and 107 graduate students, making a total of 330 Black students).[36] Black students became determined to increase their numbers and refused to allow the university or the new chancellor any more time to adjust.

Responding to the urgency created by King's death and public pressure from BSA, faculty, a segment of the white student community, and a newly formed group called Citizens for Racial Justice, Illinois altered its enrollment program.[37] The university's new plan was presented to the public in a news release dated 2 May 1968—less than one month after the assassination and two months after the Spencer Report. Instead of admitting two hundred students, "working in close cooperation with the Black Students Association, the Chancellor announced that substantial efforts will be made to increase the program to hopefully enroll at least 500 students for September 1968."[38] The university used knowledge gained from previous programs to cleave together a new program, and with the support of the board of trustees, SEOP was born. By admitting such a large number of students, SEOP became one of the largest programs initiated by a predominantly white university in attracting low-income Black high school students. Clarence Shelley, the Black director of an economic opportunity program in Detroit, Michigan, was recruited and appointed dean of the program in July.

The university put forth five objectives in implementing SEOP: (1) to provide an educational opportunity for students who may not otherwise have had the opportunity to attend college; (2) to increase the number of minority students on the campus; (3) to develop educational programs and practices to aid the disadvantaged students in their academic careers; (4) to expose non-SEOP students to the cultural and social experiences necessary in understanding different cultures; (5) to develop information to deal successfully with educational and sociological problems affecting students from disadvantaged backgrounds.[39] Since affirmative action programs were new and not wholly accepted, the administration carefully crafted the public face of SEOP and attempted to assuage public concerns. The administration had previously discussed affirmative action in terms of compensation for past discrimination and as a remedy to contemporary discriminatory practices and conditions. In its statements to the public in 1968, the university focused on rectifying current discrimination and the worth of a diverse student body for the entire campus.[40] Further, the university carefully explained that SEOP was predicated on economic disadvantage rather than race and that African Americans would dominate the program only because their economic situation was worse than any other group's. However, public perception was that SEOP was for Black students only—a misperception that would plague the program from its outset.

At the time the university was organizing SEOP, the campus was under siege. It faced aggressive antiwar protests by white students and faculty, legal battles brought by students over free-speech issues, vivid remembrances of the riots across the street from the Chicago branch during the summer of 1966, and Black students' opting out of interracial campus groups in favor of race-exclusive organizations. Many Illinois residents and legislators already believed the university was out of control. The initiation of a special admissions program for disadvantaged (Black) students could lead to a public relations disaster, particularly since the university also faced an increasing number of applications for enrollment, entertained higher admission standards, and had limited space. In a move to justify the program, downplay race, and soothe concerns, the university issued a report discussing the economic and social sense of the program, in which it stated, "Not only will the SEOP students contribute through their trained services to society, they will pay taxes rather than requiring services from public taxes. . . . Their contribution to the state and national income over their years of productive life will far outstrip the relatively low financial investment required to provide them with a college education."[41] The university would have to prove to the public and to campus constituents that SEOP was proper, valuable, and the appropriate way in which the university could play a role in societal improvement.

In particular, the university combated the sentiment that the disadvantaged (Black) students admitted through SEOP were not qualified and that the program would lower standards and take admission slots from qualified (white) students. The university defended itself by explaining that SEOP students would not take the place of qualified students; they were enrolled in *addition* to the usual freshman class instead of filling the special reserved slots described in the Spencer Report. Plus, SEOP students still fit the combination of admission criteria set forth by the university—a strong combination of high school percentile rank, ACT score, and subject pattern requirements—the university only weighted the combination differently by placing less emphasis on the ACT. The university explained the revision of admission criteria by questioning the accuracy of the ACT for students from underprivileged and culturally deprived backgrounds and asserting that the university had always found that high school percentile rank was more predictive of college success than was the ACT anyway.[42] Moreover, the university was only doing what other campuses across the country were doing—diversifying the campus through aggressive recruitment.[43]

University administrators took steps to make SEOP a permanent feature of the campus one year after its initiation and broadened its scope to include retention issues. Students would be allowed five years, rather than the conventional four years, to complete a baccalaureate degree. The university defended the need for SEOP in a broader framework of special programs, preexisting policies of nondiscrimination, and university responsibility in societal reform. Illinois formally legitimized it as an ongoing program in 1969:

Since its inception, the University has provided special programs (in agriculture, for veterans and rehabilitation students, etc.); these programs have been initiated in the belief that a university must be sufficiently flexible to change as society, educational, and student ability change. The request of the Advisory Committee thus merits approval in view of the University's commitment to nondiscrimination, its concern for service to community and state, and its recognition that educational leadership requires, perhaps as never before, re-definition, renewal, exploration, initiative, and tolerance.[44]

The university continued to defend itself and its new program despite the program's tenuous beginnings. But the racialization of the admissions issue would lead to an explosive situation and a public relations disaster in the near future.

Enrollment Issues

To "facilitate the social class mobility of poor and disadvantaged youth," the university broadened its admission policies in admitting the SEOP students.[45] It was not the only time admission standards had been altered at the university, but SEOP was the first time the university created a racially based admission *category* for incoming students.[46] The requirements for SEOP admission reflected the university's faith in a combination of factors for enrollment and included students who met the high school subject pattern requirements for the appropriate college and curriculum and who ranked in the top half of their graduating class; students who met the subject requirements, ranked in the third quarter of their class, and had an ACT score of at least 19; and students who ranked in the bottom quarter of their graduating class and had a composite ACT score of at least 21. Students not meeting the above requirements could qualify for special admission.[47] At the end of registration, approximately 1,300 students had applied to participate in SEOP. Predicting that only two-thirds of high school seniors to whom it extended offers would actually register, the university approved 768 students for admission. However, the university misjudged. Almost three-quarters of those admitted, 565 students, registered. These included 502 freshmen and 63 transfer students.[48] SEOP students constituted approximately 10 percent of the incoming freshman class—a goal the university had not planned to reach until four years later.

True to the university's definition of disadvantaged, not all SEOP students were Black. A small number of white and Puerto Rican students enrolled through the program and constituted approximately 5 percent of the SEOP class. Also, not all Black freshmen were SEOP students. Some were admitted to the university before the initiation of SEOP. In the total group, women slightly outnumbered men, and most students were Illinois residents.[49] Students from outside Illinois were primarily from Holmes County, Mississippi, and Philadelphia, Pennsylvania, though enrollment was restricted to Illinois students in subsequent years. Most SEOP students met SEOP standard admission criteria; 87 percent met the minimum combination of high school rank, test score, and transfer grade point average. The others were admitted on a special admission basis when they were able to offer other evidence of academic success and promise.[50]

As well as filling the academic requirements, the students had to need financial aid to qualify for SEOP admission. For the fiscal year beginning 1 July 1968, the U.S. Department of Health, Education, and Welfare defined disadvantaged students as "Americans of college-going age whose family income and number of siblings, as well as the conditions of his home, school, and community, restrict his opportunities to develop socially, culturally, and economically toward becoming a useful member of society."[51] Students had to qualify for a federal equal opportunity grant (EOG), which meant their family's gross income could not exceed $7,500, or they had to have an unmet need of at least $1,200 in campus expenses.[52] Soon, however, the family income criteria for SEOP qualification changed, partly because of the high number of institutions applying for EOG funds. The federal government initiated a change in award criteria for the 1970 fiscal year as a response to the program's popularity but shrinking budget for higher education. EOGs were to be given first to students from families whose annual gross income was $6,000 or less. Other students would qualify if the number of dependents in the home, combined with the family's gross income, translated into a small family contribution. These guidelines applied only to the initial year of college attendance. The objective for the 1970 fiscal year was to have at least 80 percent of all these initial awards going to freshmen. The remaining grants were distributed among transfer students, sophomores, and juniors. No EOGs were given to seniors.[53]

Other forms of federal, state, and university financial aid were available to Illinois students. Students whose family income met a certain criteria could apply for guaranteed student loans, a creation of the Higher Education Act of 1965, or national defense education loans. Students could repay such loans over approximately ten years at a low interest rate and could wait to repay until they graduated or left school. Students participating in the College Work-Study Program, another creation of the Higher Education Act of 1965, worked part-time during their undergraduate career to defray the cost of college. Those who could not offset the difference between federal financial programs and parental contributions relied on a combination of Illinois state scholarships, tuition waivers, and grants from agencies outside the University of Illinois.[54] The 1968 and 1969 cuts in federal funds severely impaired SEOP efforts, and various campus units made attempts at fund-raising.[55] For instance, the American Association of University Professors solicited faculty contributions for a discretionary fund available to students for emergency purposes, and the Division of Rhetoric sponsored several events, including a bake sale to finance academic services, such as tutoring, and the purchase of supplies.[56] However, many SEOP staff, physical plant, and other resource needs continued to exist.

Both faculty and students participated in other, more coordinated campus fund-raising initiatives. A few faculty volunteers established the Human Resources Investment Fund into which they contributed 1 percent of their salaries to help offset the costs of college for disadvantaged students.[57] A student-initiated fund-raiser was named the Martin Luther King Fund. The fund committee solicited all faculty and graduate students to contribute to the fund "to help their institution do its part to begin to work on a national problem." In its letter to the campus, the committee explained the objectives of SEOP and urged people to contribute to the fund because "extending our facilities to talented people who would otherwise not have a chance to develop their capabilities is nothing more than sensible economic, social, and moral policy."[58] Although the members of the Martin Luther King Fund and the Human Resources Investment Fund made aggressive appeals to the campus community, the contributions were not enough.[59] Despite their efforts, the university continued to operate on a financial-emergency basis.

In October 1968, the university decided to offer four hundred SEOP students admission for the 1969–70 academic year. However, by March 1969, recruitment efforts were halted because of federal cutbacks in financial aid. The university was notified that 40 percent of the requested national defense education loan dollars would not be available. Likewise, 40 percent of the EOG funds had been cut. Without the two primary sources of financial aid used by the 1968 class, the university decided to reduce the number of SEOP participants for 1969. Instead of the original 400, 175 students were sent letters of acceptance by May 1969.[60] An additional 69 were admitted and enrolled for the 1969–70 academic year.[61] The university attributed the decline to shrinking financial aid sources. Administrators encouraged potential students to tap alternative resources, such as Illinois state scholarships and grants from outside agencies, and attempted to increase the resources available through the Martin Luther King Fund.[62]

Black students attributed the decline in numbers to other possibilities. In September 1969, BSA accused the Office of Admissions of discouraging potential students with militant or activist views from applying or rejecting them when they were otherwise qualified. The Office of Admissions responded by stating that it did not concern itself with the political leanings of applicants; the numbers were reduced because of financial aid issues.[63] This climate of distrust affected relations between Black students and administrators for several more years and had implications for future policies and programs initiated by the university.

Though the number of Black freshmen admitted to Illinois continued to vary, SEOP did substantially increase the number of Black students on campus (see table 1, which demonstrates the changing number and percentage of Black undergraduates from 1967, the year before the program, to 1975, two to three years after the first SEOP students graduated). In 1970, Illinois ranked first in the Midwest in Black student enrollment.[64]

Soon after hammering out SEOP admission issues, the university sought to recruit students to participate. During the short month between King's 4 April assassination and the 2 May public announcement of SEOP, Chancellor Peltason met with the BSA executive committee to discuss the need to revise the target numbers presented in the Spencer Report and BSA's involvement in recruitment of the new Black fresh-

Table 1. Black Undergraduate Student Enrollment, 1967–75

	Number of Black Students	Black Students as a Percentage of Total Undergraduates
1967	223	1.0
1968	690	3.0
1969	767	3.2
1970	944	3.9
1971	1040	4.5
1972	1094	4.4
1973	968	3.8
1974	856	3.2
1975	927	3.6

Source: D. J. Wermers, *Enrollment at the University of Illinois by Racial/Ethnic Categories: Fall Terms, 1967–1975* (Urbana: University Office of Academic Policy Analysis, December 1976), 12, obtained from the University Office of Academic Policy Analysis.

men.[65] BSA had been critical of the university, but Black students valued the education they received and were determined to expand the opportunity to others. Also, the university secured a grant from the Ford Foundation for recruiting, counseling, tutoring, and carrying on orientation activities, which was important because the university faced a shrinking budget and had few extra funds to support a large new program.[66] At the same time and with university sanction, BSA invited approximately eighty Black high school seniors from Chicago, East St. Louis, and Holmes County, Mississippi, to the Illinois campus and sponsored tours, discussions, dances, and other activities.[67] In May, after the public announcement of the program, the university solicited high school counselors to identify prospective students and encourage them to apply to SEOP, and it arranged a series of Illinois regional conferences with counselors working in schools with large numbers of disadvantaged students. At the meetings, admission and financial aid applications were distributed, questions answered, and problems discussed.[68] But the administration relied most heavily on BSA recruitment efforts because BSA members had proven themselves committed to the task even before King's assassination and the initiation of SEOP. In February 1968, the university praised their early efforts in a memorandum and foreshadowed the role BSA would play in SEOP recruitment during the summer: "We are highly encouraged by this evidence of interest on the part of a student organization and regard it as a most effective means of recruitment. We shall continue to encourage their efforts and to cooperate in every way. The activities of this group will be an important aspect of the total program of identification and recruitment."[69]

After the public announcement of SEOP, BSA members remained not just involved but pivotal in the recruitment efforts. BSA recruiters believed the university doubted their ability to recruit five hundred Black freshmen and sought to prove the administrators wrong.[70] They valued the opportunity to attend a quality institution and believed the addition of more Black students would help transform the university for the better. Hired as university employees during the summer 1968, BSA recruiters canvassed for prospective students across the nation, especially Chicago, New York, Philadelphia, and downstate Illinois. Recruiters returned to their hometowns and worked in neighborhoods with which they were familiar. The authenticity they were able to bring to their positions—Black undergraduates returning home as representatives of the university—meant they could be trusted by potential students. The university recognized the worth of such status. As a memo stated, "Besides the factual information about admission, these students can answer questions about the University tone from the particular perspective of a student 'telling it like it is.'"[71]

BSA recruiters impressed administrators with their results, particularly in Chicago. After a visit to the BSA Chicago headquarters for SEOP recruitment, administrators commended their organization, dedication, energy, and resourcefulness. BSA had been able to tap so many sources and publicize the program so well that community leaders routinely sought them out and submitted unsolicited names for SEOP consideration. That they took their jobs seriously was obvious to one administrator, who reported, "Apparently, there are two recruiters who are not making a 100% effort. I understand that these recruiters have been severely chastised [by fellow Black recruiters] and told to shape up or get out."[72] BSA efforts also were successful in New York and Philadelphia, hometowns for a few continuing Black students. BSA recruiters were less successful in downstate Illinois and Champaign-Urbana, but they did make a considerable effort. BSA assistance was invaluable in reaching the university goal of five hundred students.[73]

Black graduate students in BSA, with the assistance of the dean of the Graduate College, also played a large role in recruitment efforts through the Black Graduate Recruitment Committee. Black graduate students canvassed historically Black and predominantly white institutions searching for applicants to Illinois graduate programs and often traveled to institutions where they had received their baccalaureate degrees. They arrived on the different campuses with all the necessary materials for application and returned the applications to their Illinois graduate departments for consideration. They then followed up with the academic departments regarding the applicant's status and financial aid package. They were very successful in their efforts and brought a record number of Black graduate students to campus, thereby further increasing the number of Black students at Illinois.[74] In 1967, the university counted 107 Black graduate and professional students, 1.3 percent of the graduate population, but that number conflated African students and African Americans. By 1972, the Black Graduate Recruitment Committee's efforts helped more than triple the number of *African American* students to 345, 3.8 percent of the graduate student population.[75]

BSA recruiters were very proud of their part in the recruitment program, and their leadership role created an investment in the undergraduate SEOP students and the program. They had declined summer jobs with higher pay and had sacrificed the chance to attend summer school in order to help make the program, first, a reality, and second, a success. Their investment in the program translated into a high degree of commitment. Students involved with the SEOP recruitment efforts later described the experience as personally gratifying and exciting. As Yolanda Smith Stanback-Williams, a sophomore at the University of Illinois at Chicago who began as a recruiter but eventually enrolled as an SEOP student at the Urbana campus, put it, "I don't know if this is just a rumor, but they had always told us they had a quota of 100 or less Blacks at U of I Champaign. This particular year, 1968, there were going to be 500 Black faces, and I was going to be a part of it. To me, it was wonderful."[76] The idea that they would play a part in bringing five hundred Black freshmen to campus was tremendous, especially since there had never been five hundred Black students total.

However, the arrival of the SEOP students fostered conflicting feelings in some continuing students. They were excited to receive the new Black freshmen but worried that the label "special," with its connotations of lowered admission standards and financial duress, would be applied to *all* Black students. Some indicated that they had worked hard, had excelled in high school, and had been admitted to Illinois through regular channels and resented the fact that they would be associated with the altered admission standards for SEOP students. Some who came from middle-class households and had a relative who had attended college perceived a distinction between their economic backgrounds and those of the SEOP students, many of whom came from working-class families and often were the first in their families to attend college. The continuing students had ambivalent feelings about the possible tension economic class distinctions would engender and mean for Black student relationships. However, those former students who noted the revised admission standards and the differences in economic background were careful to comment that neither should have precluded the admittance of the SEOP students. Continuing students supported the enrollment of the SEOP students and believed they had a right to attend college.[77]

SEOP students arrived on campus one week before the rest of the student body to attend a week-long, pre-college workshop. Students were housed in Illinois Street Residence Hall (ISR), a popular and relatively new residence hall. One objective of the orientation was to resolve unfinished issues in SEOP student enrollment. The BSA staff's lack of recruitment training and unfamiliarity with Illinois admission procedures caused quite a bit of confusion, as did the fact that some staff members believed they had the sole authority to admit students.[78] Unprepared and understaffed housing and financial aid offices exacerbated the situation. By 7 August 1968, the Office of Admissions had received only 167 acceptance letters from prospective students, and the Housing Office estimated that only a hundred SEOP students would apply for residence hall accommodations.[79] Hugh Satterlee, the new director of financial aid, did not arrive on campus until early September.[80] Other university staff members were on summer vacation, partly because the university had underestimated the number of students in the program and the amount of work it would take to get them enrolled. Attesting to the sometimes haphazard nature of recruitment, many students who arrived for the orientation still had not taken the ACT or the required math diagnostic, reading, rhetoric, biology, or chemistry placement tests used to assign students at different academic levels. Many were still not assigned permanent housing and had to complete housing forms and contracts. Some had not completed the physical examination required by the university prior to enrollment.[81] All such matters were scheduled during their first week on campus.

BSA members assisted in the orientation program's second objective, acclimating the new students to the campus. BSA representatives took seriously their job of introducing the students to the university and the university to the students. BSA volunteers sponsored the welcome session at the orientation, lived and ate meals with the students, conducted tours of the campus, and provided such social activities as bowling, billiards, and dances.[82] BSA members were thrilled to participate. There was not necessarily an overt agenda to politicize the students during the orientation program, but Black Power attitudes were not absent in BSA-SEOP interaction. Continuing students were more concerned with the academic success of the SEOP students than with their extracurricular and social involvement on campus. As BSA's newspaper stated, "BSA has made an effort to get as many 'brothers' here as possible. The task which we must all undertake at this time is to get everyone through."[83] Since social interaction was inevitable, continuing students focused on preparing the freshmen for the academic rigor of Illinois. They warned the incoming students, "Beware, or the Chief will get you, too."

Retention Issues

After the university succeeded in attracting students, it turned its attention to retention issues. The experience of previous Black and disadvantaged students indicated that the SEOP students would encounter academic and social difficulties. The university sought to provide a safety net to ensure that their successful recruitment program would not result in a disastrous attrition rate. The campus braced for this new population of students who were considered less academically fit. Administrators and department heads encouraged faculty to restructure several courses to emphasize "content appropriate to students with scholastic deficiencies."[84] These restructured courses did not make up the bulk of any SEOP student's semester schedule, and the students took a maximum of one or two of such courses at a time.

The Department of Mathematics created Math 101, the purpose of which was to bring students to a level of competence in high school algebra. The department administered a special diagnostic math test as well as the standard math placement exam at the SEOP orientation to determine course placement. Approximately 150 SEOP students were placed in Math 101, while more than 100 enrolled in higher-level courses. Instructors noted that student difficulties stemmed from general problems, including improper organization of time, inefficient study habits, and trouble translating English into mathematical language. To improve their chances for success, Math 101 students attended smaller classes and had optional tutoring services. No special grading procedures were established for the course. "Apparently the SEOP students are proud of the fact that the University is not lowering its standards for them but rather providing them with an opportunity to compensate for the lack of an adequate mathematics background," a report noted.[85] Students who succeeded in Math 101 advanced to upper-level math courses.

After examining records of pre-SEOP Black students in the standard introductory psychology course, Psychology 100, and discovering a high percentage of unsatisfactory grades, the Department of Psychology developed a new course, Psychology 105, which attempted to address the needs of Black students. The primary difference was that the standard course was taught as a lecture course with approximately 350 students, while the SEOP sections had approximately fifteen to twenty students each, with time allowed for discussion. Also, the Psychology 105 course included topics of "particular interest to black students." Many students expressed misgivings about the course when they realized it was composed of only SEOP students. They worried that they were being placed in a remedial course and given an easier academic load. However, many chose to remain in the course when instructors explained that the exact same psychological concepts and theories were taught in Psychology 105 and the standard introductory psychology course. Many instructors were impressed by their SEOP students. According to a progress report, "Students in Psychology 105 are less inhibited, ask more questions, and seem to become excited about learning. . . . The instructors find that their students' responsiveness stimulates them, creating a more dynamic classroom atmosphere than is typical of a Freshman psychology class." As with the introductory math course, standard grading practices were used.

And, again, the instructors were impressed with their SEOP students and believed that the students would encounter "no exceptional difficulties during their course of study at the university."[86]

Approximately 330 SEOP students enrolled Rhetoric 101, designed by the Division of Freshman Rhetoric to assist disadvantaged students. The course was established "to deal specifically with atypical writing problems arising from inadequate preparation in secondary schools." The SEOP rhetoric objectives were the same as the standard freshman rhetoric, but the teaching method differed. While standard rhetoric classes were based on a comparison between individual student writing and professional writing found in textbooks, SEOP rhetoric classes focused on the student's own writing and stressed content rather than form. The Division of Freshman Rhetoric also created a writing laboratory where tutors assisted students who had writing problems. Students could attend the laboratory two hours a week and receive one hour of credit for the course. Again, instructors were impressed with the SEOP students' "vitality, enthusiasm, . . . and desire to learn." SEOP students received no special grading consideration, and their instructors predicted their success in further rhetoric courses. Most students did not object to being placed in the SEOP rhetoric, but, a report noted, "they want to learn what all the other sections are learning, keep up with them, and be expected to produce the same quality of work. Their main concern is that they are being shown favoritism as a precaution against their 'flunking-out'; most students resent this and want to be challenged to find out what their potential actually is." At the end of the first semester, the experimental rhetoric class was described as a success by both students and instructors.[87]

In the College of Education, all SEOP students enrolled in the Alternative Teacher Education Program (ATEP). In ATEP, students received first-year classroom experience in a local school rather than fourth-year exposure, as was typical for education majors. Their first two semesters of coursework included participant-observation in a local school, a foundations of education course, physical education, rhetoric, and another academic subject. Students also met with faculty in small groups to devise curriculum materials, discuss teaching pedagogy, and link their experience in the local schools to educational theory. Seventy-eight SEOP students (seventy-seven Black and one white) and twenty regularly admitted students (ten Black and ten white) participated. No additional salaries were paid to professors teaching ATEP courses; all volunteered to work on a course overload basis. Though faculty noted deficient writing skills and study habits, they agreed that the outcomes of the program were largely positive. Students particularly enjoyed the close working relationship with professors, graduate assistants, and public school teachers. The public school administrators and teachers were impressed with the students, and all asked to remain in the program for a second year, although they did note that the students' enthusiasm often exceeded their competence.[88] ATEP became known nationwide, and requests for information on the program were received from across the country from academics interested in improving teacher education.[89]

The SEOP courses were successful to a large extent, but a few administrators saw cause for concern. Too often course offerings were spotty and hastily conceived. Because SEOP was devised and implemented so quickly, problems were inevitable. The university had to turn its attention to anticipating future problems and programmatic planning. As an assistant dean of the College of Liberal Arts and Sciences, the college in which most of the SEOP courses existed, stated, "We cannot afford to muddle along, meeting crises with ad hoc solutions forever." He further questioned the commitment of individual departments in supporting SEOP aims and goals: "It is all too easy to believe that because one has set up a special course or provided departmental tutors that one has discharged one's responsibility."[90] The university had taken a large and bold step in devising SEOP, but it had underestimated the difficulties in making the program coherent. A class here and a tutor there did not go far enough. The university had to be more proactive about creating a comprehensive program.

The university created support services beyond the restructured courses in an effort to address the students' academic problems more holistically, but university efforts sometimes met with mixed results. For instance, the Tutoring Office was created to assist SEOP students in a variety of academic subjects. Students having academic difficulties could make an appointment to see a tutor, usually a graduate student or an undergraduate taking the same course. At one point, there were nine hundred tutors, far exceeding the demand.[91] However, the number of tutors did not translate into success for the program. Approximately half of the SEOP students were assigned tutors in their first semester, and about half that number participated during the second semester. Only one-third of those participating during the fall were reassigned tutors in the spring; the rest were new participants.[92] Administrators were enthusiastic about the Tutoring Office and remained committed to it, but they were distressed because Black students did not seem to appreciate their efforts.

The university hired graduate students as graduate assistants to monitor student academics, finances, and social adjustment. Many of the graduate assistants were Black. Since there were not enough Black graduate students in 1968 or 1969 to fill the demand, white graduate students filled the positions.[93] Graduate assistants met with the student every two weeks to discuss problems and solutions and to give advice. The graduate assistants received instructor evaluations, progress reports, and absence notices to better serve the SEOP students.[94] Many SEOP students resisted. They did not have a problem with Black graduate assistants, but some SEOP students resented having to report to white graduate students regarding their academic work and social adjustment.[95] One administrator noted, "At times, there appears to be an almost suicidal determination to make it on one's own. . . . Perhaps it is a matter of black pride; perhaps it is a matter of distrust of us; perhaps it is an unwillingness to cooperate with an establishment which has been less than kindly disposed toward them in the past."[96] He observed that their resistance often had dire consequences in the form of academic failure, and he and others attempted to devise ways to make the system more beneficial and productive. Black students did take advantage of university-initiated tutoring and advising programs and benefited from them in important ways, but many looked to fellow Black students for academic guidance and support.

Interpreting Black student resistance to university support as suicidal determination or Black pride missed the mark for many Black students. The fact that Black students did not take greater advantage of university-sponsored programs did not mean they considered their college efforts to be individual endeavors or that they allowed Black Power ideology to interfere with their academics. Black students were well aware of their inferior Chicago high school education and what that would mean at Illinois. They knew that tutoring was important and necessary for their academic success. CORE had initiated a tutoring service as early as 1966, and Black students continued the practice through the first years of SEOP.[97] Although the pairing of tutor and tutee was a much less formal process than that of the Tutoring Office, Black students considered the informal tutoring network a success. In part, Black students gravitated to the informal network because it did not come with patronizing overtones and a cultural deprivation notion of their academic difficulties, a feature of some university initiatives crafted as a result of the Spencer Report. An extra benefit was the camaraderie a study group could provide. Black students used the time to discuss complicated concepts, complete homework assignments, and prepare for exams away from the critical eye of the university.

Black students also developed their own advising system called BSA Partners. Upper-class students kept in contact with a small group of SEOP students to make sure they received proper academic assistance and to help them adjust to college life.[98] The arrangement felt more like a concerned friendship than a probationary program. Black departmental organizations also performed the role of adviser. Such groups as the Black Pre-Law Club, the Association of Black Engineering Students, and the Black Architectural Students Association fulfilled academic and social needs.[99] Older students used the organizations to equip their ill-prepared peers with vital information and strategies for success. Bolstered by the knowledge gained at organizational meetings, Black freshmen and sophomores returned to classrooms with important scholastic information as well as a renewed spirit and sense of confidence.

These academic and social support programs initiated by the university and Black students had a positive influence on SEOP students. Although studies found that regularly admitted students outperformed SEOP students and that SEOP students took an average of two semesters longer to graduate, SEOP students outperformed pre-SEOP students.[100] Black students arriving at Illinois before SEOP attributed their low success rates to a lack of academic assistance and isolation on campus. Before 1968, few support programs for Blacks existed. Paul Brady remembered, "When I walked in there they told me, 'Look on both sides of you. That person is not going to be here at the end.' They told everybody that."[101] With the academic support systems devised by the university and Black students, the SEOP students were able to get a handle on their studies. Also, the 1968 influx of Black students allowed for a cohort of peers. They now had friends with whom to study, attend class, and unwind. As the university had hoped, by 1973, approximately one-third of the SEOP students graduated.[102] Of the students who did not graduate, 15 percent later returned to Illinois to complete their degrees, and 27 percent transferred to other institutions to pursue their studies.[103] Both administrators and Black students considered SEOP a worthwhile undertaking and a successful beginning to affirmative action at Illinois.

The university, however, got more than it anticipated with the influx in Black students. It initiated SEOP to increase Black representation on campus—and it succeeded—but, as a consequence, the late 1960s call for Black Power also was magnified on the campus. The addition of more than five hundred Black students meant they no longer *hoped* for anything; instead they *demanded* everything. The SEOP arrival and the confusion caused by the program's short life span, combined with the newly elected and more aggressive BSA executive council in May 1968, fueled the Black student movement that significantly influenced the nature of higher education reform at Illinois.

David Addison, president of
the Black Students Association,
1968–69. (Courtesy of Illini
Media Company)

Black Power poster. (From the
Illio, 1972; courtesy of Illini
Media Company)

Black students
being loaded
into a police van
after their arrest
on 10 September
1968 for an
"alleged unau-
thorized mass
demonstration"
at the Illini
Union.
(Courtesy UPI /
Telephoto)

Students leaving Memorial Stadium, where they were taken
following their arrest for mob action on 10 September 1968.
Some 250 were arrested, filling the county and city jails and
forcing officials to use the football stadium to process the
students. (Photo by Robert Arbuckle; courtesy of the *News-
Gazette)*

Dean Clarence Shelley and Black students. (From the *Illio*, 1971; courtesy of the Illini Media Company)

Clarence Shelley, director
of SEOP. (From the *Illio*, 1971;
courtesy of Illini Media
Company)

Robert Eubanks,
faculty adviser for the
Black Students Asso-
ciation, 1967–68;
chair of the Faculty-
Student Commission
on Afro-American
Life and Culture,
1969; and interim
director of the Afro-
American Studies
Commission, 1970.
(Photo by Illini Stu-
dio; courtesy of Harry
Hilton)

Chancellor Jack Peltason. (From the *Illio*, 1972; courtesy of Illini Media Company)

Miriam Shelden, dean of women. (From the *Illio*, 1971; courtesy of Illini Media Company)

Black Students Association residence hall representatives. (From the *Illio*, 1971; courtesy of Illini Media Company)

Terry Townsend, Black Students Association member. (From the *Illio*, 1971; courtesy of Illini Media Company)

Tony Zamora, director of the Afro-
American Cultural Center, 1970–71
(From the *Illio*, 1971; courtesy of
Illini Media Company)

Black student meeting. (From the *Illio*, 1972; courtesy of Illini Media
Company)

Coalition of Afrikan People demonstration. (From the *Illio*, 1975; courtesy of Illini Media Company)

4   The Launching
of a Movement

The new SEOP students, like many beginning freshmen, eagerly anticipated the start of the academic year. The continuing students were excited to see their new recruits and ready to get them acclimated to campus. SEOP students and BSA volunteers lived together in Illinois Street Residence Hall (ISR), a highly coveted residence hall, during SEOP orientation week. Though placement tests occupied much of their time, the week spent together fostered a sense of closeness and cohesiveness. The initial intent was not to politicize the SEOP students, but together the new and continuing students would have a baptism by fire a full week before classes began. Disputes over housing arrangements and financial aid packages erupted 9 September 1968, the first day of New Student Week, and ended in a mass arrest of Black students. The arrest energized BSA and validated the organization's call to close ranks. Previously a small group of students, BSA became a major force for change on campus. Although not all Black students participated in BSA and BSA rhetoric alienated some potential allies, the arrests galvanized most of the Black student population and inaugurated the Illinois Black student movement.

Prior to September 1968, Black students created structures that would enable them to maintain coordinated protest, including a well-developed organization, experienced leaders, and communication networks.[1] On 15 May 1968, BSA held its second official election and elected graduates and undergraduates, men and women to the executive committee. The involvement of graduate students, most of whom had attended historically Black colleges in the South for their baccalaureate degrees and had either watched or participated in the southern civil rights movement, helped BSA become more savvy in its protest tactics and its negotiations with the administration. The spontaneous protest on 9 September created conditions through which Black students would aggressively disrupt the social order at Illinois and demand institutional reform. However, the arrests proved a double-edged sword. On one hand, they invigorated the Black student population, and BSA issued a list of demands for institutional reform. On the other, the arrests precipitated a backlash against Black students and SEOP. Illinois residents, campus constituents, and legislators demanded harsh punishments for the arrested students and indicted them for tarnishing the name of the university. The verbal attacks on Black students made the need for Black student unity even more urgent, and BSA sought to provide a working definition of Blackness. At times the definition became incredibly restrictive and created strife among Black students on campus. BSA recognized the dangers of a narrow understanding of what it meant to be Black, but the organization believed the need for unity in the face of attacks outweighed the need for a fluid definition even if the organization's rhetoric alienated potential Black student allies. By the end of the spiral of effects, the arrests would have a far-reaching influence on personal and institutional levels.

The Arrests

As indicated in chapter 3, a state of total confusion existed when the SEOP students arrived on campus. Miscommunication between BSA members and recruits exacerbated the fact that the university was unprepared for the number of students that would enroll through SEOP. The result was that many arriving students had not taken the appropriate tests for college admission or course placement, did not have room assignments because of incomplete housing paperwork, and were awaiting news of their financial aid status. Administrators assured students that the remaining housing and financial aid issues would be resolved during New Student Week or the first few weeks of school and encouraged the students to focus on such matters as course selection, registration procedures, the activities of New Student Week, and books for their classes.[2] On the last day of orientation, Saturday, 7 September, administrators instructed the SEOP students to move out of ISR and into their permanent room assignments in the residence halls across campus. The general student body was arriving for the beginning of the academic year, and many would be moving into their assigned rooms in ISR.

A sense of Black student camaraderie alleviated some of the tension produced by the academic, financial, and housing uncertainties. BSA members and SEOP students began to form a community during their orientation week on campus. The excitement of the continuing students cannot be overstated. Many longed for expanded friendship opportunities and remembered a time when they would not see another Black student during an entire day and would have to bid friends farewell because they could not academically compete. That they had helped increase the Black student population buoyed their spirits. Together with their recruits, they spent an entire week on campus prior to the arrival of the general student body, which meant that Illinois felt like a Black college campus to many students. SEOP recruits also reveled in the environment. They worried about the examinations they had to complete, but they thoroughly enjoyed the attention they received and their opportunity to attend the university. As the SEOP orientation week came to a close, Black students were optimistic about the upcoming academic year but worried about how to maintain the sense of cohesiveness and community fostered during orientation.

Before removing their belongings from ISR, many SEOP students surveyed their permanent rooms in other residence halls. A number of female SEOP students were dissatisfied with the size and condition of their permanent rooms. Others were told they did not have a permanent room assigned yet and would be placed in hall lounges until space could be found. After discussing their grievances with one another, approximately twenty Black women refused to remove their luggage from their rooms at ISR and vowed to stay until some satisfactory conclusion had been reached. Yolanda Smith Stanback-Williams, a transfer student from the University of Illinois at Chicago who began as a recruiter for the program, described her reaction, "After leaving ISR and going to my assigned room, I opened up the door to the room and it was a closet. Then they said I had a roommate. . . . I didn't like my little cubbyhole, and I started raising hell about it."[3] Also, many SEOP students were informed that the financial aid packages offered them (perhaps prematurely by BSA recruiters) were nonexistent and that they would have to apply for a loan or work to offset college costs. Housing staff, SEOP director Clarence Shelley, and David Addison, the new BSA president who was a law student and a former SNCC worker in the South, met with approximately seventeen dissatisfied female students on 7 September to discuss their concerns. Another meeting with additional housing staff was scheduled for the next day. The women remained in ISR that night.[4]

On the evening of 8 September, the housing staff and female students met in ISR, and the women drafted a list complaints about their room assignments. The women objected to being assigned temporary housing in lounges and the condition of their permanent rooms. They also wanted the opportunity to live with the roommate of their choice. Arnold Strohkorb, director of housing, described the meeting as constructive until Yolanda Smith (now Stanback-Williams) arrived. At that point, she took control of the meeting and explained that the Black women deserved better housing to compensate for their disadvantaged backgrounds. She declared that Black Illinois residents had been paying taxes to support the University of Illinois for years without representation on campus, and it was time for Black students to reap the benefits. Housing staff attempted to explain that the university regularly experienced an overflow in housing and that, regardless of ethnicity, it was common for several students to be placed in hall lounges until permanent rooms could be found. The women rejected the administration's explanation and demanded they be immediately placed in permanent and adequate rooms for the academic year. Administrators were aware that regularly assigned students had arrived to claim their rooms but believed that removing the Black women would take physical force. They were not willing to take such action. Instead, they moved the regularly assigned students into other rooms. Nineteen Black female students remained in ISR that night to protest their room assignments.[5]

The next day, housing staff, Shelley, and the Black female students met in ISR to further discuss complaints and to find the students permanent living quarters. Administrators presented the women with a list of available rooms. The women found certain rooms acceptable but realized that one of their demands—that they be able to choose their own roommate—was not met because some of the available rooms already had an occupant. They rejected all rooms in an effort to remain a cohesive group and announced that they would unpack and remain in ISR for the entire year. Administrators tried to calm the students and assure them that the housing staff would continue to work toward a solution, but they told the women that if they did not vacate their rooms by 2:00 P.M. the next day, they would face disciplinary action and not be able to register for classes. In a letter hastily drafted late that evening and meant to be distributed the next day, 10 September, John Briscoe, vice chancellor for administrative affairs, told the women that they were jeopardizing the status and success of SEOP. He further warned, "If you are seriously interested in an education, we want to work with you in a spirit of cooperation. If instead, you insist upon making your own rules and dealing through group force and disruption without regard for the rights of others, then this institution will have no place for you."[6] The letter never reached the students. Before the end of the evening, many were in jail, and SEOP was under heavy scrutiny.

As the number of Black students assembled in ISR grew, BSA members arrived to assess the situation and participate. The students moved from ISR to outside the Illini Union at approximately 9:00 P.M. The large group, estimated at between 100 and 150 at the time, attracted attention. Other Black students and Black community residents joined the crowd, where they were informed of the confrontation between the Black women and university administrators. Though clearly agitated, the students remained calm. Fatefully, it began to rain, and the students were forced inside, where they congregated in the South Lounge of the Illini Union. Wary of such a large group of Black students, Illini Union staff contacted administrators and advised some sort of intervention. At midnight, while most students remained in the lounge, a group of administrators met with the BSA officers, who had adjourned to the BSA office on the third floor of the Illini Union to discuss a course of action. BSA officers reiterated the female students' complaints, described the financial aid situation as unacceptable, and demanded that Chancellor Jack Peltason come and address their grievances.

After the meeting with the BSA officers, university administrators went to the South Lounge to address the group at 12:30 A.M.—half an hour after the Illini Union's closing time. Administrators explained that they were doing everything possible to remedy the situation, but the students refused to leave en masse. With rumors of property damage, theft, and physical assaults on white passersby, administrators decided that it would not be safe for the chancellor to come to the Illini Union and continued to try to reason with the students. By 2:00 A.M., a few students had gone home, but most remained for a variety of reasons, not all of which had to do with political consciousness and a desire to confront the university. Many students chose to stay for the sake of unity and to support the women protesting their room assignments. Some of the women were afraid to walk home so late at night and doubted they could get in their residence halls after curfew. When rumors of a growing police presence spread, many students reported they were afraid they would be injured by billy clubs and dogs if they left the security of the lounge. Some actually thought the chancellor was going to arrive at any minute to address the group. Others were not aware of the fact that they were violating university regulations by remaining in the Illini Union after closing hours. Some students remembered being coerced into staying by BSA members, nonstudents, and older students. Some students simply were asleep. By

3:00 A.M., it was apparent that most students had resolved to remain in the Illini Union, for whatever reason, until some action was taken on the part of the administration.[7]

Meanwhile, several administrators and staff were gathered at the Student Services Building, one block from the Illini Union. Shelley remembered that "they were trying to decide what to do, arrest them, make them leave, or let them sit all night until they got tired."[8] It was established that the students had violated university regulations by remaining in the Illini Union after closing, but the reports of property damage and attacks on white students precipitated their decision to arrest the students. The decision was not an easy one, but Chancellor Peltason remembered feeling compelled to take action: "As much as one hates to call the police the alternative was to let them stay there for a week. Then the State will be breathing down our neck, the program will be in trouble, and everybody will say, 'you shouldn't have done it.' So, let's clean it up."[9] At 3:03 A.M., ninety Urbana, Champaign, state, and university police were called to the scene. The police moved in quickly, and the students, after being assured they would not be injured, left peacefully. By the early morning hours of 10 September 1968, the Illinois campus was inaugurated as the scene of the first student "riot" of the 1968–69 academic year. Almost 250 Black students were arrested on counts of mob action and were charged with "being an inciter, leader or follower of an alleged unauthorized mass demonstration."[10] Nineteen were continuing students, three were SEOP transfer students from the University of Illinois at Chicago, but most, 218, were SEOP freshmen. All students were released from jail on bond, with considerable help from the Champaign-Urbana Black community—concerned community residents guaranteed the bonds of the students who did not have the money to post it themselves.[11]

The arrests terrified many SEOP and continuing students. Many were Black Power advocates, but they wanted to get a college education, not simply spread Black Power principles to central Illinois. The whole incident left many students in a state of disbelief and completely stunned. They had been on campus only one week, and the beginning of the academic year was still one week away when they already had been arrested, charged with mob action and unlawful assembly, faced legal hearings, and confronted the possibility of being dismissed from the university and sent home.

Some SEOP students believed they were being used as pawns in a conflict between BSA and the administration. "The leadership of BSA felt they had been hung out to dry and they didn't want to look bad in front of their constituents. The University wasn't about to give on anything. You had these two forces come together and the students got caught in the middle," one former student remembered.[12] The SEOP students were new to campus and were unfamiliar with the existing tension between BSA and the administration. They went to the Illini Union to show support for their fellow SEOP students, not for a mass demonstration. However, BSA saw the large number of new Black students as a possible source of strength in dealing with the university and attempted to use them as a tool of intimidation. The university refused to be coerced, and the unwitting students were arrested.

News of the 9 September 1968 incident spread across the country. The headline in the *New York Times* read "Classes to Begin at U. of Illinois: Tension Pervades Campus after Monday's Protest"; in the *Wall Street Journal*, "Black Student Revolt: Colleges' Bid to Enroll 'Disadvantaged' Brings Problems and Protests; Feeling Strange at Illinois"; in the *Los Angeles Times*, "College Plan for Negroes Passes Test; But 'Project 500' at Illinois U. Meets Obstacle"; in the *St. Louis Globe-Democrat*, "300 Negro Students Charged in U of I Row"; in the *St. Louis Post-Dispatch*, "Illinois University Officials Meet Negro Group's Housing Demands"; and in bold letters in the local campus newspaper, the *Daily Illini*, "Blacks Occupy Illini Union."[13] The articles chronicled the goals of SEOP, the students' arrival on campus, the fact that whites were barred from the South Lounge where the Black students met to discuss their grievances with the administration, the vandalism of the Illini Union, and the number of Black students arrested.

The *Chicago Tribune*, under the headline "Negroes Riot at U of I; Negroes Go on Rampage after Row," painted a particularly vivid but grossly incorrect picture of the student sit-in. The article described "the wave of violence" and the "rampage" precipitated by the Black women's refusal to leave ISR. Citing police officials, the article estimated the damage at $50,000, a figure far exceeding official estimates. The newspaper also falsely represented the financial assistance SEOP students received, which increased resentment toward SEOP participants: "The students, most of them Negroes from Chicago and East St. Louis—but some of them from as far away as Philadelphia—were to receive free tuition and free room and board."[14] A *Tribune* editorial published the same day corroborated the article's representation but went further, using racist imagery to describe the sit-in. The editorial described how "black students and outside supporters went ape" and "swung from chandeliers in the lounges of the beautiful Illini Union." Declaring such behavior unconscionable, the editorial lamented that these "slum products" responded to the benevolence of the university and Illinois taxpayers "by kicking their benefactors in the groin."[15]

Some Illinois administrators aggressively attacked the *Tribune,* long considered a conservative newspaper, for its recklessness. David Eisenman, a former Illinois student, SEOP staff member, and Martin Luther King Fund organizer, aggressively sought to correct misinformation about the incident and went so far as to contact a professor at Harvard University about a piece the professor had written that included reference to the incident. "The *Tribune's* 'coverage,'" Eisenman wrote, "was very effective: most people in Illinois still think that 200 rampaging black savages sacked the Union after being given a 'free ride' at the University—a ride at taxpayer expense, barring 500 deserving sons and daughters of the middle class from attending the University of Illinois. If scholarly articles are perpetuating this gross and costly fiction, I shall be very discouraged."[16] Eisenman's concerns were well founded, and the media attention garnered Illinois even more unwanted publicity than it previously received. University administrators were compelled to issue damage control statements as news of the incident spread.

The Illinois state legislature worried about both the image and the sanctity of the university and took cues from other states' dealings with student protest on public campuses. On 24 July 1968, less than a month before the arrests, the Illinois senate passed a resolution "that the presidents of our institutions of higher learning in this State, continue to take immediate and decisive measures to discipline any student who disrupts the orderly conduct of the educational function; and that such discipline include the expulsion of students in appropriate cases and the forfeiture of all privileges granted by the institution."[17] White student protests precipitated the resolution, but Black students would be the ones to put the university to the test. State senators and representatives contacted President David Dodds Henry about their concerns and implored him to maintain order. Senator Karl Berning wrote him about an article in *Time* that carried a statement to the effect that the university had agreed to accept five hundred students in SEOP each year for four years. According to the senator, such a move would be unwise, particularly since the university had not demonstrated it was ready to handle such a large group of Black students, as evidenced by the demonstration and arrests. President Henry responded and assured the senator that the numbers cited in the *Time* article were incorrect but reaffirmed the university's commitment to SEOP.[18] Senators Paul Stone and E. R. Peters and the university's most vocal critic, Representative Charles Clabaugh, also discussed the consequences of the arrests. Clabaugh predicted state intervention if President Henry did not take immediate and punitive steps to regain control of the campus. The other senators registered concern but left the university to deal with university business.[19]

The university defended SEOP and addressed the concerns of the legislators as well as contributors to the Martin Luther King Fund, alumni, and tax-paying citizens of Illinois.[20] The highest ranking administrators were involved in the damage control. Chancellor Peltason confirmed that a disruptive and coercive mass demonstration occurred and that approximately $4,000 worth of damage was done—a much smaller figure than the *Tribune*'s estimate—but he refused to call the incident a riot. He and others accused the media of exaggerating the incident and unnecessarily alarming Illinois citizens.[21] President Henry refused to justify the behavior of the guilty students but added that "it would be grossly unfair to the Project 500 students who were not involved, and to some who were . . . to evaluate the Special [Educational] Opportunities Program through an assessment of the events of September 9, 1968."[22] The board of trustees issued a similar statement. It applauded the creation and purpose of the program and advocated similar programs for the future, but it condemned "acts of violence, disruption and interference with the rights of others [as] wholly antagonistic to the spirit and purpose of the University of Illinois."[23] However supportive these statements, university administrative efforts to dispel rumors were spotty.[24] The general public instead relied on skewed media reports of the incident and grew more angry and frustrated with the university.

The parents of the arrested students also had to be allayed. Some parents were furious their children involved themselves in such a protest. Many reminded their children that they were the first in their families to have the chance to attend college. That their children would not embrace such an opportunity and would be arrested was an outrage. SEOP director Clarence Shelley remembered heated confrontations between parents and students in his office. Parents arrived on campus and demanded to know why their child participated, and their child's plea to higher principles sometimes fell on deaf ears.[25] Edna Lee Long-Green recounted how she called home to explain that the university was "denying the Black students their rights" and that she planned to protest. Her mother was less than understanding and reminded her daughter that she was sending her money to attend classes, not to protest.[26] Such parental attitudes did not necessarily reflect passivity or accommodation. Parents rightfully worried about the environment in which their children were now living and the consequences of their actions. Conversely, students rightfully worried about parental opinions of their participation in protest, particularly since the consequences could send them back home before attending even one class. Anticipating their concerns, Shelley sent a letter to all SEOP parents. He assured them that legal assistance would be provided, that all students were permitted to register and attend classes as scheduled, and that the university maintained confidence in SEOP and was dedicated to it.[27] The efforts calmed some parents, but they remained concerned about the sentencing of the students.

The arrests caused a backlash against SEOP on campus and in the community as well. Letters to the editor in the *Daily Illini* and the *News-Gazette,* the local newspaper, chastised the SEOP students for their actions. One of the women who was kept from her room in ISR by protesting women SEOP students described her encounter with the Black women as hostile and wondered why "the privileged 500" thought they automatically deserved the covetous room assignments in ISR. She then asked, "Are these the 'culturally deprived' for whom I contributed $10 to the Martin Luther King Fund?" She speculated that the Illini Union incident "may turn many people against the entire Project 500."[28] Her sentiment was echoed in other letters and articles following the incident. One article in particular, though undoubtedly overestimating the situation, suggested that the Illini Union incident would "probably even have an impact on the November Presidential elections, with George Wallace gaining votes," would lead other institutions to decide against initiating similar affirmative action programs, and would make fund-raising for future affirmative action programs virtually impossible.[29] An even more hostile letter sent to Shelley called the students "black apes," "black pigs," "dregs of society," and "hoodlums."[30] Appalled by the damage to the Illini Union and the nature of the sit-in, both of which were exaggerated in the press, many people recommended harsh sentences for those students involved. One suggested, "It's about time you college officials start cracking some heads, as that is what is wrong with this country."[31] The tone of many critics revealed an assumption that SEOP students should be grateful for their opportunity to attend such a prestigious institution, and many could not fathom why the "underprivileged students" would come to campus and not gladly accept their new status. One article warned the university that if it did not properly and adequately punish those arrested, "the prospects for order and peaceful protest during the 1968–69 academic year on the UI campus are dim."[32]

Defense of the arrested students came from many directions. Black alumni in Chicago organized the Concerned Alumni of Illinois to support them. Led by Chicago aldermen A. A. Rayner and William Cousins Jr., the group requested a meeting with Dean Shelley and Chancellor

Peltason and sponsored a rally in Chicago to support the students. They did not defend the damage done to the Illini Union, but they did support the students' grievances and were interested in the kind of disciplinary action that would be taken against them.[33] Various white student groups supported the Black students and often offered assistance. The National Students Association sent a telegram to Illinois students decrying police conduct on the night of the arrest: "The National Students Association pledges legal assistance and advice to the students involved. . . . We are ready to continue the struggle against the use of such police tactics in the educational environment."[34] In a letter to faculty, the University of Illinois Graduate Student Association made a veiled threat of violence if students were dismissed.[35] Many white students also rallied around the arrested Black students. According to the *Daily Illini*, Peace and Freedom Party members circulated a petition during a rally to support the arrested Black students and collected approximately seven hundred signatures. Speakers at the rally included Black and white students, faculty, and a church pastor.[36]

Meanwhile, BSA put its own spin on the arrests in order to defend itself. In their newspaper, *Drums*, and in a policy statement meant for the university community, they placed blame squarely on the university, charged the university with acting in bad faith, and accused certain administrators of deliberately sabotaging the program. The special edition of *Drums* addressed itself to the *Tribune* article and sought to correct misinformation. First, BSA identified financial aid issues as the crux of the problem rather than the housing issues publicized by the press. Second, it retraced the establishment of SEOP and identified problems in the university's bureaucratic machinery that precipitated and justified the sit-in. Third, it emphasized that the protest was nonviolent and registered its resentment of how the sit-in was portrayed.[37] BSA also addressed the issue of student versus community involvement in the destruction of property on 9 September—all reports from administrators and students pointed to a handful of Champaign-Urbana residents as the perpetrators.[38] BSA refused to "divide its loyalty" and "rat out" community members who participated in the destruction. It assured administrators that "all actions taken by participants in the confrontation were collective actions," and it presented a "united front against the racist bungling, intentionally halfhearted and lackadaisical attitudes" of the university.[39]

However united and strong a front BSA attempted to display, this posture did not represent or reflect the thoughts of all Black students, including some of those who identified themselves as participants in Black Power. Students were appalled by the destruction of property and did not want to be associated with such behavior regardless of cries for group unity. Others indicated they were afraid to identify the members of the community who caused the destruction because of possible reprisals. Black students were not a monolithic group on how to manage the aftermath of the arrests. Many felt a tension between loyalty to the Black student cause and fear of being dismissed from the university for further protest activity. Some Black students reconciled the tension by finding a way to support BSA with less aggressive tactics and rhetoric. A few barreled ahead with the BSA fight regardless of possible ramifications on their student status. Others were too afraid to jeopardize their college careers and too offended by BSA rhetoric to remain involved and instead opted out of the movement. Those that remained committed to the movement continued to push the university and challenge the validity of their arrests.

On-campus hearings were conducted by Subcommittee A of the Senate Committee on Student Discipline and lasted well into the spring semester. Subcommittee A, composed of faculty and students, was split on how to handle the students' academic status. Some committee members recommended expulsion; others recommended suspension; still others recommended more lenient procedures. Initially, the University Senate on Student Discipline recommended expelling the instigators.[40] The Black students, as well as various white student groups, demanded that the charges be dropped and that the students retain full academic status. After a long period of deliberations, most incoming SEOP students were issued "reprimands of record" based on reports of their alleged involvement. Lack of evidence that they were involved in destruction of property, threats, or coercion figured in their lenient sentences.[41] Of the students not issued a reprimand of record, one received conduct probation, one received a reprimand not of record, and several were acquitted since they were found not to have knowingly participated in the event.[42] Continuing students in general and particularly David Addison, the president of BSA and a law student, did not receive such lenient treatment. The university contended that because they were continuing students, they should have been aware of university rules and regulations regarding mass student disturbances.[43] Addison's campus hearings dragged on for over a year. Eventually, he and the other continuing students received sentences similar to those of the SEOP students. The university did not protest when the Champaign County state's attorney dropped the charges against students in the summer 1970.[44]

In general, the 9 September crisis fostered a strong sense of solidarity and reinforced the cohesiveness many Black students remembered experiencing during orientation. Their shared experience of the mass arrest served two functions: unity and a catalyst for activism. According to Jeffrey Roberts, who was a student then, "It actually brought people closer together. It really brought things into focus for me personally. After that experience, we knew we really had to watch each other's back. I don't think, prior to the arrest, that we would have been that close. We wouldn't have known each other that well. It was a beginning bond that brought a lot of people together."[45] Also, the arrests spurred many students to action and confirmed that the university did not want them on campus and would not act in good faith with Black students. For some, the arrest jolted them out of their "Negro" reality and pushed them toward Black Power ideology. As Clarence Shelley stated, "A lot of kids who wouldn't have been active spent all their time trying to get even for [the arrests]."[46] Likewise, Jeffrey Roberts remembered, "I think it turned a lot of people into activists. People who were sitting on the fence and didn't know what to do got pushed into, 'I need to participate.'"[47]

The 9 September arrests thus contributed to the growth in BSA membership and Black Power sentiment. Though BSA existed before the SEOP students arrived, the arrests energized the organization, as Dr. King's assassination had done months earlier. At the 9 September rally, BSA leaders attempted, in Clarence Shelley's words, "to use this mass of students as a mobilizing entity. They were trying to politicize these kids."[48] During orientation week, BSA members had focused on acclimating SEOP students to the campus, but the demonstration and arrests caused them to redefine their situation as political. The arrests bolstered BSA's call to become involved in the organization and Black issues on campus and, according to David Addison, radicalized the student population. With this newly energized and politicized group, Black students reaffirmed their connection to the Black Power movement sweeping the nation in the late 1960s and found themselves a place in it.

Though BSA often declared itself the Black student voice on campus, some Black students were not involved in BSA and did not ascribe to BSA ideology. A few Black students withdrew from BSA after the arrests. For instance, according to a letter written by a faculty member to Chancellor Jack Peltason, one particular student arrested at the Illini Union regretted his actions and vowed to no longer participate in BSA or disruptive behavior. The letter stated that the student got caught in the middle of a clash between "young firebrands" and the administration. The faculty member assured the chancellor that the student was not "a youth out to disrupt—or even to reform—the 'establishment', but . . . [was] one who, until Monday night, saw his way clear to 'making it' in the status quo." This may or may not have been an accurate interpretation of the Black student's beliefs and attitudes, but some Black students did feel caught between BSA and the administration and, as the faculty member's letter stated, felt they were left "holding the bag."[49] Rather than participate in future protests, they opted out of the Black student movement during their years at Illinois.

A significant proportion of Black students were, however, involved with the Black student movement at Illinois, whether through publishing, public speaking, boycotts, rallies, or workshops. No membership lists were kept, but former students believed that more Black students than not participated in BSA and Black Power in some way, shape, or form. For example, a large number of the Black freshmen admitted in 1968 engaged in direct-action protests against the university during their first week on campus. Many did not go to the Illini Union or remain there with a specific political purpose in mind, but the arrests catapulted many Black students into campus activism. Not all the students embracing Black Power ideology were members of BSA. BSA tactics and rhetoric turned them away from the organization, but they continued to practice Black Power principles consistent with the mission of the Black student movement at Illinois. Also, the arrival of the SEOP students allowed for a critical mass of Black students on campus. The fact that they were still a relatively small percentage of the student population was less significant than the fact that the absolute number of Black students swelled.[50] SEOP provided the numbers; the arrests provided the catalyst for activism.

Demands and the Drive for Unity

Tension between the Black students and the administration had not subsided, and the sentences from their involvement in the 9 September 1968 incident had yet to be handed down when BSA delivered a list of demands to the administration on 13 and 14 February 1969. The demands included dropping all criminal charges against those who participated in the Illini Union incident, establishing "a Black Cultural Center large enough to accommodate all Black people which will be run by the Black Students Association," hiring 50 Black residence hall counselors by September 1969, admitting 15 percent Blacks in the incoming graduate student class, hiring 500 Black faculty within a four-year period beginning with 150 by September 1969, establishing an autonomous Black studies department with a major emphasis on Afro-American and African studies, and fulfilling the university's financial commitment to the SEOP students. Demonstrating its link to Champaign's Black community, BSA demanded that the university address community concerns. Of the thirty-five demands published in the 18 February 1969 issue of the *Black Rap,* twenty dealt with student issues, while the others dealt with Black residents' issues, including granting a minimum wage increase for all janitorial and food service staff, forming a committee to assist in increasing the employment of Black residents, and extending access to university buildings, such as the Illini Union and the Intramural Physical Education Building, to Champaign residents. Though BSA demands centered on Black students and Black Champaign residents, BSA members did recognize the value of certain white allies and included white employees of the university in their demand for a wage increase.[51]

A letter from Chancellor Peltason to Robert Rogers, dean of the College of Liberal Arts and Sciences, demonstrated that the university anticipated some kind of demands from Black students as early as May 1968—prior to the SEOP students' arrival. Though BSA had only a very small number of students before SEOP, the university recognized the link between BSA's role in SEOP recruitment and the possibility of an increase in BSA activity. The chancellor warned, "Sooner or later, and probably sooner rather than later, some group or other will 'demand' that we provide courses in African history, Negro history, Negro culture, Negro music, etc." The letter explicitly asked that Rogers "quietly discuss this matter" with several department heads to develop appropriate courses and then discuss it with BSA "rather than have them hear about it from the newspapers or other sources." Dean Rogers responded to the letter after meeting with various department heads and informed Peltason that one course in history, one course in English, and a lecture series were feasible—though not in the budget—at the time.[52] Peltason encouraged the dean to move quickly.

Although administrators anticipated some sort of requests, they were not prepared for the scope of the BSA demands or the manner in which BSA pursued them. After receiving the demands, university administrators privately evaluated the situation. Melvin Rothbaum, director of the Institute of Labor and Industrial Relations, wrote a confidential letter warning the chancellor that the militant students were deliberately seeking a confrontation rather than negotiation and that the strategy employed was "keeping the university completely on the defensive." He suggested framing a set of proposals reviewing previous university efforts on Black student issues, endorsing certain demands considered reasonable, and broadening the discussion to include other student organizations, such as the Student Senate and the Graduate Student Association.[53] Administrators attempted to diffuse the situation, but BSA's public debate with the university and the increasing pace of events forced the university to respond rather than initiate certain reforms.

BSA representatives and various university officials met over the next week in an attempt to discuss the feasibility of the demands. Meanwhile, BSA rhetoric became increasingly aggressive, hostile, and incendiary. On 15 February 1969, BSA representatives met with the Faculty Senate Council to discuss the demands. After approximately two hours of debate, BSA representatives walked out of the meeting and attributed the meeting's failure to racist sentiment and university intransigence on BSA demands. "In a surprise show of bigotry the Faculty Senate Council refused to take a vote on any of the 35 demands," a BSA press release reported.[54] BSA acknowledged that faculty members had little power to initiate many of the demands but decried their lack of support. BSA also refused to hold further talks with the council until it publicly stated that it would take positive action on the demands. In a BSA press release, the organization invoked violence: "Recent events on the U of I campus have created an atmosphere which can only lead toward violent racial confrontation if negotiations are not effectively established to discuss Black demands."[55] Again resorting to scare tactics and attempting to demonstrate the gravity of the situation, BSA entered talks with Chancellor Peltason on Monday, 17 February, and stated that it was convinced that "the meeting with Peltason is the final chance to avert racial confrontation at the University of Illinois."[56] BSA continued to request meetings with the chancellor and other high-ranking administrators, only to sever talks throughout the month, citing the university's unwillingness to negotiate.

BSA leaders and the Black student body understood BSA statements as rhetoric. Black students were willing to protest and demand concessions from the university, but most were not willing to resort to violence or other coercive means. But the BSA leaders' public statements were useful for promoting the cause of Black unity on campus. By placing themselves in opposition to the university, they sought to unify Black students in a fight against the "Man," vilify the university, and demonstrate their righteousness—tactics that mirrored the general tenor of Black protest on white campuses nationwide. Their rhetoric certainly was incendiary, but BSA charges of university intransigence were not unfounded. Certain faculty and administrators were not receptive to Black student concerns and were offended by the idea that students could demand any form of institutional reform. Others questioned their academic right even to attend the university.[57] Black students used their demands as a way to sensitize the university to their concerns and to make the university more receptive to negotiation. They considered the demands *real* solutions to *real* problems.

Adding to the tense campus atmosphere were events occurring over the weekend and during the BSA negotiations with the administration. On 15 and 16 February, vandals removed and burned thousands of card catalogs from the university library. University officials estimated it would take years and tens of thousands of dollars to replace the cards. Investigators never found the perpetrators or accused any group or individuals of the crime, but they did state that it was "an effort to disrupt the university's operation, and any group interested in that could have done it."[58] Though the university was careful not to publicly name any particular group, letters to the editor in the *Daily Illini* revealed the tone of disapproving students, faculty, and the Champaign-Urbana community and indicted Black students for the vandalism. Evidently the 9 September arrests, the BSA demands, and the hostile negotiations between BSA and administrators remained fresh in their minds and in their newspapers.

One letter chastised the administration for entertaining the BSA demands and asked the university "to quit tolerating infractions of its rules and regulations and disruptive action (especially in light of the recent library vandalism) on the part of a few and return to the task of educating those eager to learn."[59] Another reminded the vandals that their destruction "hurt every student attending Illinois—black and white," an odd statement since the university never introduced race as an issue in the library incident.[60] A third letter called the BSA demands discriminatory and asked "Black students, why don't you attend classes now and work toward advanced degrees so some of your dreams will be fulfilled by your efforts and not handed to you on a silver platter?" It also admonished BSA to act in a "civil manner" when dealing with its "rational" demands and accused Black students of vandalizing the library.[61] In this environment— where SEOP received increasingly bad press, where almost 250 Black students were arrested on campus before the start of the school year, where BSA presented the university with a list of demands and continually severed talks with the administration, and where library card catalogues (the only record of book holdings at the university) were burned—BSA members increasingly stood in opposition to the university administration, and Black-white, student-administration tension intensified.

The arrests and resulting demands made the development of BSA ideology more urgent, and BSA and Black students in general hashed out their ideas in their publications. In poems, short essays, and articles, they advertised their definitions of Blackness and became part of the burgeoning Black arts movement, an offshoot of Black Power. The development and celebration of a Black aesthetic, based on African American cultural traditions, provided an instructive frame of reference. Through it, African Americans could best express themselves and their unique perspective. No longer would Black artists and writers be content to create art within the confines of white standards. Black art would reflect Black beauty; Black literature would reflect Black writing style; Black music would reflect Black rhythms. The creators of culture would be the armies of the people advancing liberation themes and building the knowledge and creative base on which to launch a Black cultural revolution.[62]

At Illinois, BSA used such newspapers as *Drums, Black Rap,* and *Yombo* (a traditional Swahili greeting) and the yearbook *Irepodun* (Swahili for "unity is a must") as forums for Black arts and expression.[63] Poems and articles became major vehicles for disseminating Black Power themes on the campus. Like writers in the larger movement, many BSA authors regarded themselves as the cultural arm of the Black revolution. Similarly, they sought to redefine Blackness by rejecting negative images perpetuated by whites; asserting Afro-centric values, images, and perspectives; and replacing stereotypes and historical inaccuracies with a body of work generated by African Americans.[64] Evidence of Black Power sentiment in BSA publications began before King's assassination and the SEOP students' arrival. Black students already contemplated new definitions of Blackness in 1966 and 1967. However, after King's assassination, the arrival of the SEOP students, and the arrests at the Illini Union, Black Power sentiment grew, as did its representation in BSA publications.

The campus definition of Black consciousness was far from monolithic and reflected the disparate conceptions of Black Power in the broader Black Power movement.[65] Years later, former students and administrators remembered cultural nationalists, Marxists, Pan-Africanists, and a host of other categorizations within the Black student movement at Illinois. Many students did not find the variant definitions problematic as long as students were able to work toward similar goals. As stated in the 1973 yearbook *Irepodun,* "No one view completely right, and yet, no one view completely wrong. What we have concluded is that there are different visions but all with the same end objective—Uhuru [unity]."[66] However tolerant of variant definitions, BSA did attempt to impose a set of behavioral and psychological constraints on students so that they would conform to a certain conception of Blackness. Articles and poems in BSA publications often were used to communicate such constraints.

One manner in which to communicate proper conduct was to contrast the Black Power movement's ideology and goals with those of the civil rights movement, and BSA often attempted to demonstrate its ideological break with previous liberation struggles. An editorial published in the October 1968 issue of *Drums* juxtaposed the Black parent and Black student/child and mirrored the perceived split between Black Power and the civil rights agenda. The author characterized the older generation as apathetic, ignorant, and "white-washed." Frustrated by their parents' inaction, the younger generation decided to take the reins. The author commented that "it appears that the days when black students waited for their parents to take action against the racist school policies are over." While their parents engaged in "habitual things," such as cooking, cleaning, reading the newspaper, and watching television, their children "organiz[ed] themselves to form a united front against the system to which their parents had become so well adjusted."[67] This view, of course, distorted the Black liberation struggle. In fact, some of the Black students at Illinois attributed their social justice concerns to the influence of their parents and other civil rights activists of the 1940s and 1950s.[68] Nonetheless, this view of a new generation was useful for breaking with the mainstream civil rights movement to launch the Black Power movement and the Black student movement at Illinois.

This break with the civil rights movement had implications for the redefinition of Negro and Black, and the act of "becoming" Black or the Negro-to-Black conversion experience was a very common theme running throughout BSA publications. For instance, a 1971 edition of *Yombo* included two poems, one entitled "Negro" and the other entitled "Black." The author characterized the Negro as an "aged" person afraid to take a step forward and emasculated, "a Negro not a man . . . a Negro, boy, not a man."[69] Blacks, in contrast, no longer sought integration. They wanted to revel in their culture and remain autonomous. This was the correct manner in which to gain liberation. "Black is like a treasure inside of a chest . . . beautiful, sweet, loving, and strong. . . . Black is where it's at, it's about time we should realize that," the author declared.[70] Negroes had outlived their usefulness; Blacks had to take the reins. The conversion process was a rebirth, and death necessarily preceded life: kill the Negro, kill the white influence, and Blackness was possible. The search for true Blackness and its attainment produced a resurrection of the mind and soul. Awareness, both political and cultural, was the means to the end.[71]

BSA also used its publications to attack the Black students they felt were not participating in or ascribing to their notion of Blackness. BSA and Black students tolerated disparate thoughts on Black Power but only to a certain degree and within a narrow framework. A poem meant to

chastise those who did not fully participate in the celebration of Blackness was indicative of the era:

> Black enough to belong to BSA
> but too white to come to meetings
> Black enough to have lived in the ghetto
> but too white to return
> Black enough to understand our lingo
> but too white to speak it
> Black enough to wear an Afro
> but too white to appreciate it
> Black enough for your Honky friends
> but too white for me.[72]

In this way, BSA students made clear the physical and behavioral components of Blackness. Blackness was deeper than pigment and organizational affiliation; it was a wholehearted commitment to Black liberation,
celebration of the Black aesthetic, and immersion in Black culture. Black
students who only superficially participated in Black Power by attending meetings and wearing an Afro revealed themselves through their association with whites and were ostracized by the BSA community.

BSA chastised Black students with white friends but harangued Black
students participating in interracial relationships. A poem illustrated the
disdain for Black men in relationships with white women:

> Rappin Black/Sleepin white
> That's his type,
> Rappin he's black n' proud
> Oratin real loud
> Layin up with a Sally and
> Tellin other bloods to rally
> Wearing a fro/and a black dishiki
> Doin two thangs
> One in the daytime—black
> One at night—white[73]

True brothers would never date a white woman or voluntarily socialize
with whites rather than Blacks. The desire for Black liberation and the love
of a white woman could not coexist in the heart of a *real* Black man. The
poem, in addition to being a rejection of assimilationist practices, created an in-group understanding through the use of Black vernacular terms.
The reader had to know Black expressions to understand the poem, but
again, understanding the "lingo" was not enough. Blacks students had to
accept Blackness and totally participate in it or risk being labeled a Negro and alienated from a large segment of the Black student community.

In their search for a more fully developed Black identity, many Black students participated in invented traditions—traditions constructed, instituted, and popularized in a fairly short period of time. The objectives of invented traditions included socialization, the inculcation of beliefs, and the provision of behavioral conventions.[74] According to the Black nationalist scholar Sandra Hollins Flowers, "In meeting these objectives, the traditions and their accompanying symbols provided nationalists and their followers with a sense of historicity that they did not feel in the observance of traditions and symbols in the context of the dominant society."[75] Wearing African jewelry, the Afro hairstyle, and such African-inspired clothing as dashikis, raising a clenched fist to symbolize Black Power, celebrating Kwanzaa, following the Nguzo Saba, and waving the red, black, and green Black nationalist flag were all manifestations of such traditions and symbols.[76] Black students reproduced such images in their publications and in their own behavior. Yolanda Smith Stanback-Williams provided an example of how an invented tradition infused Black students with a sense of power and pride:

> Our Blackness led me to create a 6' x 5' Black nationalist flag a few nights before graduation, June 1970. Many of the Black graduates preferred to march into [the auditorium] together with our flag in tow. At first, we weren't allowed in with the flag. We were told we couldn't bring it into the building. We refused to go in without it. Finally, after about twenty to thirty minutes, someone came up to us and said, "If you wrap the flag around the pole and keep it lowered—don't wave it or anything—have it your way." They let the flagged group in. We went in together and then went to our seats. To us, that was Black Power.[77]

They also created their own traditions on campus. In an effort to create events with a Black focus and center, Black students initiated annual events that paralleled university-sponsored activities, such as Black Homecoming and the election of a Black king and queen, Black Mom's Day, and a Black congratulatory ceremony held in addition to the university's graduation ceremony.

The growth of Black Power ideology further fractionalized the already tense student body. Black students never participated in the campus (white) activities to a large degree. But the increase of Black Power sentiment made crossing racial boundaries almost impossible without being ostracized from the Black student community. Leftist white student groups, such as the campus chapter of Students for a Democratic Society, sometimes supported Black student protests and sit-ins that occurred throughout 1969 and 1970. However, rarely did Black students support or participate in protests initiated by white students against university complicity in the Vietnam War effort. Black students often considered white student issues remote from more urgent and pressing problems facing Black students and the Black community in general. As David Eisenman stated in a February 1968 article, "Black [students] had no patience with discussion of any issues not directly affecting them. They say Vietnam is a 'safe' issue for white radials to take up, because it allows no direct personal involvement."[78] Increasing Black and white student activism often strained relationships between Black and white students, and both groups were wary of each other. In 1970, the university itself addressed the seriousness of racial tension on campus by conducting the "Hearing Panel on Black-White Relationships," in which the panel recognized that "even in the areas of the campus where there is no open conflict there is an uneasy and awkward climate."[79]

The sentiment of a small number of faculty, administrators, and students exacerbated racial tensions on campus. Some openly doubted the Black students' ability to compete at Illinois and believed their increasing activism reflected their academic frustrations. Such a discussion reached a national audience in a letter written by Lloyd Humphreys, a professor of psychology at Illinois, and published in an October 1969 issue of the journal *Science*. Humphreys never mentioned SEOP by name, but he did identify his university affiliation and a "crash recruitment program" begun in 1968. In the article, he stated that "recent events at my own university have produced in me a strong pessimism about the future." He proceeded to characterize Negroes as less intelligent than Caucasians and attributed the difference to biological factors and "deficiencies in the home and neighborhood." His major contention was that affirmative action programs brought intellectually unqualified Negroes to campus, which had a negative impact on student quality. He then connected Blacks' academic difficulties to their activism on campus: "A group of young people who are newly imbued with pride in race are placed in a situation in which they are, by and large, obviously inferior. . . . The causal chain from [*academic*] frustration to aggression is well established. A large ability difference as a source of aggression cannot be ignored. The universities are damned if they don't admit more Negroes, but they are also damned in another sense if they do."[80] Humphreys's sentiment was far from universal on campus, and his statements were countered by other faculty members who supported the Black students' rights to attend Illinois.[81] However, anecdotal evidence substantiated Black students' assertions that they encountered a hostile environment inside and outside the classroom. Certain Black student claims of racism may have been exaggerated, but those that did face hostility found their psychological well-being deeply affected.[82]

Furthermore, the link Humphreys made between poor academics and aggressive campus activism was a dubious one.[83] First, the majority of SEOP students met standard qualification requirements. Though they received lower GPAs and graduated at a lower rate than white students, SEOP students consistently outperformed administrator expectations and succeeded more often than they failed. Second, white student activities, not Black student protest, brought the National Guard to campus on two occasions, caused more than $20,000 in damage to the university and nearby campus-town, and precipitated the need for the Rumor Center, through which the university could control and correct misinformation during times of campus unrest.[84] The Black student sit-in at the Illini Union and the $4,000 worth of damage paled in comparison. If violence and campus activism were related to academic difficulty, as Humphreys argued, then white students must have been even less academically fit and more racially proud than Black students.

Why, many whites asked, did Black students attend Illinois instead of a historically Black college if they felt that the university was not supportive and provided a hostile environment? BSA did not publish answers to this question in its publications because they would have been counterproductive in negotiations with the university about the institution's failings. Even though Black students saw room for institutional improvement, they were fully aware of the valuable opportunity Illinois offered. Tangible reasons often made the decision to attend Illinois an easy one. Some students, especially those in SEOP, recognized the generosity of Illinois financial packages. Some had to apply for loans to offset the cost of attendance, but the aid packages were more generous at Illinois than at other institutions. Others believed the quality of education offered at Illinois exceeded that possible at historically Black institutions. The academic reputation of the university was attractive and beneficial for future career pursuits. Still others interpreted attendance as their right as tax-paying citizens in the state of Illinois. As Terry Cullers stated, "Since we're paying taxes for this institution, we felt we should be able to take advantage of it."[85] Also, the campus was only an hour and a half from Chicago, home for most Black students. Black students reconciled the perceived dissonance in attending a predominantly white institution and practicing Black Power ideology and did not consider the matter a primary concern. As Terry Townsend remembered, "We were more concerned with trying to pressure this university into being all it could be."[86]

Unity through Conformity: Pitfalls of a Narrow Definition

The development of a campus-appropriate Black Power understanding was useful. It invigorated self-reflection, brought Black students together, and produced demands on which the university would act. However, the definition of Blackness could be very constraining, and Black students policed one another regarding the acceptance of Black Power principles. Peer pressure to conform in college was not new, but the development of the proper racial identity became overwhelmingly important in the late 1960s. Who had the authority to determine who was Black enough to be called Black was a question left unanswered, and the criteria for true Blackness were often stringent and narrow. The in-group and out-group dichotomy often was falsely and hurtfully drawn. If a certain individual did not fit all the criteria expected of a true brother or sister both physically—by wearing an Afro and forming personal relationships with other Blacks—and psychologically—by appreciating the Afro and wanting to pull away from white influence and integration—the individual was called a Negro, sell-out, or Uncle Tom. This tactic often pushed away potential allies and alienated others.[87]

Certain BSA members and Black Power adherents practiced this Blacker-than-thou philosophy, and maintaining one's status as truly Black could be both difficult and demanding. Black students were expected conform to the physical, psychological, and behavioral conceptions of Blackness and then to translate them into campus activism. Students did recognize the value of academic success but paired it with activism in an evaluation of a true brother or sister. The degree of conformist pressure students felt varied. James Eggleston acknowledged there was pressure, but he did not consider it a factor in Black students' relationships.[88] Other students, such as Sandra Norris Phillips, remembered being able to slip in and out of the movement.[89] However, others did experience a significant amount of pressure that negatively influenced their psychological well-being. SEOP director Clarence Shelley remembered "lots of pressure on students for them to behave in a certain way. You could see the dissonance in how they were expected to act and how they really wanted to act."[90] A confidential memorandum from the Student Counseling Service and the Mental Health Division of the Health Service addressed this tension. The memo described Black students who had visited counseling services and how the students had "been subtly threatened with harm if they did not allow their hair to grow au natural, if they ate with whites, or if they did not become active members of a particular group."[91] The memo attested to the fact that not all Black students at Illinois followed BSA or its ideology of Blackness and that those who did not were sometimes harassed or coerced into participating.

Blacker-than-thou sentiment influenced participation in other organizations, including Black Greek societies, which suffered as a result of narrow conceptions of Blackness. Black students continued to join Black fraternities and sororities but often did so under the disapproving eye of a segment of the Black student population. Yolanda Smith Stanback-Williams, a member of a Black Greek sorority, Sigma Gamma Rho, described the influence of Black Power ideology on the Black Greek fraternities and sororities: "We were pressured to get involved in BSA and not other things, especially Greek life. BSA would say to be Greek is to be white."[92] Other members of Greek organizations expressed similar sentiments. BSA publications chastised Black Greeks for defeating the purpose of the collective Black community by promoting elitism and actively imitating whiteness. Whereas in the early twentieth century membership in a Black Greek organization brought prestige, in the late 1960s a number of Black students considered it antithetical to the cause of Black liberation. Black Greeks resented such implications. Some worked to dispel the stereotype, while others did not care, but the popularity of Black fraternities and sororities was affected.

BSA publications walked a fine line between providing a working definition of Black Power that was neither too broad as to be meaningless nor too narrow as to be prohibitively restrictive. Sometimes they failed and provided incredibly rigid understandings, but the organization recognized the implications of defining Blackness too narrowly and admonished individuals who used attacks on others to demonstrate their commitment to Black Power principles and the Black community. Such individuals became known derogatorily as Super Blacks more concerned with the appearance of Blackness than an internalization of it.[93] In an article entitled "Blacker Than Thou," Super Blacks were warned not to alienate potential allies and told to rein in their divisive rhetoric. The author reminded Super Blacks that "the person you level a charge of 'Tom' at may in fact be more with it than you are." In a plea for unity, the author also urged Black students to "temper the fervence that can be so much better channeled at our real adversaries than at those among us who fall at a different point on the continuum."[94] A later issue of *Drums* further insulted such individuals by calling them Super Niggers and characterized them as a "coloured man with a six foot natural and custom made dashiki who sits in the snack bar and other places rapping about what other folk ain't doing. They are the authorities on Blackness and the upcoming revolution who wouldn't know a revolution if it hit him in his face. He is a super Hip hopper on Black Power whose total reading time has been limited to half of Brother Malcolm's autobiography."[95] The attack on Super Blacks demonstrated the nuances in the psychological component of Blackness. Black students performed Blackness all the time on campus through their publications, policing of one another, and dealings with the university. But they frowned on demonstrating Blackness in front of an audience by insulting other students. Only when individuals came to a true knowledge of self through an internalization of Blackness did they experience a feeling of inner security that allowed them to move beyond divisive rhetoric and mere physical notions of Black Power.

Blacker-than-thou sentiment had a very personal and hurtful impact on Black students. For Dan Dixon, the tension between Black Greek life and campus activism was not necessary, and he deeply resented having his Blackness and social consciousness questioned: "I had white boys chanting 'two, four, six, eight! We don't want to integrate!' in high school. Now you have these supposed Black people tell me they were Blacker than me? . . . Having come up in a cauldron of racism, I knew what it was. I didn't have to read the book." Dixon considered his tenure as BSA president during the 1967–68 academic year "in name only" since non-Greeks controlled the executive council as well as the newspaper. He ran against David Addison for BSA president the following academic year but lost. He soon withdrew from campus activism and attributed his withdrawal to the pressures and alienation of Blacker-than-thou sentiment.[96]

Yolanda Smith Stanback-Williams, one of the primary agitators in the ISR housing struggle who later created the Black nationalist flag under which graduating students marched, also described her experience with Blacker-than-thou attitudes. She identified several factors, including her arrest on 9 September 1968, that led her to withdraw from campus activism. While watching how BSA handled the arrests and the nature of its demands, she began to reevaluate her participation and later disapproved of BSA ideology and tactics. "A lot of us didn't go to BSA like we thought we would. A lot of kids felt BSA led us the wrong way. . . . They demanded as opposed to compromise. I had had enough of demanding."[97] She remembered that the pressure to conform was so intense that she removed herself from campus activism and shied away from BSA. Instead, she gravitated toward Black Greek life and within a year of her arrival organized a chapter of her sorority on campus. Although some students like Yolanda Smith Stanback-Williams and Dan Dixon disassociated themselves from BSA and BSA politics, they maintained a belief in Black Power. BSA membership was not a prerequisite for Black Power ideology. Though some students pulled away, they found other outlets for Black Power, forums to celebrate Blackness, and ways to protest racism on campus.

Another divisive issue on the Illinois campus was that Black often meant Black *man*, with Blackness being a reclamation of Black masculinity. The emphasis on race pushed issues of gender to the periphery.[98] At Illinois, men and women acknowledged such masculine definitions, but the sexism in the Black Power movement never was discussed in BSA publications in an effort to keep this dirty laundry and potential source of disunity behind closed doors. Private discussions between Black men and Black women were held, but rarely did discussions of sexism become public discourse—at least in the presence of non-Blacks. However, both Black men and Black women did address gender roles in BSA publications and sometimes advocated very traditional and conservative views. This prose often exhibited posturing and symbolism in which men and women honored each other with laudatory words and paid homage. But their written text should not be confused with an acceptance of a gender hierarchy. Rather, they were wary of revealing dissension in the racial ranks. Though racial concerns took center stage, Black students, particularly women, did not allow gender to be completely ignored, and the conservative ideas expressed in print did not always translate into practice on campus.

Black men and women did gently chide one another about what they expected, but never did they attack one another in their publications. A major goal identified by both men and women was racial unity and the creation of a healthy relationship between Black men and Black women. For his part, "a brother," as it was signed, wrote a letter to all Black women in which he expressed his confusion regarding the "collage" of different opinions about Black women: he was told to respect and protect her, while at the same time he was told that she would effectively castrate him if he displayed emotion and weakness. In his "gyrational merry-go-round" of confusion, he solicited Black women for guidance and symbolically prostrated himself in his plea with such phrases as "although I am a man, I am still a child." By the end of his letter, the author realized that Black women should be treated as queens, held in high esteem, and considered equals in the Black liberation struggle. Together, men and women would forge the path to the future.[99]

In the same publication, a Black woman offered her own thoughts on Black men and the need for racial unity. Addressing the theme of interracial relationships, she suggested Black men "search your soul and mind to find yourself" and reminded them that their pursuit of white women was detrimental to the struggle. In her plea to Black men, she stated that Black women wanted to facilitate the male search for awareness but could not do so if the man did not initiate the search of his own volition. "Brothers, help us help you," she exclaimed. For her, the revolution was impossible without a positive relationship between Black women and Black men, and unity was imperative. At the end of her plea, she solicited men to "come home" and help establish a strong and united Black nation: "Learn to love us brothers, because we are you, and you are us."[100] Men and women desperately sought unity and did not want gender issues to divide the community and derail their collective racial goals.

In print, Black students advocated conservative gender roles, a posture not atypical in Black student movements across the country. One article in the *Black Rap* summarized a speech on gender made at the 11 February 1969 BSA meeting by Al Booker, a former Black student activist at Wisconsin State University. According to Booker, the role of women was the socialization and education of Black children, while her function was to make the man God of his house and be subservient to his needs. The Black man was to dominate his household, help reproduce the "new Black nation," and protect "his" women.[101] BSA members offered no editorial comment on Booker's speech. However, Black women did write articles with similar themes. In an article entitled "Black Womanhood," one Black woman student acknowledged that Black men "needed" to reclaim their masculinity and applauded their empowered sense of self in a symbolic prostration of her own: "One who, for too long depended on woman and who now projects his manhood in full force—Black man, you are my GOD!" Reminiscent of Booker, the author asserted that a man's duty was to protect "his women" and reproduce a Black nation, while a woman's duty was to socialize children and make the home comfortable for her husband.[102]

Such conservative views of gender roles were sometimes tolerated by Black women at Illinois. As Jacqueline Triche Atkins stated, "It was understood that this was the first opportunity [for Black men] to really strut their stuff. Maybe we should support them and back them up."[103] However, Black women were neither absent nor subservient. They actively asserted themselves in every phase of the Black student movement at Illinois. It was a group of women that, by defying university policy and remaining in ISR, provided the catalyst for the Black student movement. Almost half of those arrested on 9 September 1968 were women. They were on the BSA executive council before and after SEOP and contributed to BSA newspapers. Black men and women may have discussed the worth of conservative gender roles in the publications, but many did not practice them on campus. While Black women acquiesced to men at certain times and for particular reasons, they at no point wholeheartedly accepted their prescribed role in either male-female relationships or the Black liberation struggle.[104]

Moreover, women often initiated and dominated the discussions on gender roles. Discussions about the relationship between Black men and Black women and their roles in the Black liberation struggle occurred before BSA was formed, but the conversations became institutionalized soon after the organization's inception. The November 1967 issue of *Drums* advertised a BSA-sponsored forum to discuss "problems between Black men and women on this campus."[105] By late 1969, Black manhood and Black womanhood classes were held on a regular basis and were well attended. When first conceptualized, the workshops were held jointly. According to Curtina Moreland-Young, a leader in the womanhood workshops, "the whole emphasis at this time was to try to develop a new kind of Black person. . . . One of the ideas was that this society had negatively impacted our ability to understand what we needed to be as men and women, and particularly what we needed to be to each other."[106]

After deciding that combination workshops were counterproductive because of frequent arguments between the sexes and accusations of culpability—which completely dispels the notion of Black women students as subservient—the workshops were held separately. Sandra Norris Phillips taught in the womanhood workshops and described the atmosphere as primarily friendly: "Some of the discussions got virulent at times. But it was still a very supportive environment."[107] Themes included how to successfully manage a relationship with a Black man, how to raise children properly, and the role of Black women in the Black Power movement. According to Antonio (Tony) Zamora, one-time director of the Black cultural center where the workshops were held, the manhood workshops revolved around understanding how to respect and protect Black women, being responsible for your actions, taking proper care of your family, and ensuring widespread participation in Black events on campus. As Zamora described them, "It was about nation building. How do we create something that's better for our people."[108] A primary goal of the workshops was to create a situation in which people learned how to function in a partnership. The workshops continued into the mid-1970s, demonstrating Black student interest in gender even though it remained secondary to racial concerns.

Blacker-than-thou sentiment and a masculine definition of Blackness were not unique to the Illinois campus. The Black student movement was a part of the larger Black Power movement and was therefore subject to the same shortcomings and potentially divisive issues. Both in the broader movement and on the Illinois campus, Black people hashed out Black Power as they went along, often devising competing notions and restrictive definitions. But Black people, including Black students at Illinois, were conscious of the contradictions in their rhetoric. For instance, Black students desperately sought a coherent definition of Blackness and demanded a high degree of conformity in public and private, but at the same time they recognized the worth of different perspectives on Blackness and chastised individuals who deliberately alienated possible allies in an attempt to prove themselves. Similarly, they recognized the importance of gender issues and discussed their thoughts and opinions on it in private, but they pushed gender to the periphery to protect their racial unity. The overwhelming desire for racial togetherness precipitated by Black Power ideology was exacerbated by the fact that Black students felt under siege from the university, the Illinois legislature, and Illinois citizens. Many felt they could ill afford a conception of Blackness so broad that it would dissolve their movement into an incoherent mess. Instead, they adopted the predominant Black Power sentiment, warts and all.

BSA matured as an organization after the SEOP students arrived and the large number of Black students were arrested at the Illini Union. Beginning in May 1968, annual executive council elections were held. Its newspapers were printed on a regular basis and became longer as more students participated. The mass arrest in September of 1968 and the resulting list of demands provided the organization with a concrete set of goals into which members could channel their energy. The creation of committees, including the Black Graduate Committee and the Recruitment and Retention Committee, enabled a division of labor that would allow different groups to agitate and initiate discussion on different sets of BSA demands.

BSA also matured ideologically. The 1968 arrests made the need for a common group understanding more critical. Unity sometimes came under the guise of forced conformity, but BSA believed that a coherent definition of Blackness, constraining though it could be, provided a powerful tool for negotiating with the administration. SEOP students participated in this construction of Black identity on campus. They brought with them additional energy, ideas and perspectives on Blackness, and ways to demonstrate and advertise Black issues in the publications. It was the SEOP students who provided BSA with the numerical support it needed to negotiate their demands. It was also this group of students who, after the original BSA members graduated, took over BSA and advocated Black student issues. Together, the new and continuing Black students sought to make their understanding of Black Power a tangible reality on campus by forcing the university to address Black student concerns and initiate institutional reform.

5 "We Hope for Nothing; We Demand Everything"

The federal government, individual states, and various colleges and universities responded to the rise in youth activism on campuses with various forms of legislation in the late 1960s and early 1970s. The new bills, laws, and amendments differed from state to state and from university to university, but all were created to deter and punish certain kinds of activism. Black *and* white students were the targets of the legislation.[1] Campuses across the nation exploded, and the American public questioned the ability of university administrators to maintain control. Illinois created its own protocol for dealing with disruptive students and sought to maintain order. The university did not approve of certain legislation and publicly registered disagreement, but as federal and state bills became law, the university was compelled to comply.

However, the university did not simply bow to public pressure, squash student activism, and ignore BSA demands. The university realized there was room for campus improvement and recognized the worth of some BSA demands. Administrators and faculty had entertained ways to improve the quality of life and academic success of Black students on campus before 1969, but the university had focused on compensatory education and support programs to help Black students that required only cosmetic changes to campus. The BSA demands focused attention on the university's complicity in Black student underachievement. The university moved forward and publicly demonstrated its dedication to two of the demands—the creation of a Black studies program and a cultural center—and even asked Black students to participate in bringing them to life. The negotiation was difficult and stressful, but both BSA and university administrators and faculty stayed the course despite public pressure to the contrary.

Unintended Consequences

After issuing their demands, Black students at Illinois experienced a backlash similar to the aftermath of the September 1968 arrests. Illinois residents and university alumni wrote letters to university officials expressing their distress with how Black student activism was handled. A member of the class of 1934 wrote President David Dodds Henry, "It seems where a minority group wants something, they demand it, and if they don't get it, they take it. It is high time the University puts up a fight against this sort of behavior."[2] Media coverage of the demands and Black student negotiations over them incensed others. One individual from as far away as Kentucky wrote a letter to university officials and referenced an article in the *Daily Illini* that discussed negotiations between BSA and the Undergraduate Student Association (UGSA). The article documented a meeting between the groups where BSA blocked entrances and exits and attempted to intimidate UGSA members into increasing the amount of money funneled to BSA. The author of the letter suggested that the university prosecute BSA members for their actions. Vice Chancellor George Frampton responded, assuring the author that the *Daily Illini* exaggerated the situation. According to Frampton, Dean Robert Brown was present at the meeting and reported that "no one appeared to him reasonably intimidated or fearful. No members of UGSA ever stated or complained that they were threatened or intimidated, and on the contrary they have stated that any tension during the evening resulted only from the heat of negotiations."[3] Other concerned citizens registered their distress in phone calls to the Rumor Center. The nature of the calls evidenced a general state of racial wariness. For instance, on 28 May 1969 alone, a typical day, over twenty calls to the Rumor Center concerned Black unrest. Individuals asked a variety of questions from "Will we have any racial problems tonight?" to "Are there any Black Panthers in town?" to are there "Blacks from Chicago with machine guns and 400 Black militants from St. Louis" coming to Champaign?[4] The queries attested to the tense climate on campus and in Champaign-Urbana as well as to the fact that the Rumor Center was desperately needed.

The university not only worked to dispel rumors and provide accurate information but also tightened regulations regarding proper conduct.

In a February 1969 report to the board of trustees, Chancellor Jack Peltason cited deficiencies in university policy regarding the regulation of student demonstrations and advocated the "removal of any ambiguity about University policy toward disruptive actions and about the appropriate role of disciplinary subcommittees."[5] President David Dodds Henry, in his report to the trustees, outlined four initial measures correcting the inadequacies. One, the Senate Committee on Discipline issued a clarifying statement regarding "what is a disruptive or coercive action" and established that a specific cease and desist order did not need to be given to discipline a student for participating in a demonstration or protest. The new regulations would be distributed to incoming freshmen and highly publicized across campus for those already enrolled. Two, a single hearing committee would be used for all students cited for discipline in the same incident. This would reduce the faculty hours involved in hearing and deciding the cases. Three, the Senate Committee on Discipline would not be permitted to make changes in procedure once charges were filed (such changes had lengthened the trials of those arrested at the Illini Union and had made the process more confusing). Four, the Ad Hoc Senate Committee on University Disciplinary Authority and Procedures was established to examine other discrepancies in the disciplinary process and was asked to submit a permanent plan for handling massive defiance of university regulations.[6] These changes in policy were a direct response to the 9 September aftermath and were an attempt to simplify future proceedings and hearings. All new undergraduate and graduate students for the 1969–70 academic year received a letter from the chancellor notifying them of the policy changes.[7]

In 1969, the Illinois legislature also responded to campus unrest by initiating several legislative bills. House Bill 1894 directed state colleges and universities to adopt a policy on demonstrations to maintain order on campus. The legislature would require that universities clearly outline rules and regulations on student conduct with "special attention to firmness, to insuring that the civil rights of others are not infringed and to establishment of a step by step approach to secure the reasonable operation of university or college activities in case of any disruptive activity."[8] The University of Illinois already had begun down this path, but the bill would force the university to submit its policy to the State Board of Education and the governor. Senate Bill 1144 provided for the criminal prosecution of students who remained on state-supported land after being told to depart by a representative of the state. Those who interfered with or impeded the movement of persons or the use of facilities could be charged in a court of law. The consequence for defying the new law would be a fine, jail time, or a combination of the two.[9] Senate Bill 191 would revoke any scholarship funded wholly or partly by the state if the holder participated in an unlawful disturbance directed against the administration of a college or university. The chief executive officer of the institution at which the student was enrolled made the final determination if the scholarship would be revoked but only after the student was afforded the opportunity to present evidence against revocation.[10]

The university lobbied the Illinois legislature about the proposed acts. As the chair of the Illinois Joint Council on Higher Education, President David Dodds Henry wrote a letter directly to the governor. The Joint Council supported only Senate Bill 1144 that provided for the prosecution of students who remained on state-supported land after being told to depart or who impeded persons or facilities. In particular, the Joint Council agreed that responsibility for determining guilt or innocence should lie with the court system, not the institution where the student was enrolled. The Joint Council agreed with the spirit of Senate Bill 1894 that required institutions to file a policy on demonstrations. However, the Joint Council maintained that the bill duplicated already established campus regulations, and it resented having to submit policy statements to the State Board of Education and the governor for approval. The Joint Council argued that such action was "unnecessary and a departure from the legislative tradition of allowing the lay boards to manage the institution's internal affairs without the kind of surveillance the Bill contemplates."[11] Nonetheless, both bills passed and became law in September 1969.

The Joint Council and President Henry reserved their harshest criticism for Senate Bill 191, which would revoke state scholarships when a student was found to have participated in an unlawful demonstration. The state legislation was consistent with federal legislation enacted under the Higher Education Amendments of 1968 and the Department of Health, Education, and Welfare Appropriations Act of 1969. Both federal and state legislation threatened to revoke financial aid if students were found guilty of participating in disruptive protest. The appropriations act read, "No part of the funds appropriated under this Act shall be used to provide a loan, guarantee of a loan or a grant to any applicant who has been convicted by any court of general jurisdiction of any crime which involves the use of or the assistant to others in the use of force, trespass or the seizure of property under control of an institution of higher education to prevent officials or students at such an institution from engaging in their duties or pursuing their studies."[12] The seizure of property clause was a direct warning to those students participating in sit-ins, one of the most popular forms of protest employed by activists at the time.

The higher education amendments enumerated the kinds of financial aid to be revoked if students were convicted. Among the federal monies to be withheld were national defense education funds, equal opportunity grants, and work-study funds.[13] The Illinois bill piggybacked on federal initiatives and threatened to revoke state aid under the same principles.

The Joint Council completely disagreed that revocation of state financial assistance should be used as a disciplinary mechanism because "it operates to treat the needy student more severely than his more affluent counterpart in connection with the same misconduct." The Joint Council also argued that responsibility for the conviction should lie outside the university. The scholarship should be revoked not at the institution's discretion but only upon a court conviction. It was improper of the legislature to ask that universities determine if the student's actions violated the state or federal constitution. The question should be left to those trained in constitutional law.[14] Despite these efforts, the Illinois bill passed in September 1969. Administrators at the university did not relish their newfound power, but they were forced to comply with the law.

Black students at Illinois were particularly influenced by the threats to revoke financial aid. Most SEOP students held a combination of national defense student loans, equal opportunity grants, work-study incentives, and Illinois state scholarships—precisely the forms of financial assistance the state and federal government threatened to revoke. These new laws could have a major impact on Black student attendance if Black students were convicted of participating in campus unrest.[15] Black students attended Illinois to receive an education, an opportunity that they did not take lightly. The threat of having to leave the institution because of a loss of financial aid curtailed aggressive protest activities. Instead, they funneled their energies into the creation of the Afro-American Studies and Research Program and the Afro-American Cultural Program. Their dealings with the university were still heated, but they took place inside commission meetings, not on the campus streets.

Illinois legislators assured President Henry that they did not want to usurp the autonomy of universities and that their actions had taken place against the backdrop of an angry citizenry demanding that the state government do something to protect the integrity of higher education in Illinois.[16] Though some legislators eschewed a government role in higher education, further intervention occurred with the creation of the Illinois Bureau of Investigation on 1 January 1970. The head of the new office wrote university officials and notified them that the bureau was "charged with the responsibility of enforcing all the laws of the State of Illinois." So that the bureau could conduct its job and investigations properly, the director asked the dean of students to complete a questionnaire with such leading questions as "Do you feel that a university or college campus should be a sanctuary to those in violation of the law, or should the laws be enforced equally on campus just as in any other public place?" and "Are there any laws which you would oppose having enforced on your campus?"[17] Answering such questions could prove awkward considering that the university was bound to obey the laws of the state of Illinois. The president and chancellor of the university and the president of the board of trustees had all publicly registered their disagreement with particular acts. Now the legislature, through the Illinois Bureau of Investigation, ensured that university disagreement did not translate into flouting the law.

The U.S. Congress also spent an inordinate amount of time worrying about higher education. With the possible exception of appropriations bills, student unrest and campus disorders occupied the most legislative time during 1969.[18] The federal government initiated commissions to study the problem and make recommendations. In June 1969, the National Commission on the Causes and Prevention of Violence issued a report on campus unrest across the nation. The commission lamented "the violence and disorder that have swept the nation's campuses. Our colleges and universities cannot perform their vital functions in an atmosphere that exalts the struggle for power over the search for truth, the rule of passion over the rule of reason, physical confrontation over rational discourse." The commission attributed the campus unrest to societal issues rather than specific campus causes. Students protested the perceived gap between professed ideals and actual performance, injustices that remained unresolved, the inequality of opportunity, and involvement in the war in Vietnam that "most of them believe is unjustified." Student efforts to improve the democratic system were encouraged, but the destruction of existing institutions was considered counterproductive and rash.[19]

The commission was disturbed by public and legislative reaction to the campus unrest that "would punish colleges and universities by reducing financial support, by passing restrictive legislation, or by political intervention in the affairs of educational minorities." It cautioned university administrators in their dealings with students and offered advice. Faculty, administrators, and students needed to reach a broad consensus on permissible methods of presenting ideas, proposals, and grievances and the consequences of going beyond them. The administration had to prepare and review contingency plans for dealing with campus disorders in an effort to determine the circumstances under which institutions should use disciplinary procedures, police action, and court injunctions. Universities also needed to develop decision-making bodies that provided a rapid and effective deterrent to campus unrest as well as redress for grievances. Lastly, the commission recommended that universities improve communication with students, alumni, and the general public to avoid misinformation and misunderstanding.[20]

Approximately one year later, Alexander Heard, the chancellor of Vanderbilt University who had been appointed as a special adviser to President Richard Nixon, issued a separate report on campus unrest. Like the National Commission on the Causes and Prevention of Violence, Heard placed campus unrest in a context beyond the campus borders, "The condition cannot be conceived as a temporary, aberrational outburst by the young, or simply as a 'campus crisis' or a 'student crisis.' Because of its immediate and potential consequences the condition we face must be viewed as a national emergency." The U.S. involvement in Vietnam, the invasion of Cambodia, and the student murders by police at Kent State and Jackson State intensified antiwar sentiment and frustration with the federal government. Students were becoming increasingly convinced that the United States had become a highly repressive society that was intolerant of dissent. To increase confidence in the government, Heard proposed that the president take initiatives in welcoming young people in the political process and increase meaningful, two-way communication with campus constituents. Heard implored the president to listen to student opinions: "The young may be trying to tell us things we ought to hear. You should have the chance to evaluate firsthand the assumptions of those who reach different conclusions from yours about Southeast Asia. The views of youth and the trends they represent have grave political and social consequences. Effective execution of foreign policy and maintenance of respect in the world are both hampered by dissent at home."[21]

The Heard report treated Black students in a separate section and placed their concerns in the context of the broader Black community and the rise of Black Power. The Black liberation struggle had shifted from a focus on legal remedies to more aggressive and confrontational methods of redress. Black students translated the new mood into campus demands. Racial equity and increased economic and educational opportunities were at the forefront of the agenda, while Vietnam and international concerns remained secondary. "If the war ended today [and] the draft the day after that," Heard wrote, "it would not significantly reduce the feelings of cynicism and distrust among black college youth or the potential for more unrest. In fact, the ending of the war without some accompanying dramatic attention to their historic problems would increase their feelings of doubt that the basic institutions in the society will be responsive to their needs." Heard recommended that President Nixon make a more public and concerted effort to address Black community and Black student issues. He also suggested the president increase contact with representatives of the Black community, use the moral influence of his office to reduce racial tensions and increase racial understanding, and immediately provide additional student financial aid for economically disadvantaged students. According to Heard, the federal government had a large and potentially positive role in improving conditions at campuses across the country.[22]

The National Commission on the Causes and Prevention of Violence report and the Heard statement spoke directly to what was happening on the Illinois campus.[23] In particular, Black students linked their struggles to those of the wider Black community and demanded an end to unresolved racial injustice and unequal opportunity. The increasing frustration with the pace of societal reform fueled dissent on and off campus as African Americans embraced the concept of Black Power. The Vietnam War and U.S. intervention in Southeast Asia were secondary concerns. Rather than throw the weight of BSA behind white student protests against the war, Black students demanded the reconciliation of domestic racial issues and focused their energy on injustice in Champaign and on campus. At Illinois, they sought to improve conditions through the development of racially based campus programs and engaged the administration in discussions regarding campus reform.

Afro-American Studies and Research Program

Despite campus, state, and federal pressure to remain quiet on campus, Black students barreled forward. After issuing their demands in February 1969, BSA moved quickly and publicly to engage the university in reform. Certain demands—for instance, that the university hire five hundred Black professors by 1972—were improbable. However, even outlandish demands highlighted areas for university improvement, and concerned administrators worked to improve the situation. Other, more feasible demands became university foci immediately. A few days after BSA issued its list of demands, the university's Senate Council produced recommendations lifted directly from the list: "the establishment of a Black cultural center as a supportive unit to SEOP and active consideration of matters relevant to the organization of an African American studies program."[24] On the heels of the BSA demands and Senate Council recommendations, Chancellor Peltason appointed the Faculty-Student Commission on Afro-American Life and Culture on 27 February 1969.[25] The university was not intimidated into inviting students to join the commission, but the administration fully understood the potentially volatile consequences of not including Black students and valued their constructive input. In this way, Black students played a large role in campus reform. Rarely were students asked to sit on such an important institutional body and never had they been given such power.

Members of the university community had made individual attempts to initiate Black-centered courses before the creation of Faculty-Student Commission on Afro-American Life and Culture and BSA demands. CORE initiated the call for a Black history course in 1966.[26] In 1967, the Illinois legislature passed the ethnic group bill, which declared, "The teaching of history shall include a study of the role and contributions of American Negroes and other ethnic groups."[27] Although the bill was meant for primary and secondary schools, Department of History faculty at the university attempted to integrate such material in the history survey course offered to undergraduates. Faculty members also discussed the merits of such inclusion at the Third Annual Conference on Afro-American History held at Illinois in November 1968.[28] As early as October 1968, one month after the arrests at the Illini Union, certain faculty and administrators discussed the possibility of a center for the study of the African American experience under the auspices of the College of Liberal Arts and Sciences.[29] Meanwhile, the college developed an Afro-American lecture series in which prominent Black figures were invited to campus and asked to give public lectures for students and the Champaign-Urbana community. The lecture series organizers deliberately sought the assistance of BSA in choosing speakers and invited BSA to host receptions for the guests.[30] These individual attempts appeased some Black students, but the BSA demands and the creation of the Faculty-Student Commission on Afro-American Life and Culture accelerated the development of a cohesive Black studies program.

However, the development of an academic program proved difficult at Illinois. Formed three years after the first Department of Black Studies at San Francisco State College, the Faculty-Student Commission looked to other campuses for clues and direction for its developing program. Most programs at other institutions were hastily organized in response to Black student demands, and the lack of preparation time translated into problems with longevity, direction, purpose, and institutionalization. Their marginal position on campus, absence of a well-devised program philosophy, and fiscal realities undermined their status on campus, and many Black studies programs floundered.[31] The Faculty-Student Commission gleaned what it could from other campuses and attempted to learn from their example. In March 1969, one month after its inception, the commission developed a working definition in an attempt to start down the right path: "The field of Afro-American studies is defined as an interdisciplinary area of scholarly study which includes the humanities, the law, the arts, and the behavioral sciences insofar as they pertain specifically to the American Black but also insofar as they are directly related to the particular problems of Afro-American life."[32] Students majoring in Black studies would be equipped with the basic tools and techniques necessary to attack the problems "engendered through centuries of social, psychological, and economy tyranny."[33] The commission was confident about its first step and eager to put the program philosophy in place. But staffing and structuring the program would be a different and more difficult matter.

A separate committee was convened to choose a director for the program. Like the Faculty-Student Commission, the committee included students designated by BSA's executive council and faculty members. The committee established guidelines for the prospective candidates that revealed the concerns of students and faculty regarding both the quality and legitimacy of the program. The individual had to be deeply concerned with Afro-American studies and identify with the Black experience and community, be a scholar acceptable to the academic community, and be "a vigorous and forceful personality able to conduct the affairs of the program in the context of student, faculty, and administrative pressures." The committee planned to gather recommendations and vote on candidates. Never had students been granted positions on committees that created and determined the leadership of an academic program. BSA even had veto power over any nomination and threatened to use it if necessary.[34]

Meanwhile, the university realized there was a shortage of professors (both Black and white) with the academic background to teach courses for the program. The Faculty-Student Commission proposed a three-pronged approach. First, it encouraged departments to recruit permanent specialized faculty (this can be tied directly to the BSA demand for more Black professors, though non-Black professors who could teach Black-centered courses were also recruited). Second, it advised the use of visiting professors to develop and teach the new courses. Third, it looked to graduate students as a future pool of professors. By recruiting graduate students with an interest in Black studies and developing their talents, the university could deepen its pool of possible faculty (the recruitment and admission of more Black graduate students also was a BSA demand).[35] The Faculty-Student Commission offered to assist departments in their efforts to recruit professors and create new courses. However, Robert Eubanks, an African American professor in civil engineering who chaired the commission, was careful to indicate that the creation of Black-centered courses did not mean that Black issues should not be integrated in traditional courses.[36] The Black contributions to and experience in America needed to be included in traditional American history, literature, and art courses, not simply in courses created solely for Black studies.

The most successful first attempt at increasing course offerings was the Afro-American lecture series institutionalized in the form of History 199 under the auspices of the College of Liberal Arts and Sciences in the 1968–69 academic year. Students enrolled for one credit hour and wrote a paper on a lecture given by a visiting scholar or an aspect of African American culture. The university opened the lectures to the public and hosted them in the auditorium to accommodate students, faculty, Champaign-Urbana residents, and interested others. Speakers represented a variety of disciplines and discussed a myriad of topics. Reverend Channing Phillips, who placed fourth in the presidential balloting on the Democratic ticket in 1968, gave a talk entitled "Being Black in America"; Val Gray Ward, a Black dramatist, presented an address entitled "Concert Voice of the Black Writer"; Percival Borde, a scholar of Caribbean and African culture, gave a lecture entitled "The Talking Drums"; Alex Haley, editor of *The Autobiography of Malcolm X*, spoke about his work-in-progress, *Roots*; Wardell Gaynor, an associate producer of a television show, spoke about his program *Of Black America*; Reverend C. T. Vivian, a member of the Southern Christian Leadership Conference, gave a lecture entitled "The Black Church in Transition"; and A. B. Spellman, author and participant in the television show *Black Heritage*, gave a talk entitled "Toward a Saner Base for the New Black Music." Over three hundred Black and white students enrolled in the course.[37] An estimated 1,300 to 1,800 people attended various individual lectures. Anticipating the drawing power of the author James Baldwin, administrators relocated his lecture to the basketball stadium.[38]

The Department of History and the College of Liberal Arts and Sciences conducted a survey to gauge student satisfaction with the lecture series. Seventy-six students (25 percent of those enrolled in the course) ranked the series as outstanding. Students liked the idea of taking the course for credit, using papers as the primary determinant of grades, and believed they were graded fairly on their papers (although four indicated that the grading was too easy). Most said they would have liked a regularly scheduled discussion section in conjunction with the lectures. Most appreciated the variety in lecture topics. Approximately half enjoyed the predominantly cultural nature of the lectures, while the other half would have appreciated a more "sociological-political approach." The main criticisms of the series included the lack of discussion groups and the discontinuity of lecture topics. When asked to report who should be included in future lecture series, the top four choices were, in order, Jesse Jackson, Chicago civil rights activist and leader of Operation Breadbasket; Eldridge Cleaver, Black Panther Party Minister of Information; Stokely Carmichael, one-time SNCC chairman; and Fred Hampton, chairman of the Illinois chapter of the Black Panther Party. All eventually came to campus as part of the lecture series or as BSA-invited speakers. Although one student wrote, "After getting a B+, I would not recommend this course to anyone no matter what it's worth," series planners considered the following statement more typical: "I can sincerely say that this was the best course that I have taken at this University or anywhere else. If more courses were structured similarly, perhaps institutionalized education would not be so irrelevant and useless. This is the first time I have ever wanted to thank anyone for a course."[39]

In the 1969–70 academic year, the course was renamed LAS 199. Heeding the advice of previous students enrolled in the class, coordinators of the series altered the course. Lecturers continued to arrive from across the country, but students also attended discussion sections, read three books by Black authors, and took a final exam.[40] According to one report, 310 students enrolled in the course and received three hours credit;[41] 285 students completed the course; and the average grade (not including those students who deferred their grade) was a 3.25 on a 4.0 scale.[42] SEOP director Clarence Shelley recognized the importance of the lecture series beyond its academic worth and reflected on its broader significance in helping allay Black student concerns and frustration on campus. Shelley applauded the college's efforts and commented in a letter to the dean of the College of Liberal Arts and Sciences, "I think more than any other single activity on campus this program has been responsible for the intellectual and cultural growth of the SEOP students for experiences in light of the social and political pressures to which they have been subjected."[43]

While individual new courses were being devised and offered, the Faculty-Student Commission continued to discuss the administrative structure of the future Black studies program and its institutionalization. The commission debated the merits of creating a department, center, or program and knew the decision would have consequences for its autonomy and funding. The BSA demands issued in February 1969 called for "the immediate establishment of an autonomous Black Studies Department," but BSA grew wary of university commitment to creating and supporting an autonomous program and in spring 1969 demanded that the program *not* be institutionalized as an independent unit. Commission chair Robert Eubanks agreed with the second version of the BSA demand: "My overwhelming reason is the difficulty which an Afro-American Studies Department would encounter in the acquisition of University of Illinois level staff."[44] He doubted that Black professors who specialized in Black issues would want to be segregated in a department outside their discipline. Consequently, the program would hire a full-time director, but its faculty would have joint or courtesy appointments in other academic departments across campus.

The commission cast the net widely for qualified individuals to teach relevant courses, but BSA and faculty on the commission sometimes differed over the definition of *qualified*. BSA members had been exposed to exciting and informative individuals through the lecture series and BSA-sponsored visits. Few if any of the speakers held the requisite degree to teach at a university, but some had bachelor's or master's degrees, and all identified with the Black experience and Black community—a quality Black students admired most. However, the instructors and particularly the director had to be respected and accepted by the university faculty. Hiring "unqualified" individuals or individuals without proper credentials could leave the program vulnerable because it would be the only academic unit on campus staffed by people without doctoral degrees. Chairman Eubanks addressed this concern: "We have refused to insult the students or the faculty by attempting to fill these [positions] with people who will lower the caliber of the faculty at the University of Illinois. This does not mean that we are hung up on degrees." He and others preferred candidates with doctoral degrees, but the lack of a doctorate did not preclude faculty appointments.[45] Eubanks's concern was not unfounded, but it sometimes came into conflict with BSA demands and certainly slowed the institutionalization of Black studies at Illinois. The disagreements over faculty hires ignited a tense relationship between Eubanks and BSA that would further slow the process.

A year and a half later, in fall 1970, the Black studies program remained in the planning stages. Although African American undergraduates constituted only 3.9 percent (944 students) of the Illinois student population at the time, their numbers did not deter the popularity of the lecture series, the development of Black-centered courses, or constant pressure for a Black studies program.[46] Black students were not concerned that they were a minority on campus, particularly since the call for the initiation of a Black history class was made by CORE when less than three hundred Black students attended Illinois in late 1966. The number of Black and white students enrolled in the lecture series course ballooned to 875 in 1971, making it one of the largest courses offered on campus.[47]

In the spring of the 1970–71 academic year, the university responded to the popularity of LAS 199 and proposed a follow-up course, LAS 291, "The Black World: Perspectives." Enrollment was open to sophomores, juniors, and seniors with prior relevant coursework.[48] The sheer number of students enrolled in the few Black-centered courses offered demonstrated an interest in these courses and a desire for similar ones, and the need for a coordinated program grew.

Tensions within the Faculty-Student Commission reduced its effectiveness and preempted meaningful action, however. BSA and the commission interpreted the pace of events differently. BSA believed the slow pace was a deliberate attempt to undermine the program and push it to the periphery, and the organization questioned the commitment of the commission and the university to Black students. According to Chairman Eubanks, the growing number of commission participants (Champaign-Urbana residents were invited to participate) hindered fruitful discussions and action, and the intransigence of BSA representatives on certain issues precluded compromise and therefore lengthened the process of institutionalization. Frustrated that the commission refused to adopt "a more meaningful organization and 'vote itself out of business,'" Eubanks resigned as chair in December 1969 and recommended to the chancellor that the commission be reorganized.[49]

Accordingly, the chancellor disbanded the Faculty-Student Commission and established the Afro-American Studies Commission in January 1970. The new commission now integrated the creation of a cultural center into its mission and created a hierarchy. Program directors would run the cultural center and the academic program and would report to the executive director of the Afro-American Studies Commission, who acted as a liaison between the directors and the vice chancellor. One of the old commission's primary objectives—the development of a program philosophy—was reached, but the institutionalization of a Black studies program remained unfinished, and a director had yet to be found. On 16 February 1970, the Reverend Dr. Renford Gaines became interim executive director of the new commission and interim director of the academic program that would work to implement the Black studies program.[50] He tendered his resignation only a few months later, in August 1970. Delano Cox, an assistant dean in the College of Liberal Arts and Sciences, became the director of the academic program on a third-time basis.[51] Robert Eubanks, now the nemesis of BSA, became the interim executive director of the Afro-American Studies Commission.

In September 1970, angered by the reinstatement of Eubanks in a central role and by the slow pace of program development, BSA demanded that the commission be eliminated immediately and that the program directors report directly to the vice chancellor. "In this structure we have eliminated a useless body which only served as an unnecessary buffer zone," BSA declared.[52] Black students doubted the university's commitment to a quality Black studies program and pointed to the pace of events and Eubanks's lack of expertise in Black studies as proof. Eubanks resigned on 16 October 1970 and removed himself from the institutionalization of Black studies. "It is clear that misinformation, frustration and poor communication have caused a large number of black students to feel that the present commission structure is ineffectual, and that I have been a major impediment to progress," Eubanks stated. He implored the university to move forward with its plans for Black studies and to encourage academic departments to include content on Blacks in their courses, but he commented he would no longer play a major role in Black campus affairs.[53] The chancellor reluctantly accepted his resignation, and the Afro-American Studies Commission was disbanded. With university sanction and consistent with BSA demands, program directors now reported directly to the vice chancellor.[54]

Before the commission's demise, it did formulate a set of proposals that further defined the role of a Black studies program in higher education: its mission was to be corrective, descriptive, and prescriptive.[55] First, the commission asserted that a Black studies program was useful for instructional purposes. Offering new courses with previously absent African Americans at the center would expose Blacks and whites to the richness of Black culture and insert the African American in American history, literature, etc. Second, the commission maintained that research on Black Americans and Blacks in the diaspora was necessitated by "events of recent years [that] compelled an often previously uninterested academic community to focus on the many phases of the Black American." To facilitate and promote this new research interest, Illinois library holdings needed to be expanded. Third, the commission evoked the public service role of a public institution. Commission members recognized the "urgent need" for the university to commit itself to social change in the economically and educationally underdeveloped communities of Illinois. This more complete understanding of the role and purpose of Black studies brought the program closer to reality, but a coherent program was yet to be initiated.[56]

A high turnover rate in leadership plagued the start of the Black studies program. After two years as director of the academic program, Cox resigned to become chair of an eight-member advisory committee on SEOP. In 1972, the Afro-American Studies and Research Program became an institutional reality with Walter Strong, a graduate student in political science, as the director. After one year, Strong resigned, and Ora Brown became interim director. By 1974, the program had yet another director, Dr. John Stewart.[57] That directors often had to divide their duties and could not commit themselves full-time to program development undermined the status of the program. For instance, Cox's duties were divided between the College of Liberal Arts and Sciences, SEOP, and the Afro-American Academic Program (that was soon to become Afro-American Studies and Research Program). Likewise, Strong was a graduate student, an instructor in political science, and the vice chancellor for academic affairs while acting as director. Stewart was the first full-time director and the first director to hold a doctorate.[58] In the early to middle 1970s, the program was organized in the sense that it became a reality, but its institutional future remained shaky.

BSA and the university remained committed to Black studies. The organizing process was tense and strained, but both groups believed the fight was worth it. Its advocates pushed forward and refused to be swayed from the task. By the late 1970s, the Afro-American Studies and Research Program had grown stronger and more viable. Its original structure remains intact in the year 2003. The program maintains an interdisciplinary focus and is staffed by faculty members with joint or courtesy appointments in a variety of departments on campus. But the goal of having a major in Afro-American studies was never reached. In the 1970s, the university explained that the lack of courses and adequate organization meant that only a minor was feasible. Over thirty later, the situation remained the same. The number of Black-centered courses has grown over the years, and the program maintains a full-time director, but the University of Illinois has not created a formal major for those interested in Black studies.

Afro-American Cultural Program

As the Afro-American Studies and Research Program was becoming a reality, so, too, was the Black cultural center. Black students already had created dance and choral groups on their own and were supported in their endeavors by university staff in student services, but they sought a more coherent body though which to participate in cultural creation.[59] Initially included in BSA's list of demands, the creation of the center was assigned to SEOP administrators and staff in the fall of 1969. However, after realizing it would put an undue strain on SEOP, the Faculty-Student Commission took over its development and institutionalization and assigned the task to a committee composed of both faculty and BSA representatives. Perhaps because its purpose was the creation and investigation of Black culture and was not an academic enterprise or because administrators were much less concerned with hiring a cultural center director with a doctorate degree than with staffing the Black studies program, the cultural center faced fewer obstacles in becoming institutionalized.

In the fall semester of the 1969–70 academic year, the Afro-American Cultural Program opened with Val Gray Ward, artist, dramatist, and former History 199 guest lecturer, as its first director. Robert Eubanks, who at the time was still chair of the Faculty-Student Commission, said her duties entailed the coordination of cultural and artistic activities on campus. In a university press release, Ward explained that her duties included "making Black students aware of their heritage, and sharing our rich Black culture with those who are not aware of our contributions."[60] The Afro-American Cultural Program was located in a small university-owned house until larger accommodations could be found. All students were welcome at the center since the creation of a separate social activity space only for Black students would have violated Title 6 of the Civil Rights Act of 1964. However, racial tensions on campus, the Black students' sense of ownership of the center, and separatist sentiment meant that only Black students and Black Champaign-Urbana residents used the cultural center facilities to its fullest.

The cultural center was not just a recreation center or meeting place for Black students and Champaign-Urbana Black residents. Under Ward, the center sponsored several culturally centered workshops, including a writer's workshops, where students read, learned about, and wrote poetry and essays; a dance workshop, where students learned and performed African dances; and manhood/womanhood workshops, where issues of gender roles and male-female relationships were discussed. Often, workshop participants would showcase their talents in shows or publications. The center became the campus locus for creating and exulting Black culture and the Black aesthetic and was extremely popular with Black students. Many considered it a haven from the hostile academic and social atmosphere of the campus. According to Jeffrey Roberts, "It was a place you could go and you didn't feel like you were being beat-up on by the University. Every place else you went had such a negative situation. At least for that hour you were at the cultural center you felt like you were in a positive situation where people were reinforcing whatever needs you had."[61]

Ward was very popular with Black students, but her relationship with the chair of the Faculty-Student Commission was strained. Eubanks lauded her for her efforts and her artistic ability but described her as "difficult to work with and hard to help." He attributed part of the problem to her lack of administrative experience. In his opinion, her uneasiness about her lack of college experience (she did not have a college diploma) and her assumption that the faculty did not respect her further exacerbated the tensions. To compensate, "she mislead and incensed the students to get their support," he contended. Eubanks also cited disagreements over control of the budget. As of 1969, the Faculty-Student Commission controlled the funds for the cultural center. Ward argued for autonomy and, according to Eubanks, resented the fact that she had to have his approval for expenditures.[62]

In the opinion of BSA, Eubanks precipitated her resignation. BSA members accused Eubanks of collusion with university administrators in disparaging Ward and a lack of dedication to the cultural center. In their September 1970 letter to the vice chancellor, they angrily discussed the fact that the director did not have fiscal autonomy but had to ask the Afro-American Studies Commission executive director for permission to spend money.[63] Just a few years earlier, Eubanks had been the BSA faculty adviser (1967–68) because he was one of only two or three Black professors on campus. But now BSA questioned his "sensitivity and rapport with Blacks" and depicted him as an autocrat who refused to share power. Robert Ray, director of the center from 1971 to 1973, remembered that Ward felt the university had created the center as a "token" gesture to appease protesting Black students and doubted its dedication to supporting it.[64] Amid the turmoil, Ward announced her resignation near the middle of her term and officially resigned on 31 August 1970.[65]

Eubanks, at this time the interim director of the Afro-American Studies Commission, helped form a search committee to replace Ward. He cautioned against appointing a director not acceptable to Black students: "The strong interest and involvement of Black students in the Cultural Program makes it imperative that the Cultural Program Director be acceptable to them and be able to work with them." According to Eubanks, he submitted the names of two possible candidates to BSA as the "sole organized voice of Black students on this campus." BSA rejected both and tendered its own list of candidates, including graduate students and undergraduates matriculating in June. The only candidate Eubanks and the administration thought possessed the requisite maturity and skills already had a previous commitment and could not fill the position.[66] Again, Eubanks drafted a list of possible candidates. Antonio (Tony) Zamora, a professional musician, student of music, and former LAS 199 guest lecturer, was acceptable to the students and became director in the fall semester of 1970.[67]

Black students felt intensely connected to and invested in the cultural center and were prepared to defend it at any cost. For instance, BSA sent a letter dated 23 July 1970, to Black freshmen preparing to attend the university in the fall of 1970. Addressed to "Brothers and Sisters," BSA apprised incoming Black students of the campus situation. The letter stated, "We have begun preparing for the fall semester and would like to acquaint you with the *political* situation of Blacks at the University of Illinois." Students were made aware of the status of the newly opened cultural center, the difficulty in retaining a director, and the center's lack of autonomy because of certain administrators (most likely Eubanks, though he was not mentioned by name). Autonomy was declared a must because the center housed and initiated cultural and political activities for Black students. The new Black students also were made aware of BSA as an organization, its upcoming elections, and possible programs. Just as it opened, the letter closed with an example of the influence of Black Power on the students: "[U]moja and Uhura."[68]

At the same time the search for a cultural center director occurred, the university sponsored the "Hearing Panel on Black-White Relationships." During the 1969 and 1970 calendar years, the university experienced escalating violence between Black and white students. Many of the disturbances occurred in Illinois Street Residence Hall, the same residence hall that Black women refused to vacate in September 1968. The residence hall became the locus since it had an attractive and large multipurpose room where Black students enjoyed hosting dances and other social activities. The panel sought to understand the conditions igniting the disturbances and to make recommendations on how to improve the situation. One of the panel's recommendations was the expansion of the cultural center and the university's rededication to the center. "The Panel is under the impression that the facilities currently used for a Black Cultural Center were provided as an immediate step, in recognition of the fact that it would only serve temporarily while a more adequate facility is constructed or located. Black students are less certain than we are that the University views it as a temporary solution," the report stated.[69] A permanent cultural center would give Blacks a place to congregate and feel at home, rejuvenate their spirits, and allow for time to investigate the African and African American heritage. It would also demonstrate university commitment to Black students and Black student issues.

George Frampton, the vice chancellor for campus affairs, addressed the panel's recommendations. According to Frampton, the university remained committed to the cultural center and Black students. He reported that the university's budget request for 1971–72 included $400,000 to be used to house the cultural center (as well as the Black studies program). He acknowledged that the amount allotted was not enough to support the center but cited an inability to convince the State Board of Higher Education to improve the facility. President David Dodds Henry, Chancellor Jack Peltason, and Earl Hughes, president of the board of trustees, had all made personal appeals to the State Board of Higher Education for funding for a permanent "Afro-American facility" but had been denied. Frampton stated, "We do not intend to give up. Only a first phase of the battle is over." Frampton believed that Zamora's appointment was a step in the right direction. Now that the cultural center had a director who could act as an advocate and continue to pressure the board for funding, "the prospects for the future of this center begin to look more hopeful now than at any time so far this year," he said.[70]

Zamora did not share the administration's faith in university efforts. Frustrated over the lack of autonomy for the cultural center (especially with regard to its finances) and the strained relationship with Eubanks, Zamora resigned after only three weeks. Students accused Eubanks of having greater loyalty to the university than to the cultural center and Black students. BSA used the example of Ward's tense relationship with Eubanks and her early resignation to prove their point. It refused to see another director "chased out," rallied around Zamora, and demanded his reinstatement. In conjunction with the letter written in September 1970 that indicted Eubanks for his role in the slow pace in the development of a Black studies program, BSA circulated a petition in which the organization openly doubted Eubanks's commitment to Black students and called for his resignation on the following grounds:

1. Dr. Eubanks is not and never has been attuned to the problems and ethos of the Black students of this university;
2. We have never considered Dr. Eubanks our representative; he is the representative of the university administration. We require a representative who is ours, not someone else's!
3. Dr. Eubanks has failed to work cooperatively with two former Directors of the Afro-American Culture Center [Val Gray Ward and Tony Zamora], resulting in their resignations. These directors had achieved great rapport with the Black students and community.[71]

Days after the petition was circulated, Eubanks resigned as interim director of the Afro-American Studies Commission. Zamora was reinstated as director as per the students' demands.

Under Zamora, the cultural center's institutional structure grew, as did its programs and workshops. His efforts brought the center closer to the administrative nature and structure of other units on campus. For

instance, when first organized, the center's only staff position was director. Zamora brought in a significant number of staff members, usually
graduate students, to facilitate in coordinating cultural center activities,
including two assistant directors, a receptionist, a typist, an accountant,
a historian, and two librarians. Undergraduates sometimes filled the roles
of workshop coordinators. Using his musical talent, Zamora organized
the Lab Band, which included students and nonstudents from Champaign-Urbana, Chicago, New York, and Ghana, and he sponsored a student singing group called the Black Chorus.[72] Both groups performed on
campus, in local schools and other institutions of higher education in the
state of Illinois, and at various penal institutions. The center also published its first pamphlet in which the purpose of the cultural center was
described: "Our purpose is to bring about self-awareness, self-apprecia-
tion, and Black unity through our culture. We emphasize the use of traditional and contemporary trends in African and Afro-American life
styles, showing similarities which point to the oneness of Black culture.
It is aimed at establishing a natural and scientific basis for the Black approach to life."[73] During this formative period, the cultural center took
the first steps toward establishing its longevity on campus.

Zamora also established the character of the cultural center in that
he helped mold it into a reflection of the Black arts movement sweeping
the nation. The Black aesthetic became a conduit through which Black
Power themes evolved and demonstrated the emancipatory nature of
Black culture. Its development provided, in the words of the journalist
and historian Lerone Bennett Jr., "a new frame of reference which tran-
scends the limits of white concepts."[74] Through it, African Americans
could best express themselves and their unique perspective on reality.
Black students emulated the writing style of such poets and dramatists
as Haki Madhubuti and Amiri Baraka, participants in the Black arts
movement. At the cultural center, they created art, literature, and music with Blackness at their core.

Zamora described his interaction with students as fruitful and rewarding. He enjoyed interacting with them, delighted in watching and
assisting them create cultural products, and considered them extremely
bright. However, the stress of being torn between university commitments and concern for Black students, working to establish a solid foundation in the cultural center in an environment he considered hostile, and
taking on administrative duties unfamiliar to him caused Zamora to re-
sign permanently as director in 1971 and distance himself from the university.[75] Robert Ray, an instructor in the Department of Music, became

Zamora's successor. Under his direction, the center continued to focus on the arts, including drama, dance, photography, and music. Ray resigned in mid-1973. His reasons for resigning were unclear, but in 1972 he had indicated that if the cultural center's budget was cut, he would leave: "That would tell me that the University does not have a commitment to the program and that I should look elsewhere for a job because in a few years they are going to phase the program out."[76] He had also reiterated the Hearing Panel on Black-White Relationships' two-year-old-charge that university attempts to relocate the center needed to be accelerated and had openly expressed doubt that the center would relocate for another two to three years.[77] Bruce Nesbitt, an African American from Champaign and the coordinator of the Student Relations Program for the Office of Campus Programs and Services, became interim director in August 1973. He was appointed director in 1974. Not until the late 1970s would the cultural center acquire a permanent facility.

By the early 1970s, the Afro-American Studies Commission's support for the Afro-American Studies Program and the Black cultural center began to take root. Budget constraints, frequent changeover of directors, and the hasty nature of their conceptualization were early obstacles in ensuring program longevity. However, the university and students remained committed to their survival, and both programs continued to eke out an existence. The cultural center continues to provide several different workshops and activities, including Omnimov (a dance group), the *Griot* (a newsletter), and WBML (a radio station run by students). Students continue to minor in Afro-American studies and take a variety of courses on the African American experience. None of these activities could have occurred without BSA and its demands.

Black students and BSA do not deserve all the credit for reform efforts at Illinois. The administration contemplated different ways in which to bolster Black student retention and satisfaction prior to BSA's demands. However, the university understood Black student attrition as a mark of cultural deprivation, and the reforms it proposed were geared to improve individuals, not alter the structure of education at Illinois.[78] The Black Power movement and the resulting Black student movement shifted the focus to reforming the university. BSA forced the university's hand and precipitated aggressive and far-reaching reforms that the university had not previously entertained. The interaction of initiatives helped change the campus forever.

6   A Lasting Influence

By the mid-1970s, Black student attempts to use Black Power ideology and principles to reform the University of Illinois bore fruit and changed the campus permanently. Their efforts had increased Black student enrollment and led to the creation of the Afro-American Studies and Research Program and the Afro-American Cultural Program. Moreover, Black students were able to force the university administration into more aggressive action on other issues, such as creating a commission to hear Black student grievances, hiring Black faculty, reexamining hiring policies for university staff, and devising outreach programs to the Champaign-Urbana community.[1] The university was not unconcerned with such issues prior to Black student demands, but the nature of the demands and the manner in which Black students pursued them produced very different results.[2] In a matter of a few years, primarily between 1969 and 1971, Black students helped precipitate institutional changes that improved the quality of education and campus life for all students. By 1974, the university administration had firmly entrenched some of the reforms in the university structure.

Black students were proud of their accomplishments, but as the decade wore on various factors began to weigh heavily on them and hastened the decline of the Black student movement. In large part, the decline paralleled the demise of the Black Power movement. In both their writings and in oral interviews, Black students at Illinois connected themselves to Black Power and understood their demands and purpose as an integral component of that struggle. By the early 1970s, the Black Power movement and its most visible supporters had come under heavy attack from government agencies and programs and faced increasingly violent repression.[3] Inside the movement, the loss of a collective purpose, factional disputes, and competition for leadership exacerbated its decline.[4] The Black student movement at Illinois—as well as at other campuses—suffered a similar fate. As the Black Power movement gained strength, Black students brought Black Power principles to campus and gained power inside the university. With its decline and dissolution, Black Power's influence faded, as did student participation in the Black student movement.

Black students at Illinois reflected on the decline of their own movement.[5] In a 1975 article printed in the Illinois yearbook, *Illio,* entitled "Black Activism Deactivates," the author identified group jealousies, internal conflicts, and petty difference as important factors.[6] Black students had never been a completely unified group, but multiplying group differences fractured the Black student community. In the late 1960s, BSA was the primary Black organization on campus other than Black fraternities and sororities. By 1975, more than thirty different organizations exclusively serving Black students existed. As graduate and professional students formed their own organizations, BSA became an explicitly undergraduate organization. The Black law students were the first to secede from BSA and form the Black Law Students Association in 1970. Black graduate students followed a short time later by transforming the Black Graduate Committee of BSA into the Black Graduate Student Association. BSA's undergraduate membership splintered into organizations housed in the different residence halls across campus. In 1973, Black students at the Pennsylvania Avenue Residence Hall formed their own organization, the Black Student Committee at P.A.R., later renamed Salongo (strong in Kiswahili). Other groups of Black students followed and created their own residence hall governments with Kiswahili names.[7] The new governments fell under the umbrella of the newly created Central Black Student Union. Though descendants of BSA, the hall governments became much more social than political.

The emergence of different residence hall governments was partly a reaction to the reorientation of BSA objectives and style, which further alienated participants and fractionalized the Black student population. In 1972, BSA renamed itself the Coalition of Afrikan People and shifted its focus to include more nonstudent and nonuniversity issues, such as independence movements in Africa and the creation of an educational facility for Black north Champaign residents called the Harambee Institute.[8] Explaining the change, members of the Coalition of Afrikan People declared, "The name BSA was felt too restrictive and not encompassing the many facets of Black people."[9] Robert Harris, an assistant professor of history at the time, hypothesized that the Coalition of Afrikan People alienated potential members by focusing on Pan-Africanist ideology "at a time when students wanted to deal with more immediate needs."[10] The separate residence hall governments took up the slack left by the organization.

More academic, social, cultural, and political organizations were created in the early to middle 1970s and further diffused the Black student population. The new organizations offered Black students something they had not had—a choice of organizations in which they felt comfortable and which addressed Black student issues. However, the sheer number of alternatives splintered the Black student population. By the mid-1970s, the Coalition of Afrikan People was only one of many organizations that purported to speak for Black students. Its membership quickly declined, and the organization finally dissolved in 1976. Politically motivated Black student groups continued to exist, but the Black Students Association did not.

Attrition through protest fatigue and graduation further exacerbated the demise of the Black student movement. The continuing students who played such a pivotal role in recruiting and socializing the first SEOP students graduated in the early 1970s. The other continuing students and even the 1968 SEOP class had graduated by 1973. The students who had the most to do with such university reforms as Black student recruitment and the planning and implementation of the Black studies program and cultural center were gone from campus. Those few who did remain were tired of battling and demanding. They wanted to be able to enjoy the college experience and college life without the rigors of protest and the threat of being sent home. Some of their demands had been met, and many wanted a break from forcing the university to entertain certain reforms. They were anxious to be students rather than agents of social change.

Those Black undergraduate students who remained at Illinois for graduate or professional school reported that the increased academic competition and racial hostility in the post-baccalaureate environment, paired with a kind of battle fatigue, lead them to focus on individual concerns. When Christine Cheatom Holtz, a former BSA executive council member, attended law school, she remembered someone attempting to get her involved at the graduate level. Instead, she focused on the academic rigors of law school (in addition, she remembered having to fight the intense racial hostility in the law school) and getting her husband paroled from a draft-resistance charge.[11] Yolanda Smith Stanback-Williams, a participant in the 9 September 1968 sit-in at the Illini Union, stated, "By the time I hit graduate school, I wasn't involved with anything." She shied away from activism and sorority commitments and concentrated on her studies and outside pursuits.[12] Delores Parmer Woodtor anticipated continuing her involvement in BSA but reported that conflicting interests with certain BSA members and personal commitments led her attention elsewhere.[13] These women and other Black students who withdrew from student activism did not necessarily give up their attitudes on Black Power or student rights and withhold support for particular student initiatives. However, the Black student movement was almost nonexistent by the mid-1970s. After 1975, most Black registered student organizations focused on academic and social support. *Yombo*, the last of the newspapers distributed by BSA/Coalition of Afrikan People, faded. *Irepodun*, the Black yearbook, ceased to exist.

In other ways, the successes of the Black student movement made their involvement unnecessary and obsolete as the university co-opted their reforms. For instance, Black students and BSA focused most of their energy on increasing Black student enrollment and establishing a Black studies program and a Black cultural center. The university agreed that these issues should receive attention and moved forward with students to make them a reality. The student role in all three projects diminished or disappeared as the university took control. Black students were first removed from the formal recruitment process. The university stopped hiring Black undergraduates as recruiters in 1970. The university recognized the worth of including continuing Black students on its recruitment staff, especially in the beginnings of SEOP, but cited problems brought about by miscommunication and lack of expertise and training as primary reasons for the decision. Similarly, Black students were removed from graduate student recruitment efforts. The initial organization created to increase their enrollment was the Black Graduate Student Committee, a group of Black graduate and professional students with university funding who traveled across the country recruiting students. In 1972, the university absorbed the duties of the Black Graduate Recruitment Committee and created the Graduate College Minority Student Affairs Office. The university hired professional staff to fill the roles continuing students had played.

Black students lost their role in the Afro-American Studies and Research Program and the Afro-American Cultural Program, and again, it was their success that hastened their disappearance from decision-making committees. By 1974, the Black studies program had become a reality with its first full-time director and a list of classes in which students could explore Black American and diasporic life and culture. Black students had helped make the program a reality and shaped its purpose and direction, but as the program became more viable Black student involvement in it faded. Students became consumers of the program rather than decision-makers. Similarly, Black student decision-making power in the cultural center faded, though they retained a much larger degree of input in the cultural center than in the Black studies program. The cultural center maintains a full-time director and staff, but students continue to initiate and run programs through it and even work in various positions. Although it is no longer the primary venue in which Black students socialize, it has retained its status as the locus of Black creative expression in its various forms.

The university also co-opted some of the support programs in which Black students participated. In the mid-1960s, the university devised its own tutoring and counseling programs, but Black students continued to use informal networks because of the paternalistic ethos of the university-sponsored support programs. In 1974, the university took cues from its previous efforts and those of Black students and institutionalized the Office of Minority Student Affairs. The new office soon took on tutoring and counseling duties and was more successful at this stage than the university had been previously. One factor that increased its success was that the office hired only Black and Latina/o graduate students as counselors—by this time the Latina/o population had grown and was experiencing some of the same difficulties as Black students. The rate of undergraduate attendance at counseling meetings improved with the shift in hiring—a derivative of Black student critiques of previous university efforts. Tutoring positions are still open to all students, regardless of race, who complete a course successfully. A large factor in its increased use is that the tutoring services took on a new ethos. Students seeking tutoring were no longer thought to be culturally deprived and in need of remediation. Rather, they requested tutoring because of the nature of challenging classes and their desire to excel.

That the university believed certain Black student demands were important enough to consider seriously and then institutionalize their suggestions demonstrates the university was not completely ignorant of or uninterested in Black student issues. However, the co-optation was a doubled-edged sword. In part, Black students welcomed the chance to step down from semi-administrative posts because they often felt that the university expected too much from them and were overburdened with their dual roles of students and program initiators. Also, their absence often was appropriate as the new programs fought for legitimacy. To become viable, the Black studies program needed a full-time credentialed staff, not students working part-time. However, Black students no longer had input on university-adopted programs. Once the university took control, it could shape and mold the programs to fit its purposes. At times the university's efforts coincided with what Black students demanded. For instance, the university continues to actively recruit Black students through a combination of the Educational Opportunities Program (the renamed SEOP) and newer admission programs and remains competitive in the Big Ten in enrolling Black undergraduates. However, the university's total control of the Black studies program meant that the demand for a Black studies major went unmet; only an interdisciplinary minor is possible.

Student activists found themselves content that the university took them and their demands seriously, but their co-optation by the university ended what some students believed would be a continued role in university business and left some activists frustrated. Other protest issues were not difficult to find, and Black students continued to see possibilities for improvement, but most were thankful for the chance to become students again and enjoy their late teens and early twenties.

―――――――――

Black students' attempts to bring the university closer to their understanding of a just and representative institution were a part of Black liberation efforts nationwide and were a pivotal part of African American social movements of the mid-twentieth century. Black students saw the creation of a cultural center and a Black studies program as an immediate solution to campus problems, but they also understood the long-term possibilities in promoting academic success for themselves and future students. The demands for increased Black student enrollment and Black faculty can be interpreted as long-term goals in an effort to increase representation, provide equal educational opportunity, and participate more fully in American institutions. Other demands reached beyond the campus boundaries. For instance, the demands that "the university deny any employer in the community access to University buildings which practices discrimination in hiring and promotion" and "that the University as an institution, or through separate departments, initiate a program designed to increase low-cost housing financed by state or federal funds for Black residents of Champaign" emerged from a long history of similar demands from the Black community in general.[14] Through their persistence and hard work, Black students were able to gain an audience with university administrators and bring Black Power principles to campus. Understood in this way, the Black Power movement becomes important when examining the nature of higher educational reform and the particular reforms of the late 1960s and early 1970s.

The Black student movement also left a more student-centered legacy on campus. Though more than thirty years have passed, various events and organizations initiated by the students in the Black Power era still exist. Since many continue to feel alienated from the larger campus community, these events and organizations provide meaning and acceptance. Black Mom's Day celebrations are still held the same weekend as the university Mom's Day celebrations. Black Homecoming activities continue to thrive. The Black Chorus grew from four students to over one hundred members and continues to perform in churches and educational institutions across the state of Illinois. The first dinner to recognize Black SEOP graduating seniors in 1972 was transformed into the Black Congratulatory Ceremony, a more personal event for Black graduating seniors, graduate students, and professional students held in addition to the university graduation ceremonies. The Central Black Student Union still offers an alternative to the university-sponsored student government. In this way, Black students continue to remind the academic and student community of the historical need for such organizations and events on campus and their role in educating Black students, acclimating them to campus, softening cultural shock, and providing a voice for Black students—an echo of the goals set forth by BSA over thirty years ago.

Also, other groups, such as Latina/os, women, and Asian Americans, followed the lead of Black students during the late 1960s and early 1970s and demanded similar concessions from the university. A Latino studies program and a women's studies program were established some years after the Black studies program. Most recently, Illinois institutionalized an Asian American studies program. Taking cues from the Black studies program emerging in the late 1960s, the new programs are broad, interdisciplinary fields. Also, Latina/o student demands regarding La Casa Cultural Latina, the Latina/o cultural center, paralleled those of Black students of the late 1960s and early 1970s. In the early 1990s, Latina/o students called for the resignation of the cultural center's director after accusing her of undermining the center's central purposes, demanded that their choice of director be instated, requested more autonomy in cultural center affairs, and accused the university of underbudgeting center programs. In their quest to be heard, Latina/o students and their supporters occupied both the Office of Minority Student Affairs and the Administration Building. Like the Black students before them, they used direct-action tactics and race rhetoric to demand an audience with the administration.[15]

Persistent discrimination experienced by Black students means that Black students themselves remain active at Illinois. In the late 1980s and early 1990s, Black students protested various issues on campus and testified to the fact that alienating experiences still exist. For instance, law students received in their mailboxes flyers containing racist epithets, derogatory cartoons, and statements calling for a ban on interracial marriage and citing Africa as the origin of the AIDS virus. In response, Black students circulated petitions and initiated forums in which to discuss the flyers and racism more broadly. When a Black female student who lived above a campus bar found racist epithets written on her apartment door, Black students rallied. On one of the bar's busiest nights of the week, a group of Black students sponsored a boycott. Two groups formed single-file lines outside the establishment so that patrons would have to pass between them to enter. The Black students inside the establishment kept the bartenders busy ordering water. Also, Black students broadened their scope and joined with other students to attack the use of Chief Illiniwek, the mascot at Illinois. Many activists described the use of such a symbol as racist and intolerable and undertook various boycotts, sponsored panel discussions, and initiated protests to ban the Chief.[16] By turning to direct-action tactics, Black students mirrored the methods used previously on campus. Though protesters were few and participation often faded with the end of a crisis, such issues galvanized students in the late 1980s and early 1990s. As long as Black students feel alienated on campus and experience racism and discrimination, activism remains a possibility.

Tangible consequences of the Black student movement are important in understanding the legacy of their efforts, but personal views of success demonstrate what the students themselves took away from their experience. When former students were asked what they thought they gained from their involvement, some commented on leadership skills and character development that spilled over into their current careers. Others pointed to lifelong friendships and a sense of community fostered during their time at Illinois. Some former students still call each other on 9 September to commemorate their arrests and reminisce. Together they survived the academic pressures, doubting administrators and faculty, and an often hostile campus environment. Former students remembered that Black students spent so much time together not because they *had* to but because they *wanted* to.

Unfortunately, the scars of their experience also linger with some former students. A few commented that they gained a strong dislike for whites at Illinois and remember the time as very painful. Some of those who attended Illinois before the arrival of the 1968 SEOP class, in particular, have mixed feelings about their time in Champaign-Urbana. Looking back, they are very proud of their accomplishments, but they remember their time at Illinois as intensely lonely. Discussing their experiences as students literally brought some to tears. The task of balancing academics, a social life, and activism felt overwhelming for some. Despite their traumatic experience, all of the former students interviewed received at least bachelor's degree, and all but one received an additional master's, law, or doctorate degree. School at Illinois was difficult, but their difficulties did not prevent them from pursuing a high quality education for future career pursuits and personal growth.

Former administrators also reflected on their time at Illinois. All of them recognize that it was a unique time in university history that has had far-reaching consequences. Walter Strong, former director of the Afro-American Studies and Research Program, stated, "In many ways it became clear to administrators that they needed to become much more aware, much more sensitive to multicultural issues and be able to develop a much better working relationship with students of diverse backgrounds. And as administrators, we began to understand the importance of participatory democracy in the student context that you just don't ask students for their opinions as an afterthought, that you involve them in the process."[17] Students have never regained the kind of decision-making power they held in the late 1960s and early 1970s, but administrators are much less likely to ignore their concerns. Clarence Shelley, the former director of SEOP, believes that the Black student movement made the campus more adaptive. Administrators learned how to react to different pressures without the luxury of time and to think in new and innovative ways about the nature of higher education. He credits Black students with precipitating institutional change that had not previously been entertained. "I have no doubt it was the students and their presentation that made the difference," he stated.[18] Black students pushed the envelope.

Like former students, former administrators are proud of their accomplishments. The Black Power era was a difficult and stressful time, one they would not wish to repeat. Administrators were pulled in different directions by Illinois residents, Illinois legislators, African American students, white students, and other groups with an interest in education at the university. They had to reconcile calls for urgency and immediate remediation with a university system structured for lengthy deliberation, discussion, and debate on programmatic changes. With their hand forced by Black students, administrators worked quickly. Some missteps were made, but they stayed the course and helped make some of the Black student demands a reality. According to former chancellor Jack Peltason, "Once we got going, we never went back. It changed the face of the University forever."[19] Though they would not repeat the experience, all the former administrators believe the effort was worthwhile.

Students during the Black Power era provided a benchmark for change at Illinois. Their time there was short and often intense, but they were able to influence educational policy and programs in ways that no students had done previously or have since then. With students and administrators forced into a closer relationship than had existed, Black students created space for dialogue on Black student issues and concerns. The dedication of students and administrators ensured that long-lasting changes came out of their collaboration on reform initiatives. Their accomplishments demonstrate the power of a social movement in an institution. For Clarence Shelley and many others, "the legacy is about the possibilities"—the possibilities for change, the possibilities for compromise, and the possibilities for growth.[20]

APPENDIX A:

LIST OF INTERVIEWEES

Addison, David. Brooklyn, N.Y. 22 March 1998.

Anderson, James. Champaign, Ill. 28 March 2001.

Atkins, Jacqueline Triche. Chicago, Ill. 23 October 1997.

Brady, Paul. Chicago, Ill. 20 November 1997.

Broom, Willard. Champaign, Ill. 20 February 2001.

Cullers, Terry. Chicago, Ill. 24 October 1997.

Dixon, Dan. Chicago, Ill. 18 September 1997.

Eggleston, James. Chicago, Ill. 24 October 1997.

Eisenman, David. Champaign, Ill. 19 February 2001.

Hammond, Rodney. Telephone interview. 29 October 1997.

Holtz, Christine Cheatom. Chicago, Ill. 18 December 1997.

Jarrell, Boyd. Champaign, Ill. 31 October 1997.

Levy, Stanley. Champaign, Ill. 22 February 2001.

Long-Green, Edna Lee. Chicago, Ill. 22 August 1997.

Massey, Walter. Telephone interview. 3 April 2001.

Moreland-Young, Curtina. Telephone interview. 1 May 2001.

Peltason, Jack. Irvine, Calif. 28 June 2001.

Perrino, Dan. Champaign, Ill. 20 February 2001.

Phillips, Sandra Norris. Telephone interview. 10 September 1997.

Ray, Robert. St. Louis, Mo. 18 February 2001.

Roberts, Jeffrey. Chicago, Ill. 21 August 1997.

Satterlee, Hugh. Champaign, Ill. 21 February 2001.

Savage, William. Telephone interview. 1 May 2001.

Scouffas, John. Champaign, Ill. 21 February 2001.

Shelley, Clarence. Champaign, Ill. 29 August 1997 and 21 February 2001.

Smith, Joseph. Champaign, Ill. 10 July 1999.

Stanback-Williams, Yolanda Smith. Chicago, Ill. 17 September 1997.

Strong, Walter. Turlock, Calif. 3 May 2001.

Townsend, Terry. Champaign, Ill. 19 October 1997.

Woodtor, Delores Parmer. Chicago, Ill. 20 November 1997.

Zamora, Antonio. West Lafayette, Ind. 12 November 1997.

APPENDIX B:

BSA DEMANDS

1. That the administration drop all charges against all Black people who were arrested September 10, 1968.
2. That the University drop all charges against Blacks who have been arrested since September 10th.
3. That the University remove all reprimands of record of Blacks resulting from the September 10th arrest.
4. That the administration immediately recognize BSA by allocating the budget which was requested in September, 1968.
5. That the University immediately begin hiring 50% Blacks in the non-academics job vacancies.
6. That the University waive civil service tests as a requirement for non-academic employment for Blacks or implement a job training program with 75% of regular pay before taking the test.
7. That the University immediately grant a minimum 20% wage increase to all persons working in the janitorial and food service capacities, (Black and white).
8. The immediate establishment of a Black Cultural Center large enough to accommodate all Black people which will be run by the BSA.
9. The immediate establishment of an autonomous Black Studies Department, with major emphasis on Afro-American Studies and African Studies.
10. The hiring of 50 Black dormitory counselors for September 1969.
11. That all Black graduate students who have been recruited by BSA be admitted to graduate school in September 1969.
12. That the Graduate College publicly state its commitment to admitting 15% Black students into the 1969–1972 entering classes.
13. That the University hire 500 Black faculty members over a four-year period beginning by hiring 150 Black faculty members for September 1969.
14. That the Illini Union be autonomously run by a board consisting of students, faculty and Blacks from the community.
15. That the University fulfill its financial commitment to all students who are receiving money for SEOP.

16. That the University make a public statement of its commitment to bring 500 students to the University in September.

17. That the Faculty Senate appoint a special committee on Black Students Affairs, consisting of five Blacks and five white faculty members acceptable to BSA who will act on Black grievances.

18. The retention of William K. Williams as one of the top administrative advisors on Black affairs.

19. An interpretation of the role of the University Planning Commission and a description of the responsibilities of said commission. This committee's budget should be accessible to BSA.

20. Immediate creation of a committee composed of members of the Black community, faculty, and the Department of Architecture to plan future construction, and location of University buildings.

21. Complete access by members of the Black community which are not specifically designated for administrative use.

22. That the University as an institution, or through separate departments, initiate a program designed to increase low-cost housing financed by state or federal funds for Black residents of Champaign.

23. That the University deny any employer in the community access to University buildings which practices discrimination in hiring and promotion.

24. That any information derived from the experimental project at Washington Elementary School, located in Northeast Champaign, or other educationally and economically deprived groups.

25. That the University actively recruit and hire Blacks as firemen and policemen.

26. That the University secure voter registration booths on campus.

27. That the University eliminate the clerical program headed by Loretta Davis or place in immediate employment graduates of the program.

28. Resumption of the Pre-Apprenticeship program operated by the University with a definite commitment from all labor unions who have received or will receive construction contracts on the Urbana campus.

28A. Elimination of the high school diploma as a requirement for employment with such unions.

29. Formation of a committee to assist the non-academic employment department in the administration of said department with the immediate aim of increasing employment of Black residents.

30. That the University provide funds for the establishment and implementation of a Black Cultural Program for residents of Northeast Champaign and to provide bus service for said residents who wish to use the facilities of the proposed Black Cultural Center.

31. The University through BGSA (the Black Graduate Students Associa-

tion) recruit and enroll 200 Black law students by 1972 and that the Black student enrollment be increased by 500 pursuant to the proposed expansion of the Law School.

32. That the University place in supervisory positions Black persons who are employed in the areas of janitorial, maid, food, and custodial services.

33. That the University exert all pressure necessary on the campus business community to actively recruit and employ Black residents and students. And that additional pressure be exerted from the various departments of the University to aid in this effort.

34. That the University actively seek and supply adequate off-campus housing for undergraduate and graduate students either through construction of such housing or policy that would prohibit discrimination and price-fixing.

35. That the present available position of Union night-time supervision be filled by Black residents of Northeast Champaign.

Source: "We Demand," *Black Rap,* 18 February 1969, BSAP.

NOTES

Abbreviations

AACL   Afro-American Culture Lecture File, 1968–71
ACW   Arthur Cutts Willard Papers, General Correspondence, 1934–46
BSAP   Black Students Association Publications, 1967–
CHAN   Chancellor's Subject File, 1967–70
CHREO   Committees on Human Relations and Equal Opportunity, 1964–
DOS   Dean of Students Subject File, 1952, 1963–84
EOP   Educational Opportunities Program File, 1964–77
HMT   Harry M. Tiebout Papers, 1941–82
LAS   Liberal Arts and Sciences Associate and Assistant Deans Subject File, 1948–72
LASDS   Liberal Arts and Sciences Departmental and Subject File, 1913–76
LCNS   Legal Counsel Numerical Subject File, 1935–83
OMBUD   Ombudsman's Subject File, 1960–92
RRP   Robert Rogers Papers, 1960–68
SEOP   Special Educational Opportunities File, 1968–70
UPR   University Press Releases, 1935, 1939, 1947–
VPAAC   Vice-President for Academic Affairs Correspondence, 1965–74

All archival material was gathered from the University of Illinois at Urbana-Champaign Archives unless otherwise noted. All newspaper articles from the *Chicago Tribune, Daily Defender, Daily Illini, Plain Truth,* and *News-Gazette* were gathered from the University of Illinois at Urbana-Champaign Newspaper Library unless otherwise noted.

Introduction

1. See, for example, Diane Ravitch, *The Troubled Crusade: American Education, 1945–1980* (New York: Basic Books, 1983).

2. See, for example, Arthur Levine, *Shaping Higher Education's Future: Demographic Realities and Opportunities, 1990–2000* (San Francisco: Jossey-Bass, 1989).

3. Sheila Slaughter, "Class, Race, and Gender and the Construction of Post-Secondary Curricula in the United States: Social Movement, Professionalization, and Political Economic Theories of Curricular Change," *Journal of Curriculum Studies* 29, no. 1 (1997): 5.

Chapter 1: Black Youth Forcing Change

1. For specific examples of internal and external pressures to exclude African Americans from various white institutions in the North, see Leon Litwack, *North of Slavery: The Negro in the Free States, 1790–1860* (Chicago: University of Chicago Press, 1961), chap. 4; and Raymond Wolters, *The New Negro on Campus: Black College Rebellions of the 1920s* (Princeton, N.J.: Princeton University Press, 1975), chap. 7.

2. For more on this, see Litwack, *North of Slavery,* chap. 4.

3. Joe R. Feagin, Hernan Vera, and Nikitah Imani, *The Agony of Education: Black Students at White Colleges and Universities* (New York: Routledge, 1996); "Enrollment in Negro Universities and Colleges," *School and Society* 28 (29 September 1928): 401–2, cited in Wolters, *The New Negro on Campus,* 313.

4. For a more thorough discussion of the New Negro, see Alain Locke, ed., *The New Negro: An Interpretation* (New York: Albert and Charles Boni, 1925); and John Hope Franklin, *From Slavery to Freedom: A History of Negro Americans,* 3d ed. (New York: Vintage Books, 1969), chaps. 24–28.

5. "Enrollment in Negro Universities and Colleges," cited in Wolters, *The New Negro on Campus,* 17.

6. Wolters, *The New Negro on Campus,* 34.

7. Ibid., chap. 2; James D. Anderson, *The Education of Blacks in the South, 1860–1935* (Chapel Hill: University of North Carolina Press, 1985), chap. 7.

8. David Sansing, *Making Haste Slowly: The Troubled History of Higher Education in Mississippi* (Jackson: University Press of Mississippi, 1990), 140.

9. Medgar Evers was one such veteran. Evers used the GI Bill to pay for his undergraduate education at Alcorn College and later attempted to enroll in the University of Mississippi School of Law in 1954. He joined the local NAACP and became the first field secretary in Mississippi in 1954. Evers agitated for Black rights until his assassination in 1963. He and other veterans important to the southern civil rights movement are discussed in Charles M. Payne, *I've Got the Light of Freedom: The Organizing Tradition and the Mississippi Freedom Struggle* (Los Angeles: University of California Press, 1995), particularly chap. 2.

10. All court case information in this chapter is from the original Supreme Court case or from Richard Kluger, *Simple Justice: The History of Brown v. Board of Education and Black America's Struggle for Equality* (New York: Vintage Books, 1977).

11. *McLaurin v. Oklahoma State Regents,* 339 U.S. 637 (1950), 641.

12. Richard L. Plaut, "Racial Integration in Higher Education in the North," *Journal of Negro Education* 23 (Summer 1954): 310.

13. Thomas W. Young to Walter White, 21 January 1927, National Association for the Advancement of Colored People Files, Library of Congress, quoted in Wolters, *The New Negro on Campus,* 315.

14. Benjamin Mays, *Born to Rebel* (New York: Charles Scribner's Sons, 1971), 65, quoted in Wolters, *The New Negro on Campus,* 318.

15. Beulah Terrell to William Pickens, 29 April 1919, National Association for the Advancement of Colored People Files, Library of Congress, quoted in Wolters, *The New Negro on Campus,* 323.

16. Wolters, *The New Negro on Campus,* 320–21.

17. Allen B. Ballard, *The Education of Black Folk: The Afro-American Struggle for Knowledge in White America* (New York: Harper and Row, 1973), 4.

18. For a complete discussion of Lucy's short time at Alabama, see E. Culpepper Clark, *The Schoolhouse Door: Segregation's Last Stand at the University of Alabama* (New York: Oxford University Press, 1993), chaps. 3–6.

19. For a full account of the rise, development, and demise of the Student Nonviolent Coordinating Committee, see Clayborne Carson, *In Struggle: SNCC and the Black Awakening of the 1960s* (Cambridge, Mass.: Harvard University Press, 1981).

20. John H. McClendon, ed., *The State of Black Champaign County* (Champaign, Ill.: Urban League of Champaign County, February 1984).

21. "Three Thousand Hear Klan Talk by Glen Young," *News-Gazette*, 25 July 1924.

22. League of Women Voters of Champaign County, Illinois, *A Community Report, Twenty Years Later: The Status of the Negro in Champaign County* (Champaign, Ill.: League of Women Voters, October 1968).

23. William C. Baker and Patricia L. Miller, *A Commemorative History of Champaign County, Illinois: 1833–1983* (Champaign, Ill.: Illinois Heritage Association, 1984).

24. League of Women Voters, *A Community Report*, 14, 16, 31. Several former administrators offered unsolicited remembrances of a "southern feel" to Champaign during the middle to late 1960s and recounted how shocked they were that Champaign practiced discrimination so overtly. See David Eisenman, interview by author, Champaign, Ill., 19 February 2001; Stan Levy, interview by author, Champaign, Ill., 22 February 2001; John Scouffas, interview by author, Champaign, Ill, 21 February 2001; and Hugh Satterlee, interview by author, Champaign, Ill, 21 February 2001.

25. *Prairie Farmer*, 11 July 1863, 17, cited in Winton U. Solberg, *The University of Illinois, 1867–1894: An Intellectual and Cultural History* (Urbana: University of Illinois Press, 1968), 81.

26. "Negro Students at the University of Illinois: An Outline of Their Enrollment, Graduates, Activities, History, and Living Conditions," 1934–35, ACW, Box 2, Folder: Colored Students, University of Illinois.

27. "Statement on the Responsibility of the University for the Housing of Racial Minorities," Board of Trustees Reports, 1946–48, 54.

28. "Just Like Dixie: No U of I Dorms for Negroes," *Daily Defender*, 4 August 1945, HMT, Box 3, Folder: SCIC Restaurant Scrapbook. The Black press has continuously commented on American institutions and their discrimination against African Americans. The first Black newspaper, *Freedom's Journal*, first published in 1827, covered a wide variety of subjects, including civil rights, education, and African events. It sought not only to publish information relevant to African Americans but also to advocate for the cause of freedom with their own voice: "We wish to plead our own cause. Too long have others spoken for us. Too long has the publick been deceived by misrepresentations, in things which concern us dearly." John Russwurm, the first Black graduate from a white institution, was one of the newspaper's editors ("The First Negro Newspaper's Opening Editorial, 1827," in *A Documentary History of the Negro People in the United States*, ed. Herbert Aptheker [New York: Citadel Press, 1969], 82–83).

29. A. C. Willard to Charles Jenkins, 2 August 1945, ACW, Box 92, Folder: Housing for Colored Students.

30. "Negro Students at the University of Illinois," 2.

31. Ibid.

32. Photographic File, Box 2, Folder: 1912–14.

33. "Negro Students at the University of Illinois," 4, 7. It is unclear if African American men were kept out of advanced military courses because of U.S. military policies or University of Illinois practice. The exclusion was probably a mixture of the two. The U.S. military did not desegregate until 1951, years after the report was written. Evidence indicates that Illinois commissioned only one African American officer in the 1930s, but "his color was so light that he was thought white" ("Negro Students at the University of Illinois," 7).

34. Ibid., 5.

35. Du Bois and Woodson, both of whom were professors, agitated for including African American content in college curriculum. Both believed an understanding of African American history and culture through an African American lens was vital to racial uplift and an important part of a college education. See W. E. B. Du Bois, "Does the Negro Need Separate Schools?" *Journal of Negro Education* 4 (July 1935): 328–35; and Carter G. Woodson, *The Mis-Education of the Negro,* 2d rev. ed. (New York: AMS Press, 1977).

36. "Negro Students at the University of Illinois."

37. *Scribbler,* March 1938, Student Organizations Publications, 1871–, Box 7, Folder: Cenacle. In 1945, African American students petitioned the university for permission to publish a "small newspaper for circulation among Negro students on the campus." There is no further mention of the African American student newspaper and no copies of it in the University of Illinois Archives. It is difficult to know if the newspaper was ever published. Regardless, the petition for the newspaper is very telling of Black student attitude and thought during the time (see "Petition for Publication of Small Newspaper for Negro Students," Committee on Student Affairs Minutes, Box 2, Folder: 1945–46).

38. Committee on Student Affairs Minutes, Box 3, Folder: 1949–50.

39. Lucy Gray, interview by Deirdre Cobb-Roberts, Champaign, Ill., 12 June 1997, cited in Deirdre Cobb-Roberts, "Race and Higher Education at the University of Illinois, 1945 to 1955" (Ph.D. diss., University of Illinois at Urbana-Champaign, 1998), 60.

40. Untitled, 1951, HMT, Box 3, Folder: SCIC Dissolution and Reorganization, 1951.

41. Various signed affidavits, HMT, Box 3, Folder: Restaurant Affidavits, 1947–48.

42. Harold Asher, signed affidavit, 18 January 1947, HMT, Box 3, Folder: SCIC Theater Affidavit, 1946–48.

43. See HMT, Box 3, Folder: Barbershop Project.

44. Quoted in David Henry to Board of Trustees, 16 February 1962, HMT, Box 4, Folder: Restaurants.

45. Harry Tiebout to NAACP, 26 August 1961, and Herbert L. Wright to Claudia Young, 4 April 1960, ibid.

46. Code on Student Affairs, cited in Henry to Board of Trustees, 16 February 1962.

47. Tiebout to NAACP, 26 August 1961.

48. M. E. Van Valkenburg to David Henry, 15 December 1961, HMT, Box 4, Folder: Restaurants; Henry to Board of Trustees, 16 February 1962.

49. Royden Dangerfield to University Council, 13 March 1961, HMT, Box 4, Folder: Restaurants.

50. Cobb-Roberts, "Race and Higher Education at the University of Illinois," 49, 50, 54, 55.

51. "Negro Students at the University of Illinois"; Cobb-Roberts, "Race and Higher Education at the University of Illinois," 116, citing evidence from Student Ledger Cards, Microfilm, 1899–1981.

52. Quoted in Cleveland Sellers, *The River of No Return: The Autobiography of a Black Militant and the Life and Death of SNCC* (Jackson: University Press of Mississippi, 1973), 166.

53. Stokely Carmichael and Charles V. Hamilton, *Black Power: The Politics of Liberation in America* (New York: Vintage Books, 1967), viii (first quote), 44 (second quote).

54. Quoted in Sellers, *The River of No Return,* 234.

55. Quoted in ibid., 231.

56. For a discussion of the national nature of the Black student movement, see Durward Long, "Black Protest," in *Protest! Student Activism in America,* ed. Julian Foster and Durward Long (New York: William Morrow, 1970), 459–82. For a discussion of the connections between Black students at Illinois and Black students at other campuses, see James Anderson, interview by author, Champaign, Ill., 28 March 2001.

57. Another contributing factor was President Lyndon Johnson's introduction of Executive Order 11246 in 1965. The order required federal contractors to "take affirmative action to ensure that applicants are employed, and that employees are treated during employment, without regard to their race, creed, color, or national origin" (President, "Equal Employment Opportunity 11246," *Federal Register* 30 [24 September 1965]: 19319). Affirmative action principles in employment soon spread to higher education admissions.

58. Marvin Peterson, Robert Blackburn, Zelda Gamson, Carlos Arce, Roselle Davenport, and James Mingle, *Black Students on White Campuses: The Impact of Increased Black Enrollments* (Ann Arbor, Mich.: Institute for Social Research, 1978), 28–29.

59. Alan E. Bayer and Alexander W. Astin, "Campus Unrest, 1970–71: Was it Really All That Quiet?" *Educational Record* 52 (Fall 1971): 308.

60. Urban Research Corporation, *Student Protests 1969* (Chicago: Urban Research Corporation, 1970), 14.

61. H. Rap Brown, *Die! Nigger! Die!* (New York: Dial, 1969), 57.

62. William Exum, *Paradoxes of Protest: Black Student Activism in a White University* (Philadelphia: Temple University Press, 1985), 42.

63. For a detailed discussion of Black student unions, see ibid., chap. 3.

64. Quoted in Richard McCormick, *The Black Student Protest Movement at Rutgers* (New Brunswick, N.J.: Rutgers University Press, 1990), 17 (first quote), 35 (second quote).

65. Nathan Hare, "The Case for Separatism: 'Black Perspective,'" in *Black Power and Student Rebellion,* ed. James McEvoy and Abraham Miller (Belmont, Calif.: Wadsworth), 234.

66. Martin Weston, "Black Studies Dead or Alive?" *Essence,* (1974): 57, cited in Alan King Colón, "A Critical Review of Black Studies Programs" (Ph.D. diss., Stanford University, 1981), 9.

67. Vincent Harding, "Introduction," in *The Challenge of Blackness,* ed. Lerone Bennett Jr. (Atlanta: Institute of the Black World, 1970), iv.

68. Colón identified and described the threefold purpose of Black studies in "A Critical Review of Black Studies Programs," 8.

69. Quoted in Harry Edwards, *Black Students* (New York: Free Press, 1970), 98.

70. McCormick, *The Black Student Protest Movement at Rutgers,* 111.

71. Cushing Strout and David Grossvogel, *Divided We Stand: Reflections on the Crisis at Cornell* (New York: Doubleday, 1970), 3.

72. McCormick, *The Black Student Protest Movement at Rutgers;* Exum, *Paradoxes of Protest;* Sandra Walker, "Transitional Experiences of Black Students at a Predominantly White University (Ph.D. diss., Washington University, 1976); Strout and Grossvogel, *Divided We Stand.*

73. Patrica Gurin and Edgar Epps, *Black Consciousness, Identity, and Achievement: A Study of Students in Historically Black Colleges* (New York: John Wiley and Sons, 1975), 350. Some historically Black institutions also experienced student unrest during the late 1960s and early 1970s. For a discussion of Black student protests at Black colleges, see Lawrence B. de Graaf, "Howard: The Evolution of a Black Student Revolt," in *Protest! Student Activism in America,* ed. Julian Foster and Durward Long (New York: William Morrow, 1970), 319–44; E. C. Harrison, "Student Unrest on the Black College Campus," *Journal of Negro Education* 41 (Spring 1972): 113–15; and Nathan Hare, "The Struggle of Black Students," *Journal of Afro-American Issues* 1 (Fall 1972): 111–30.

74. Exum makes this claim in *Paradoxes of Protest,* 172.

75. Jeffrey Roberts, interview by author, Chicago, Ill., 21 August 1997.

76. *Black Rap,* 13 October 1969, BSAP.

77. Quoted in Exum, *Paradoxes of Protest,* 61.

78. For a further discussion of the link between the sociohistorical context and the development of African American educational efforts, see William H. Watkins, "Black Curriculum Orientations: A Preliminary Inquiry," *Harvard Educational Review* 63 (Fall 1993): 321–38. In the article, Watkins described six curriculum orientations and linked them to the Black experience in the United States and the larger struggles over curriculum from the eighteenth century to the twentieth.

Chapter 2: From Negro to Black

1. Donald J. Wermers, *Minority Ethnic Enrollments at the University of Illinois Fall Terms, 1967–1973* (Urbana: University Office of School and College Relations, April 1974), 17, obtained from the University Office of Academic Policy Analysis.

2. Cobb-Roberts, "Race and Higher Education at the University of Illinois," 110, citing evidence from Student Employment Folders, 1934–74.

3. Though most campus groups were de facto segregated, Black and white students did sometimes work together. Black and white students in the NAACP and the Congress of Racial Equality drafted a resolution to condemn the Alabama church bombing that killed four young girls, went to Mississippi to register Black

voters in upcoming elections and to teach in freedom schools, participated in teach-ins, sit-ins, and marches in Champaign-Urbana, and called for a boycott of Illinois athletics, charging the Athletic Association with discriminatory practices. Examples of such activities are included in "Senate Maps Bill," *Daily Illini*, 17 September 1963; "UI Rights Workers Return from Mississippi Campaign," *Daily Illini*, 7 November 1964; "SNCC to Stage Sit-In," *Daily Illini*, 19 May 1964; "NAACP Calls for Boycott," *Daily Illini*, 13 February 1965; and James Johnson, "Bevel: Say It Long, Loud," *Daily Illini*, 10 April 1964.

4. White students were not completely unconcerned about racial issues. Some joined with Black students in the NAACP and SNCC to fight for racial justice in Champaign. Others formed their own groups to fight against discrimination on campus. One such group, the Ad Hoc Committee of Students for Human Dignity and Social Peace, is discussed in chapter 3.

5. Dan Dixon, interview by author, Chicago, Ill., 18 September 1997.

6. Charles Willie and Joan Levy found similar conclusions in their study of four separate predominantly white campuses in "Black Is Lonely," *Psychology Today* 5 (March 1972): 50–52, 76–80.

7. Christine Cheatom Holtz, interview by author, Chicago, Ill., 18 December 1997.

8. Edna Lee Long-Green, interview by author, Chicago, Ill., 22 August 1997.

9. Black student optimism is reflected in various interviews by the author and in Frank Costin, "The LAS Summer Study Program Evaluation Report," 4 December 1965, EOP, Box 1, Folder: Information on Course.

10. "Audiotapes," [1965], OMBUD, Box 1, Folder: Complaints, Anonymous, Audiotape, Racism on Campus.

11. Paula Giddings discussed both the founding of Black Greek letter organizations and the trials of one sorority during the Black Power movement in *In Search of Sisterhood: Delta Sigma Theta and the Challenge of the Black Sorority Movement* (New York: William Morrow, 1988). The number of Black students involved in fraternities and sororities is not available at the University of Illinois Archives. The statistics are not contained in the Greek Affairs Files, and the archives do not hold the records of the Black Greek Council.

12. Boyd Jarrell, interview by author, Champaign, Ill., 31 October 1997. Chicago residents were not the only ones who perceived the Willis Wagons as objectionable. The U.S. Department of Justice investigated their use and described them as a form of racial segregation (Alan B. Anderson and George W. Pickering, *Confronting the Color Line: The Broken Promise of the Civil Rights Movement in Chicago* [Athens: University of Georgia Press, 1986], 341–64).

13. Yolanda Smith Stanback-Williams, interview by author, Chicago, Ill., 17 September 1997.

14. David Addison, interview by author, Brooklyn, N.Y., 22 March 1998.

15. Terry Cullers, interview by author, Chicago, Ill., 24 October 1997.

16. Sellers, *The River of No Return*, 19. For an example of the shifting ideology of a Black student at Illinois, see William Savage, telephone interview by author, 1 May 2001.

17. For a discussion of CORE, see August Meier and Elliott Rudwick, *CORE: A Study of the Civil Rights Movement, 1942–1968* (New York: Oxford University Press, 1973).

18. "University of Illinois Undergraduate Student Organization Record," Student Organization Constitutions and Registration Cards File, 1909–81, Box 7, Folder: CORE formerly NAACP.

19. "Constitution and By-Laws of the University of Illinois Chapter of the Congress of Racial Equality," [1966], Clipped Article File of William Savage.

20. Anderson and Pickering, *Confronting the Color Line*, chap. 2. The complaints of mid-twentieth-century African American Chicago residents were remarkably and sadly similar to earlier African American complaints. See Robert L. McCaul, *The Black Struggle for Public Schooling in Nineteenth-Century Illinois* (Carbondale: Southern Illinois University Press, 1987); and Michael Homel, *Down from Equality: Black Chicagoans and the Public Schools, 1920–41* (Urbana: University of Illinois Press, 1984).

21. Otis Dudley Duncan and Beverly Duncan, *The Negro Population of Chicago* (Chicago: University of Chicago Press, 1957), 96, 95. See also St. Claire Drake and Horace R. Cayton, *Black Metropolis: A Study of Negro Life in a Northern City* (New York: Harcourt, Brace, 1945), chap. 8.

22. Quoted in *New York Times*, 10 July 1966, cited in David Garrow, *Bearing the Cross: Martin Luther King, Jr., and the Southern Christian Leadership Conference* (New York: William Morrow, 1986), 489; see also ibid., chap. 8.

23. Anderson and Pickering, *Confronting the Color Line*, 211–13, citing *Chicago Sun-Times*, 13, 15, 17, and 27 July 1966; and *Chicago Tribune*, 13 July 1966.

24. For a more thorough discussion of the radicalization of the national CORE, see Meier and Rudwick, *CORE*, 329–73, 413–14. For a discussion of campus CORE ideology, see Savage interview; and Anderson interview.

25. Former students could not recall how this racial split occurred, if white students left the organization willingly, or if white students were unceremoniously ousted, as in SNCC in 1966 (see Carson, *In Struggle*, chap. 13).

26. "CORE Touches Racial Issues," *Daily Illini*, 5 October 1966; "Plan Negro History Course," *Daily Illini*, 18 November 1966 (quote). For other *Daily Illini* articles covering the Black history course, see "Neglected History," 28 October 1966; and "Expect History Dept. Support; Requests Negro Course," 2 November 1966. History 199, "Black Culture," became a reality in the spring 1969 semester.

27. William Savage, "CORE's Purposes," *CORE Newsletter*, 27 September 1967, Clipped Article File of William Savage.

28. "Viewpoint," *CORE Newsletter*, 27 September 1967. Since reliable membership lists for CORE were not available at the University of Illinois Archives, an accurate count of participants is impossible.

29. Jacqueline Triche Atkins, interview by author, Chicago, Ill., 23 October 1997; "Audiotapes."

30. James Eggleston, interview by author, Chicago, Ill., 24 October 1997.

31. Sandra Norris Phillips, telephone interview by author, 10 September 1997.

32. Gurin and Epps, *Black Consciousness, Identity, and Achievement*, 339–51.

33. This discussion is based on various materials in LCNS, Box 5, Folder: Clabaugh Act, 1966–67; Box 43, Folder: W. E. B. Du Bois Club Newspaper Clippings and Miscellaneous Material; and Box 43, Folder: W. E. B. Du Bois Club Materials Submitted to Board of Trustees.

34. Untitled, in Robert W. Rogers to David D. Henry, 24 March 1967, LCNS,

Box 43, Folder: W. E. B. Du Bois Club Newspaper Clippings and Miscellaneous Material.

35. This discussion is based on various materials in LCNS, Box 5, Folder: Clabaugh Act, 1966–67; Box 43, Folder: W. E. B. Du Bois Club Newspaper Clippings and Miscellaneous Material; and Box 43, Folder: W. E. B. Du Bois Club Materials Submitted to Board of Trustees.

36. *Snyder et al. v. the Board of Trustees of the University of Illinois,* 286 Fsupp 927 (ND IL 1968).

37. "Statement of Facts on University Discipline and the Anti-Dow Civil Disobedients," December 1967, LCNS, Box 44, Folder: Student Discipline—Dow Chemical Co. (Miscellaneous).

38. K. Edward Renner to Jack Peltason, 8 November 1967, ibid.

39. For a discussion of the May 1970 National Guard occupation of the campus, see Clipped Article File of David Eisenman; Clipped Article File of Willard Broom; Willard Broom, interview by author, Champaign, Ill., 20 February 2001; and various materials in DOS, 1966–92, 1994, Box 31, Folder: Rumor Center Information Sheets, March–May 1970.

40. Charles Bowman, professor of law and chair of the Faculty Advisory Committee, advised Chancellor Peltason that an appeal to superior moral law did not justify interference with free speech or access and counseled that faculty participating in the Dow protest receive an official reprimand and be warned that future conduct would lead to dismissal. See Charles H. Bowman to J. W. Peltason, 21 November 1967, LCNS, Box 44, Folder: Student Discipline—Dow Chemical Co. (Miscellaneous).

41. Elise Cassel, "Student Reformers Group," *Daily Illini,* 2 March 1968; Linda Picone, "Reform Caucus Explodes," *Daily Illini,* 23 March 1968.

42. Paul Schroeder, "Why?" *Daily Illini,* 15 March 1968.

43. Cecil Cheatom to Local Board No. 71, 27 March 1968, included in "Ex-Editor of *Drums* Indicted," *Plain Truth,* 1 December 1968.

44. Chapter 1 more thoroughly examines the role of white students in the NAACP on campus and white student interest in the aims of the civil rights movement.

45. Quoted in "Encourages Negroes to Form Racial Pride," *Daily Illini,* 7 January 1967.

46. "BSA Aims and Policies," *Drums,* December 1967, BSAP.

47. "Request for University Recognition of a New Undergraduate Student Organization Not Maintaining a House," Student Organization Constitutions and Registration Cards, 1909–1981, Box 4, Folder: Black Students Association, 1967–72.

48. CORE, before BSA, had lamented the dichotomy between Greeks and non-Greeks in its first newsletter. See Terry Cullers, "A Note to the Frats and Sorors," *CORE Newsletter,* 27 September 1967, Clipped Article File of William Savage.

49. Paul Brady, interview by author, Chicago, Ill., 20 November 1997.

50. Dixon interview.

51. Ibid.

52. Delores Parmer, "Greek Coup," *Drums,* December 1968, BSAP.

53. "Black Power, CORE Intentions, What Goals They Look Forward To," *Daily Illini,* 7 January 1967.

54. Phillips interview.

55. Long-Green interview.

56. Phillips interview.

57. Psychologists devised various explanations of the Negro-to-Black conversion experience. The language in this paragraph was taken from William E. Cross Jr., "The Negro-to-Black Conversion Experience," *Black World* 20 (July 1971): 13–27; and William E. Cross Jr., *Shades of Black: Diversity in African-American Identity* (Philadelphia: Temple University Press, 1991).

58. Cullers interview; Long-Green interview; Terry Townsend, interview by author, Champaign, Ill., 19 October 1997.

59. "Unity with C-U Blacks," *Drums*, November 1967, BSAP.

60. Eggleston interview.

61. William Savage, "Retention and Recruitment," *Drums*, March 1968, BSAP.

62. Rodney Hammond, telephone interview, 29 October 1997.

63. "Goals Are Black Unity and Black Consciousness," *Drums*, November 1967, BSAP.

64. Ibid. This sentiment closely resembled that of H. Rap Brown, one-time SNCC chairman, speaking about the Black student role in the liberation struggle. See Brown, *Die! Nigger! Die!* 66–69.

65. "Revolutionary Blasts Whites," *Daily Illini*, 17 February 1968.

66. For a fuller critique of the emerging Black Power ideology, see chapter 4.

67. Christine Cheatom, "Accept What You Are," *Drums*, December 1967, BSAP.

68. Atkins interview.

69. Quoted in "Phil Cohran Here for Black Heritage Weekend," *Drums*, November 1967, BSAP.

70. For a discussion of the murders at Jackson State and South Carolina State College at Orangeburg, see Eggleston interview; Townsend interview; and "BSA Mourns Slaughtered," "Orangeburg Facts," and "Orangeburg's Blood Will Not Flow in Vain," *Drums*, March 1968, BSAP.

71. Cullers interview. Many former students remembered such sentiments. See especially Anderson interview; and Brady interview.

72. Quoted in Carolann Rodriguez, "Negroes Predict Violence," *Daily Illini*, 5 April 1968. In a 29 October 1997 telephone interview, Hammond stated he was misquoted in this article. Hammond remembered stating something to the effect of "Now that [King] has been eliminated, I would not be surprised if there was a violent reaction to his death since the power of his symbolism is now removed." Though the words may not have been Hammond's, the fact remains that many Black Illinois students held beliefs consistent with those printed in the article.

73. The information on King's assassination and its impact on Chicago is based on Donald Mosby, "Despite Guard, Cops, Federal Troops More Looting Hits Ghetto," *Daily Defender*, 8 April 1968; and "Student Reactions Mixed Over King's Death: Prayers, Plans, and Riots Are Outlets for Grief," *Daily Defender*, 8 April 1968.

74. Quoted in Dave Potter, "Rights Figures Blast Daley on 'Shoot Looters' Order," *Daily Defender*, 16 April 1968.

75. "Unity and Action" and "PIGS at Work: Incident 1," *Black Rap*, 18 February 1969, BSAP.

76. "PIGS at Work: Incident 1."

77. Roy Wilkins and Ramsey Clark, *Search and Destroy: A Report by the Commission of Inquiry into the Black Panthers and the Police* (New York: Metropolitan Applied Research Center, 1973), 6.

78. Hammond interview.

79. David Addison, president of BSA from 1968 to 1969, maintained a very close relationship with Hampton and even recalled speaking with Hampton shortly before his murder. Addison interview.

Chapter 3: The Special Educational Opportunities Program

1. President, Executive Order, "Equal Employment Opportunity 11246," *Federal Register* 30 (24 September 1965): 19319. Title 7 of the Civil Rights Act of 1964 also prohibited discrimination in federal government agencies and established the Equal Employment Opportunity Commission (*Civil Rights Act of 1964*, Public Law 88–352, 88th Cong., 1st sess. [2 July 1964]).

2. Seymour Martin Lipset and William Schneider discussed public opinion on affirmative action in higher education in "The *Bakke* Case: How Would it be Decided at the Bar of Public Opinion?" *Public Opinion* 1 (March/April 1978): 38–44. For a discussion of both sides of the affirmative action debate, see William Bowen and Derek Bok, *The Shape of the River: Long-Term Consequences of Considering Race in College and University Admissions* (Princeton, N.J.: Princeton University Press, 1998); and Nathan Glazer, *Affirmative Discrimination: Ethnic Equality and Public Policy* (New York: Basic Books, 1975).

3. The influx of students due to affirmative action programs and societal concerns was not the first time institutions of higher education had to absorb a large number of students within a short period of time. For instance, the influx of veterans returning from World War II and taking advantage of the GI Bill alarmed universities across the country. Also, the fear of a new population lowering admissions standards and the creation of "remedial" courses and support services was not new. As a group, veterans had worse academic records and lower American College Test scores than did the average student. To accommodate this new population, administrators and faculty modified admissions criteria, sometimes gave veterans preferential enrollment over nonveterans, created special "refresher" courses, and initiated special veterans' services, including a veterans' counseling office. The fear that veterans would lower academic standards was not realized. Veterans repeatedly outperformed their nonveteran counterparts in the academic arena (Keith Olson, *The G.I. Bill, the Veterans, and the Colleges* [Lexington: University of Kentucky Press, 1974], 41–56). For a discussion of the GI Bill's impact on the University of Illinois, see Cobb-Roberts, "Race and Higher Education at the University of Illinois," 28, 45.

4. The definition of disadvantaged was a slippery one that even Illinois recognized as difficult to define (see Richard E. Spencer, "University of Illinois Program for the Culturally Deprived," March 1968, EOP, Box 1, Folder: Proposals, 1968–69). Prior to 1968, Illinois understood disadvantaged as economically depressed and racially isolated. The definition became clearer by the late 1960s, and the university followed federal guidelines set by the Department of Health, Education, and Welfare in connection with Equal Opportunity Grant applications for the fiscal year beginning 1 July 1968, in which a "disadvantaged" student was

defined as "an American of college-going age whose family income and number of siblings, as well as the condition of his home, school, and community, restrict his opportunities to develop socially, culturally, and economically toward becoming a useful member of society" (quoted in Spencer, "University of Illinois Program for the Culturally Deprived," 19).

5. David D. Henry, "The State of the University, 1963–64," *Faculty Letter* 71 (14 January 1964): 5, Clipped Article File of Joseph Smith.

6. "University Committee on Human Relations and Equal Opportunity," 30 January 1964, Committee notes of Miriam Shelden, Clipped Article File of Joseph Smith.

7. University Committee on Human Relations and Equal Opportunity, Preamble, "Interim Report by the University Committee on Human Relations and Equal Opportunity," 30 November 1964, 1 (first and second quotes), 2 (third quote), CHREO, Box 1.

8. Ibid., 1.

9. Ibid., 8.

10. The faculty was not unanimously eager to recruit disadvantaged students, however. In a letter to his colleagues, Lloyd Humphreys, a psychology professor, called Blacks "inferior on every sort of intellectual ability" and worried what effect their enrollment would have on grading practices and department standing. Harry Triandis, another professor in the psychology department, countered Humphreys's assertion and argued that the tests on which Humphreys based his assessment were culturally biased and the data possibly contaminated (Lloyd Humphreys to Colleagues, 6 October 1969, and Harry Triandis to Lloyd Humphreys, 7 October 1969, VPAAC, Box 9, Folder: Equal Opportunity, Blacks, 1969–71).

11. "Report of the AAUP Committee on the University and Race Relations," 20 May 1964, 1, Clipped Article File of Joseph Smith.

12. W. Ellison Chalmers, "The U of I and the Racial Crisis: A Personal Summary and Evaluation, 1965–66," 26 October 1964, 7–8, Clipped Article File of Joseph Smith. Other faculty members agreed with Chalmers's assertions. See, for example, William K. Williams, "University Activity in the Area of Human Relations and Equal Opportunity, 1965–1966," September 1966, EOP, Box 5, Folder: Reports, University, 1965–69.

13. David D. Henry, "The State of the University, 1963–64," *Faculty Letter* 71 (14 January 1964): 5, Clipped Article File of Joseph Smith. Henry's ramp metaphor resembles a metaphor President Lyndon Johnson used regarding affirmative action in a commencement address at Howard University over a year later: "You do not take a person who, for years, has been hobbled by chains and liberate him, bring him up to the starting line of a race and then say, 'you are free to compete with all the others,' and still justly believe that you have been completely fair" (Lyndon B. Johnson, "Commencement Address at Howard University: 'To Fulfill These Rights,' June 4, 1965," in *Lyndon B. Johnson: Containing the Public Messages, Speeches, and Statements of the President; Book II, June 1 to December 31, 1965* [Washington D.C.: Government Printing Office, 1966], 636).

14. David D. Henry, "The Year Ahead," *Faculty Letter* 81 (21 September 1964): 1, Clipped Article File of Joseph Smith.

15. Samuel C. Davis, Jane W. Loeb, and Lehymann F. Robinson, "A Comparison of Characteristics of Negro and White College Freshman Classmates," *Jour-

nal of Negro Education 34 (Fall 1970): 360. Although the university had not collected racial data on registration forms prior to 1966, it was well aware of the number of Black students on campus, though it conflated Africans and African Americans in the totals (see "The University of Illinois Negro Students," 1940, ACW, Box 42, Folder: Colored Students of Illinois).

16. University Committee on Human Relations and Equal Opportunity, "Interim Report by the University Committee on Human Relations and Equal Opportunity."

17. "Report to the President, Activity in the Area of Human Rights and Equal Opportunity, 1966–67," December 1967, 4, EOP, Box 1, Folder: Research, 1968–72.

18. Information on individual campus unit efforts to increase educational opportunity was gathered from a combination of sources: University Committee on Human Relations and Equal Opportunity, "Interim Report by the University Committee on Human Relations and Equal Opportunity"; University Committee on Human Relations and Equal Opportunity, "Report to the President, 1964," December 1964, CHREO, Box 1; Miriam Shelden, "Notes from Meeting of University Committee on Human Relations and Equal Opportunity," 8 June 1964, Clipped Article File of Joseph Smith; Williams, "University Activity in the Area of Human Relations and Equal Opportunity, 1965–1966"; and William K. Williams, "Summary of Programs at the University of Illinois Related to Human Relations, May 1966," Clipped Article File of Joseph Smith.

19. See, for example, "Audiotapes"; Williams, "University Activity in the Area of Human Relations and Equal Opportunity, 1965–1966"; and Spencer, "University of Illinois Program for the Culturally Deprived."

20. Ad Hoc Committee of Students for Human Dignity and Social Peace, "Report to the Human Relations Commission," [1964], 6, Clipped Article File of Joseph Smith.

21. The idea for the program grew out of a proposal at a February 1965 conference on the education of disadvantaged youth (see "Report of the Allerton House Conference on Human Relations and Equal Opportunities Emphasizing the Education of Disadvantaged Youth," February 1965, EOP, Box 5, Folder: Reports University, 1965–69).

22. "Roll Call: An Experimental Summer Program for Culturally-Deprived Students," 19 May 1965, included in A. J. Janata to L. H. Lanier, 20 May 1965, Clipped Article File of Joseph Smith.

23. LAS Committee on Policy and Development, Subcommittee on Disadvantaged Students, "Interim Report," 1 April 1965, 2, LAS, Box 17, Folder: Admissions Policy, 1968–70.

24. Costin, "The LAS Summer Study Program Evaluation Report," 14.

25. For instance, one pre-SEOP student, Edna Lee Long-Green, participated in the summer program and remembered experiencing hostility inside and outside the classroom when she enrolled at Illinois full-time (Long-Green interview).

26. Costin, "The LAS Summer Study Program Evaluation Report," 14.

27. Miriam Shelden, "Interim Report, Special Project for the Culturally Disadvantaged," 23 February 1967, EOP, Box 1, Folder: Research, 1968–72.

28. "University of Illinois—Urbana, Special Educational Opportunities Program," attachment in Charles Sanders to Emerson Cammack, 21 February 1969, EOP, Box 1, Folder: Proposals, 1968–69.

29. Shelden, "Interim Report, Special Project for the Culturally Disadvantaged," 2.

30. "Proposal for Provisions for Students from Disadvantaged Areas," 14 February 1967, attachment in Charles Sanders to Emerson Cammack et al., "Special Educational Opportunities Program, Materials," 21 February 1969, LASDS, Box 17, Admissions Policy, 68–70.

31. Jack Peltason had been a professor of political science and dean of the College of Liberal Arts and Sciences at Illinois prior to becoming chancellor. His field of expertise included the Constitution and civil rights, and he authored a book with that theme entitled *Fifty-Eight Lonely Men: Southern Federal Judges and School Desegregation* (New York: Harcourt, Brace, and World, 1961).

32. "Report to the President, University of Illinois, Activity in the Area of Human Relations and Equal Opportunity, 1966–1967," 4.

33. Spencer, "University of Illinois Program for the Culturally Deprived," 13. The Spencer Report came to the same conclusion as the Coleman Report, one of the most influential pieces of social science research of its time, which found that achievement was related more closely to a student's family background than to the quality of the school the student attended. In many ways, it absolved schools for the continued lower status of African Americans. See James Coleman et al., *Equality of Educational Opportunity* (Washington, D.C.: Government Printing Office, 1966), 21–23.

34. Spencer, "University of Illinois Program for the Culturally Deprived," 7 (first quote), 4 (second quote), 3 (third quote).

35. 1960 Illinois data, 1970 Illinois data, and 1970 Champaign County data derived from Bureau of the Census, *Characteristics of the Population: Illinois, 1970,* prepared by U.S. Department of Commerce in cooperation with the Social and Economic Statistics Administration, Bureau of the Census (Washington, D.C.: Government Printing Office, April 1973), 15–89, 15–90, 15–252; 1960 Champaign County data derived from Bureau of the Census, *Characteristics of the Population: Illinois, 1960,* prepared by the U.S. Department of Commerce, Bureau of the Census (Washington, D.C.: Government Printing Office, 1963), 15–202.

36. Wermers, *Minority Ethnic Enrollments at the University of Illinois Fall Terms, 1967–1973,* 17.

37. The university itself attributed its swift action in part to the pressure from BSA (see "University of Illinois—Urbana, Special Educational Opportunities Program").

38. Press Release, 2 May 1968, SEOP, Box 1, Folder: SEOP, February–July 1968.

39. Jack Peltason, "The Special Educational Opportunities Program at the University of Illinois at Urbana-Champaign," *Campus Report* 2 (October 1968): 1, Clipped Article File of Joseph Smith.

40. Ibid.; Press Release, 2 May 1968.

41. "The Special Educational Opportunities Program of the University of Illinois at Urbana-Champaign," *Campus Report* 3 (March 1970): 1, Clipped Article File of James Anderson.

42. For a defense of university policies regarding SEOP, see "Program 'Not Racist'—Eisenman," *Daily Illini,* 25 May 1968; and "Specifics of 500 Student Plan: Questions Fielded by King Fund Canvassers," *Daily Illini,* 21 May 1968, Clipped Article File of David Eisenman. Eisenman also recalled hostility toward SEOP and

its students in his interview with the author. For a critique of the ACT, see Spencer, "University of Illinois Program for the Culturally Deprived," 10–11. Admissions and Records reports from the mid-1960s all state that high school percentile rank was the most predictive of college success (see Office of Admissions and Records Annual Reports, 1964–71, Admissions and Records Director's Office, Annual Reports, 1964–71, Box 2).

43. See Joseph Smith, "A 'Front Line Perspective' of the Development of SEOP," presentation given at Sixth Annual Allerton Conference on School Administration, 10–11 April 1969, Clipped Article File of Joseph Smith; and "University Activity in the Area of Human Relations and Equal Opportunity, 1965–66," *Faculty Letter* 129 (1 November 1966): 1–2, Clipped Article File of Joseph Smith.

44. "The Special Educational Opportunities Program of the University of Illinois at Urbana-Champaign," attachment in Charles Sanders to Emerson Cammack, 28 April 1969, LASDS, Box 17, Folder: Proposals, 1968–69.

45. "The Special Educational Opportunities Program of the University of Illinois at Urbana-Champaign," March 1970, 1.

46. In a program not associated with SEOP, students who did not meet standard admission criteria could be admitted after demonstrating evidence of their ability to do satisfactory work (see "University of Illinois Undergraduate Study, 1968–1969," Admissions and Records, Records and Statistics, Undergraduate Study and Undergraduate Course Catalogs, 1964–70, Box 1). The GI Bill could also fit under this description.

47. Clarence Shelley, *Annual Report, July 1, 1968–June 20, 1969* (Urbana: University of Illinois at Urbana-Champaign Office of Student Personnel, 1969), A-3, 2, Clipped Article File of Clarence Shelley.

48. Peltason, "The Special Educational Opportunities Program at the University of Illinois at Urbana-Champaign."

49. Faite Royjier-Poncefonte Mack, *A Systematic Study of the Differential Characteristics of Black and White Graduates in an Educational Opportunity Program* (Washington, D.C.: Office of Education, U.S. Department of Health, Education, and Welfare, September, 1972), 23, Clipped Article File of Clarence Shelley.

50. Peltason, "The Special Educational Opportunities Program at the University of Illinois at Urbana-Champaign."

51. The HEW definition was cited in Margaret H. Ismaila to E. E. Oliver, Charles Warwick, Robert Corcoran, and James T. Hashbarger, 28 March 1968, SEOP, Box 1, Folder: SEOP, February–July 1968; and Spencer, "University of Illinois Program for the Culturally Deprived," 19.

52. David D. Johnson [Chief of the Educational Opportunities Grants Branch of the Office of Education] to Coordinators of Student Financial Aid, "EOG Administrative Memorandum No. 2–69," 11 November 1968, 1–4, SEOP, Box 1, Folder: August–September 1968.

53. Ibid.

54. Peltason, "The Special Educational Opportunities Program at the University of Illinois at Urbana-Champaign."

55. Walter Strong to Herbert Cox et al., 15 December 1970, Clipped Article File of David Eisenman; Hugh M. Satterlee to Leonard Spearman, 8 June 1972, EOP, Box 2, Folder: Dean of Students.

56. AAUP Policy Committee to Urbana Faculty Members, 30 October 1968, and SEOP Rhetoric Program to Interested Persons, 4 December 1968, LAS, Box 17, Folder: Proposals 1968–69.

57. David Eisenman to Martin Luther King Fund Contributors, 11 April 1969, ibid; Eisenman interview.

58. Bruce Morrison and David Eisenman to All Faculty and Graduate Students, 11 June 1968, LAS, Box 17, Folder: Proposals, 1968–69.

59. Ibid. Also, a student group called Students for Equal Access to Learning proposed a flat fee of five dollars each semester to be used for unrestricted grant aid on the condition that the state legislature match the contributions dollar for dollar. The general student body approved the fee in 1970 (see Eisenman interview; and David Eisenman to Francis Keppel, 1 October 1969, Clipped Article File of David Eisenman).

60. Jack Peltason to Clarence Shelley, 13 May 1969, SEOP, Box 1, Folder: April–July 1969.

61. John E. Bowers, "The Special Educational Opportunities Program at the University of Illinois at Urbana-Champaign," 27 December 1970, Clipped Article File of James Anderson.

62. The financial backing for SEOP students remained an issue for years. For instance, financial aid officers worried how fifth-year SEOP students could be funded in their last undergraduate year with shrinking national, state, and campus budgets (see Satterlee to Spearman, 8 June 1972).

63. Both sets of correspondence were included in Office of Admissions and Records, "Admissions Procedures for Fall, 1969," 25 September 1969, Clipped Article File of James Anderson.

64. Meyer Weinberg, *A Chance to Learn: The History of Race and Education in the United States* (Long Beach, Calif.: University Press, 1970), 332.

65. J. W. Peltason to Dan Dixon, 2 May 1968, EOP, Box 1, Folder: Proposals, 1968–69.

66. William H. Nims to David D. Henry, 8 July 1968, ibid.

67. William Savage, BSA Recruitment and Retention Committee of the BSA, to Graduating Seniors, 19 April 1968, SEOP, Box 1, Folder: SEOP, February–July 1968; "BSA Holding H.S. Weekend," *Daily Illini*, 24 April 1968.

68. James T. Hashbarger to E. E. Oliver, 16 February 1968, SEOP, Box 1, Folder: SEOP, February–July 1968.

69. E. E. Oliver to James T. Hashbarger, "Memo on High School Contact Program of the Black Students Association," 16 February 1968, ibid.

70. Interviewees believing the university doubted their ability to recruit five hundred students included Dan Dixon, Terry Cullers, and Paul Brady.

71. "University of Illinois—Urbana, Special Educational Opportunities Program," 6.

72. Charles Warwick, "Two-Week Report on '500' Recruiting Program," 25 June 1968, 1 SEOP, Box 1, Folder: SEOP, February–July 1968.

73. The university eliminated the use of student recruiters and the week-long orientation for SEOP students in 1970 (see Student Personnel/SEOP, "Impact of the FY 72 and FY 73 Budgets," 11 April 1972, EOP, Box 1, Folder: Past Funding, 1971–72).

74. Reed E. Coleman, "A Proposal for the Recruitment of Black Graduate Students," [1969 or 1970?], Jim Anderson to Marie Metze, 4 November 1970, and Vincent West to To Whom it May Concern, 16 December 1969, Clipped Article File of James Anderson; Anderson interview; Curtina Moreland-Young, telephone interview with author, 1 May 2001.

75. D. J. Wermers, *Enrollment at the University of Illinois by Racial/Ethnic Categories: Fall Terms, 1967–1975* (Urbana: University Office of School and College Relations, December 1976), obtained from the University Office of Academic Policy Analysis.

76. Stanback-Williams interview.

77. Interviews by author (see appendix A for a list of interviewees). One study revealed that pre-SEOP students and SEOP students were more alike than different. Like SEOP students, pre-SEOP students were admitted to Illinois with lower ACT scores than their white counterparts but qualified for admission since the ACT was weighed with other factors. Also, pre-SEOP students were poorer than their white counterparts. Fifty-eight percent of Black freshmen in the 1966 entering class and 68 percent in the 1967 class reported family incomes of less than $7,500. Approximately 77 percent of SEOP students reported the same family income (Davis, Loeb, and Robinson, "A Comparison of Characteristics of Negro and White College Freshman Classmates," 361, 364).

78. Patricia Yeatman to Robert Rogers, 8 July 1968, LAS, Box 17, Folder: Proposals, 1968–69.

79. Paul Doebel to Jack Peltason, 7 August 1968, EOP, Box 4, Folder: SEOP, 1972–74.

80. Satterlee interview.

81. "Special Educational Opportunity Program, 'Project 500,' Pre-College Workshop," July 1968, Clipped Article File of Clarence Shelley.

82. Ibid.

83. "Hey Brother . . . 900 Brothers & Sisters Arrive on Campus," *Drums,* May 1968, Clipped Article File of William Savage. Paul Brady remembered a similar sentiment: "The last thing we wanted was for them to be political or social. They were going to do that anyway. We wanted them in tune to the fact that this was a real battle" (Brady interview).

84. "The Special Educational Opportunities Program of the University of Illinois at Urbana-Champaign," March 1970, 2.

85. William Plater, "Summary of Department of Mathematics Courses for SEOP Students," 5 December 1968, 3, in Shelley, *Annual Report, July 1, 1968–June 20, 1969,* appendix 5.

86. William Plater, "Summary of Department of Psychology Courses for SEOP Students," 4 December 1968, 2, ibid.

87. William Plater, "Summary of Division of Freshman Rhetoric Courses for SEOP Students," 28 October 1968, 1 (first quote), 3 (second quote, 3 (third quote), ibid.

88. W. L. Shoemaker and Arthur Davis, "The Alternative Teacher Education Program: One Segment of the Special Educational Opportunities Program of the University of Illinois at Urbana-Champaign," 1969, Clipped Article File of James Anderson.

89. Requests for information on the program were received from the University of Minnesota, a Chicago Public School System teacher, Indiana State University, a principal at the Middlesex (Connecticut) Junior High School, and the Penta County Vocational School in Ohio, Clipped Article File of James Anderson. Publications on ATEP include Peter Sola and Booker Gardner, "ATEP: An 'Alternative Approach' to the Training of Teachers at the University of Illinois," *Journal of Negro Education* 45 (Fall 1976): 459–71; Arthur Davis, "An Evaluation of the ATEP in College Education" (Ph.D. diss., University of Illinois at Urbana-Champaign, 1970); and Walter Feinberg and David Tyack, "Black People, Not Student Personnel: The 'Disadvantaged' in Teacher Education," *Record* 71 (December 1969): 225–35.

90. Patrick L. Miller to Clarence Shelley, 3 July 1970, EOP, Box 6, Folder: Correspondence.

91. David Eisenman, "Tutoring Office Summary," 1, in Shelley, *Annual Report, July 1, 1968–June 20, 1969*, appendix 8.

92. Michael Brady to David Eisenman, 2 May 1969, EOP, Box 1, Folder: Tutoring Office, 1969–70.

93. James Anderson, personal communication with author, 14 August 2001.

94. Richard Gaines, "The SEOP Graduate Assistant: A Job Description," 2 October 1969, LAS, Box 6, Folder: Academic Advising, 1967–71.

95. James Anderson, personal communication with author, 14 August 2001. Clarence Shelley speculated that the more militant students intimidated some students into avoiding white graduate assistants. That the graduate assistant structure was new and not well organized or conceptualized may also have contributed to Black student avoidance of it (Clarence Shelley, personal communication with author, 20 August 2001).

96. Miller to Shelley, 3 July 1970.

97. CORE actually advertised for tutors in *CORE Newsletter*, 27 September 1967, Clipped Article File of William Savage.

98. Patricia Yeatman to Brothers and Sisters, July 1968, EOP, Box 1, Folder: Background and Related Materials, 1968–69.

99. All three organizations were started in 1970. Other departmental and residence hall organizations followed. See various descriptions in "Request for University Recognition of a New Undergraduate Student Organization Not Maintaining a House."

100. Jane Loeb, "Long-Term Retention, Performance, and Graduation of Disadvantaged College Students in an Educational Opportunities Program," August 1973, 1, 5, Clipped Article File of Jane Loeb; Bowers, "The Special Educational Opportunities Program at the University of Illinois at Urbana-Champaign," 16–18: Lawrence Schiamberg, "Comparison of LAS SEOP Freshmen and a Random Sample of Other LAS Freshmen on GPA for Fall 1968–1969," attachment in Robert A. Waller to Charles Warwick, 3 March 1969, SEOP, Box 1, Folder: April–July 1969; College of Liberal Arts and Sciences, "Highlights of the Annual Report, 1969–1970," [Summer 1970], LAS, Box 17, Folder: SEOP; Mack, *A Systematic Study*.

101. Brady interview.

102. Jane Loeb, "Performance and Retention of Students in the Educational Opportunities Program," 1971, 8, Clipped Article File of Jane Loeb.

103. Mack, *A Systematic Study*, 34, 42.

Chapter 4: The Launching of a Movement

1. Aldon Morris includes similar factors in his discussion of indigenous social movement theory. See Aldon Morris, *The Origins of the Civil Rights Movement: Black Communities Organizing for Change* (New York: Free Press, 1984), chap. 11.

2. "Statement Made by Clarence Shelley; Notes regarding the Events on September 9, 1968," 23 September 1968, EOP, Box 6, Folder: Union Incident.

3. Stanback-Williams interview.

4. The accounts of 7 September 1968 are from "Security Office Report of Events, Illini Union, September 9 and September 10, 1968," Clipped Article File of Clarence Shelley. This was not the first time Illinois had dealt with major problems regarding the housing situation. According to Keith Olson, the influx of veterans enrolling at Illinois as a result of the GI Bill caused overcrowding and forced drastic measures. For instance, because of a lack of housing in 1946, three hundred veterans slept in bunk beds in the Old Gymnasium Annex (Olson, *The GI Bill, the Veterans, and the Colleges,* 76).

5. The accounts of 8 September 1968 were taken from "Security Office Report of Events, Illini Union, September 9 and September 10, 1968."

6. John Briscoe to Students, 10 September 1968, in "Security Office Report of Events, Illini Union, September 9 and September 10, 1968," 36.

7. The accounts of 9 September 1968 are based on "Security Office Report of Events, Illini Union, September 9 and September 10, 1968." A discussion of coercion tactics is included in H. G. Haile to Jack Peltason, 11 September 1968, LAS, Box 17, Folder: SEOP. For a discussion of the reasons Black students remained at the Illini Union, see Roberts interview; Clarence Shelley, interview by author, Champaign, Ill., 29 August 1997; Stanback-Williams interview; and Eggleston interview.

8. Shelley interview.

9. Jack Peltason, interview by author, Irvine, Calif., 28 June 2001.

10. "Report of Proceedings by Subcommittee A of the Senate Committee on Student Discipline," April 1969, EOP, Box 6, Folder: Union Incident.

11. "Security Office Report of Events, Illini Union, September 9 and September 10, 1968."

12. Roberts interview.

13. Headlines obtained from Clipped Article File of Clarence Shelley.

14. John O'Brien, "Negroes Riot at U of I; Negroes Go on Rampage after Row," *Chicago Tribune,* 11 September 1968.

15. "Editorial," *Chicago Tribune,* 11 September 1968.

16. David Eisenman to David Riesman, 2 January 1970, Clipped Article File of David Eisenman. Eisenman also wrote an article in the *Daily Illini* in an effort to correct misinformation presented in the media (see David Eisenman, "Report of Sit-in 'Biased,'" *Daily Illini,* 10 December 1968).

17. "State of Illinois, Senate Resolution No. 246," 24 July 1968, n.p., LCNS, Box 9, Folder: Project 500, 1968–69.

18. "Black Is Beautiful and Belligerent," *Time,* 24 January 1969, ibid.; Karl Berning to David Henry, 18 February 1969, ibid; David Henry to Karl Berning, 22 February 1969, ibid.

19. Carl Schwartz, "Union Incident 'Damn Foolish'—Rep. Clabaugh," *Daily Illini*, 13 September 1968; Ed Borman, "Peters Reports Eight 'Troublemakers' at Illini Union Are 'Counseled Out,'" *News-Gazette*, [between December 1968 and 15 January 1969], EOP, Box 1, Folder: Press, 1968–69.

20. David Eisenman, a particularly vocal advocate of the Martin Luther King Fund and SEOP supporter, wrote letters to the Martin Luther King contributors to quell their concerns, to provide an accurate picture of the events that precipitated the arrests, and to counter the false statements made by the *Chicago Tribune*. See David Eisenman to Contributors, Martin Luther King, Jr. Fund, UI Foundation, 11 October 1968, LAS, Box 17, Folder: 500 Program.

21. Jack Peltason, "Statement of Chancellor J. W. Peltason," *Campus Report* 2 (October 1969): 2, EOP, Box 1.

22. David D. Henry, "Statement of President David D. Henry," ibid., 1.

23. Board of Trustees, "Statement—Board of Trustees," 18 September 1968, CHAN, Box 14.

24. Jack Peltason to David Henry, 8 January 1969, UPR, Box 4, Folder: S; Eisenman interview.

25. Shelley interview.

26. Long-Green interview.

27. Clarence Shelley to Parents, 17 September 1968, EOP, Box 4, Folder: SEOP, 1968.

28. Mary Kathryn Fochtman, "Complaint," *Daily Illini*, 13 September 1968.

29. Diana Moore, "Sit-In Perils Future for Funding of 500 Program," *News-Gazette*, 13 September 1968. George Wallace, a presidential candidate, was the governor of Alabama and a staunch segregationist in the early 1960s. He is best known for barring the entrance to the University of Alabama in an effort to keep two African American students from integrating the university in 1963.

30. J. Theodore Engeln to Clarence Shelley, 10 September 1968, Clipped Article File of Clarence Shelley.

31. Ibid.

32. "Without Reason UI in Jeopardy," *News-Gazette*, 12 September 1968.

33. A. A. Rayner to Dean Clarence Shelley, Western Union Telegram, 5 October 1968, Clipped Article File of Clarence Shelley; William Cousins Jr., "Statement," 1 October 1968, Clipped Article File of William Savage.

34. Robert Powell [President of the National Students Association] to Bruce Morrison [President of the University of Illinois Graduate Student Association], [1968], Clipped Article File of Clarence Shelley. Though the National Students Association protested the police action at the Illini Union, administrative reports and interviews did not support the claim that police used unnecessary force to arrest the students.

35. Executive Committee of the Graduate Student Association to Members of the Faculty, Fall 1968, LAS, Box 17, Folder: 500 Program. The Graduate Student Association also wrote to the chancellor and the board of trustees to solicit funds to support BSA (see John Ronsvalle to Jack Peltason, 28 September 1969, and John Ronsvalle to Board of Trustees, 30 December 1969, OMBUD, Box 1, Folder: BSA, 1968–72).

36. "Rally Supports Black Students," *News-Gazette*, 27 September 1968.

37. "The 'Riot'? BSA Disputes the Media," *Drums*, September 1968, BSAP.

38. The university's official record of events, "Security Office Report of Events, Illini Union, September 9 and September 10, 1968," includes testimony regarding nonstudent destruction of property at the Illini Union. Also, both administrators and former students remembered the nonstudent role in vandalism in their interviews with the author.

39. Black Students Association, "Black Students Association's Policy Statement," in "Let's Make the '500' Program Work, Open Meeting for Faculty and Students Sponsored by the AAUP," 16 September 1968, Clipped Article File of Clarence Shelley.

40. Press Release, 13 September 1968, UPR, Box 4, Folder: S.

41. "Report of Proceedings by Subcommittee A of the Senate Committee on Student Discipline."

42. Peltason, "Statement of Chancellor J. W. Peltason," 2.

43. Press Release, 13 September 1968, LASDS, Box 4, Folder: S.

44. The state's attorney accused the university of frustrating his efforts to prosecute the students. The university denied his allegations but was relieved when the charges were dropped since it had already handled the situation internally (see Ed Borman, "Lack of UI Help Cited; State Drops 241 Cases," and "UI Legal Counsel Says Agreements Were Fulfilled," *News-Gazette*, [May 1970], EOP, Box 1, Folder: Press, 1968–69).

45. Roberts interview.

46. Shelley interview.

47. Roberts interview.

48. Shelley interview.

49. Haile to Peltason, 11 September 1968.

50. As scholars at the American Council on Education found in their study of 427 colleges and universities, as the absolute number of Blacks enrolled increased, so, too, did the likelihood of Black protest (Alexander Astin and Alan Bayer, "Antecedents and Consequents of Disruptive Campus Protests," *Measurement and Evaluation in Guidance* 4 [April 1971]: 28).

51. "We Demand," *Black Rap*, 18 February 1969, BSAP. See appendix B, herein, for a list of the thirty-five demands printed in *Black Rap*. With regard to white allies, one of the BSA demands included retaining William K. Williams, a white administrator, as an adviser on Black affairs. Also, many Black students, particularly women, considered Miriam Shelden, a white woman who was dean of women and had spearheaded pre-SEOP programs for incoming Black students, an asset to Black students (Stanback-Williams interview; Delores Parmer Woodtor, interview by author, Chicago, Ill., 20 November 1997). Black students also considered Peter Rasmussen, a white resident of Champaign and a contributor to Champaign's Black nationalist newspaper, the *Plain Truth*, a friend to BSA (Woodtor interview; "Racist Parole Board Sends Innocent Black Back to Prison," *Black Rap*, 17 March 1969, 1, BSAP). The BSA demands were very similar to Black student demands at other institutions. For evidence of common themes, see Exum, *Paradoxes of Protest*; Peterson et al., *Black Students on White Campuses*; McCormick, *The Black Student Protest Movement at Rutgers*; and Long, "Black Protest."

52. Jack Peltason to Robert Rogers, 22 May 1968, and Robert Rogers to Jack Peltason, 5 June 1968, LAS, Box 17, Folder: SEOP.

53. Melvin Rothbaum to Jack Peltason, 19 February 1969, CHAN, Box 24.

54. BSA, "Faculty Senate Fiasco," 16 February 1969, ibid.

55. Ibid.

56. BSA, "Blacks Meet with Chancellor," 17 February 1969, ibid.

57. See, for example, Humphreys to Colleagues, 6 October 1969.

58. Roger Simon, "Vandals Hit UI Library; Estimate $55,000 Loss," *Daily Illini*, 18 February 1969, citing statement made by Robert Downs, head of library administration.

59. Dale A. Law, "The Masses," Letters to the Editor, *Daily Illini*, 20 February 1969, 11.

60. Name Withheld, "Vandals," ibid.

61. Name Withheld, "Get with It," Letters to the Editor, *Daily Illini*, 21 February 1969, 13. For other articles and letters to the editor regarding the library card-burning incident, see *Daily Illini*, 18–21 February 1969.

62. For a discussion of the Black arts movement, see Addison Gayle Jr., ed., *The Black Aesthetic* (New York: Doubleday, 1971).

63. Africa and Africanness were common themes in BSA publications and were consistent with the national trend toward increasing Pan-African sentiment in the late 1960s and early 1970s (see Sid Lemelle, *Pan-Africanism* [New York: Writers and Readers, 1992]). BSA publications began to run articles with African themes, Black students chose Swahili-inspired names, and the organization itself changed its name to the Coalition for Afrikan People by the early 1970s.

64. This description of the role of Black artists and writers is from Sandra Hollins Flowers, *African American Nationalist Literature: Pens of Fire* (New York: Garland, 1996).

65. Stokely Carmichael, an ideologue of the Black Power movement, initially asserted that Blacks could define Black Power for themselves. However, he and other Black Power leaders vied to provide a definitive statement of Black Power as a goal and political strategy after becoming increasingly aware that other supporters and opponents also could offer their own interpretations (Carson, *In Struggle*, 215–22). Carmichael's coauthored book, with Charles V. Hamilton, *Black Power: The Politics of Liberation in America*, was an attempt to more fully define the concept, ideology, and goals of Black Power.

66. *Irepodun*, 1973, n.p., BSAP. An example of the tolerance and acceptance of various definitions is an article published in *Black Rap*. Discussing the different notions of revolution described by Julius Lester and LeRoi Jones (Amiri Baraka), the author states, "It should not worry us that Brother Jones' and Brother Lesters' concepts of revolution vary. The white man has always disagreed as to what is democracy. . . . Therefore, we, as Black people, must develop in each of our own minds, our concept of the revolution" ("Towards a Revolutionary Ideology," *Black Rap*, 17 March 1969, BSAP).

67. "Editorial," *Drums*, October 1968, BSAP.

68. Various works discuss the protest activities of the Black youth coming of age in the 1940s and 1950s, including Morris, *The Origins of the Civil Rights Movement*; Payne, *I've Got the Light of Freedom*; and Adam Fairclough, *Race and Democracy: The Civil Rights Struggle in Louisiana, 1915–1972* (Athens: University of Georgia Press, 1995).

69. Clyde Winters, "Negro," *Yombo*, 2 December 1971, BSAP.

70. 'Diane,' "Black," *Yombo*, 2 December 1971, BSAP.

71. This characterization of the Negro and birth of Blackness was adapted from Cross, *Shades of Black*, chaps. 5 and 6.

72. *Black Rap*, 21 October 1970, BSAP.

73. Albert Gray, "Who Are You," *Irepodun*, 1972, 61, BSAP.

74. Eric Hobsbawm and Terence Ranger, *The Invention of Tradition* (Cambridge: Cambridge University Press, 1983), 7, 9, cited in Flowers, *African American Nationalist Literature*, xiv, xv.

75. Flowers, *African American Nationalist Literature*, xv–xvi.

76. The adoption of invented traditions did not necessarily mean nonparticipation in dominant society's traditions. For instance, many African Americans celebrate Kwanzaa (the concept and name are African, the particular nature of celebration is African American) as well as Christmas. The purpose of Kwanzaa is to honor the tradition of African and African American ancestors, plan for the year ahead, and strengthen the Black community (Angela Shelf Medearis, *The Seven Days of Kwanzaa: How to Celebrate Them* [New York: Scholastic Books, 1994]). Also, not all African American traditions celebrated in the late 1960s began in the late 1960s. For instance, though the Black nationalist flag became increasingly popular in the late 1960s, its origin can be traced to Marcus Garvey and his Universal Negro Improvement Association during the 1910s and 1920s (Lerone Bennett, *Pioneers in Protest* [Baltimore: Penguin Books, 1968], 233–40). The clenched and upraised fist as a symbol of power can be traced to civil rights activists in the South, including Willie Ricks and Stokely Carmichael during the early to middle 1960s (Carson, *In Struggle*, 208–10).

77. Yolanda Smith Stanback-Williams added this statement to the transcript of her interview by the author.

78. David Eisenman, "PBL Taping Frustrating Experience," *Daily Illini*, 20 February 1968.

79. William K. Williams, "Report of the Hearing Panel on Black-White Relationships," 28 October 1970, 1, CHAN, Box 66.

80. Lloyd Humphreys, "Racial Differences: Dilemma of College Admissions," *Science* 166 (10 October 1969), 167. Humphreys's statements resemble those of his fellow psychologist Arthur Jensen. In 1969, Jensen published an article in which he argued that Black were genetically inferior and that neither spending more money on education nor providing more schooling would equalize society (Arthur Jensen, "How Much Can We Boost IQ and Scholastic Achievement?" *Harvard Educational Review* 39 [Winter 1969]: 1–123).

81. See Triandis to Humphreys, 7 October 1969.

82. See, for example, Atkins interview; Holtz interview; Addison interview; Shelley interview; and "Audiotapes."

83. Patricia Gurin and Edgar Epps found in their study of Black students that individual achievement goals and activism were unrelated, that grade performance was not related to activism, and that nationalist ideology was almost always unrelated to how well students performed in college (Gurin and Epps, *Black Consciousness, Identity, and Achievement*, 346, 350).

84. For a discussion of white student protest, see materials in President David D. Henry General Correspondence, 1955–69, Box 221, Folder: Campus Disruptions; Clipped Article File of Willard Broom; *Illinois Alumni News* 49 (June 1970):

1–3, OMBUD, Box 2, Folder: Demonstrations, 1969–70; and "Strike: The Student's Voice," 4 March 1970, OMBUD, Box 2, Folder Demonstrations, 1969–70.

85. Cullers interview.

86. Townsend interview.

87. For a discussion of Blacker-than-thou sentiment, see Cross, *Shades of Black,* 201–9; William Grier and Price Cobbs, *Black Rage* (New York: Basic Books, 1968), 115–17; and George Napper, *Blacker Than Thou: The Struggle for Campus Unity* (Grand Rapids: William B. Eerdmans, 1973), chap. 2.

88. Eggleston interview.

89. Phillips interview.

90. Shelley interview.

91. Student Counseling Service and Mental Health Division of the Health Service, "Confidential Draft: Suggestions for Controlling Intimidation," [1969], CHAN, Box 24.

92. Stanback-Williams interview.

93. Cross describes such Super Blacks as new converts to Blackness stalled in the immersion stage of the Negro-to-Black conversion experience (Cross, *Shades of Black,* 201–9).

94. "Blacker Than Thou," *Drums,* September 1968, BSAP.

95. "What Are You Doing, Super Cool, Super Militant, Super Niggers?" *Drums,* 17 October 1969, BSAP.

96. Dixon interview.

97. Stanback-Williams.

98. For a thorough discussion of how a masculinist definition of Blackness confined and alienated Black women in general and writers in particular, see Madhu Dubey, *Black Women Novelists and the Nationalist Aesthetic* (Bloomington: Indiana University Press, 1994). For an example of how it affected Elaine Brown, the former chair of the Black Panther Party, see *A Taste of Power: A Black Woman's Story* (New York: Pantheon Books, 1992). Individual Black women's thoughts on the masculine notion of Blackness are included in Flowers, *African American Nationalist Literature,* xx, xxi, 78, 110, 150. The emphasis on Blackness often relegated discussions of economic class to the periphery as well. According to William Exum, the denial of the reality of economic class on college campuses was partly because of shared beliefs about the negative qualities implied by being middle-class, such as "tomming" and lack of revolutionary consciousness (Exum, *Paradoxes of Protest,* 166–68).

99. "To All Black Women," *Yombo,* May 1972, BSAP.

100. "What We Have for You," *Yombo,* May 1972, BSAP.

101. "Black Nationalism," *Black Rap,* 18 February 1969, BSAP.

102. "Black Womanhood," *Black Rap,* 17 March 1969, BSAP.

103. Atkins interview.

104. Ibid.; Holtz interview; Phillips interview.

105. *Drums,* November 1967, BSAP.

106. Moreland-Young interview.

107. Phillips interview.

108. Antonio Zamora, interview by author, West Lafayette, Ind., 12 November 1997.

Chapter 5: "We Hope for Nothing; We Demand Everything"

1. The protest activities of white students heightened the need for campus policies on student protest at Illinois. In 1970, white students, many involved in the campus chapter of Students for a Democratic Society, protested the deferment of a William Kunstler campus appearance (Kunstler became famous after his defense of the Chicago Eight, who were arrested during protests at the Democratic National Convention in 1968) and the presence of General Electric recruiters on campus (GE's involvement in the Vietnam War prompted the protest). Their protests sometimes turned violent. In the two days of protest following the deferment of the Kunstler appearance, 30 students were arrested and charged with participating in a riot and defying university regulations, an air force recruiting station was firebombed, an additional 147 students were arrested, a night-time curfew was set, students initiated a week-long strike, and the National Guard was called in twice to restore order on campus. For information regarding the Kunstler appearance and General Electric protests, see materials in President David D. Henry General Correspondence, 1955–69, Box 221; Clipped Article File of Willard Broom; *Illinois Alumni News* 49 (June 1970): 1–3; and "Strike: The Student's Voice."

2. Wanda Taylor Legg to David Henry, [1969], LCNS, Box 8, Folder: Student Demonstrations, 1968–30 June 1969.

3. George Frampton to George Coil, 1 March 1971, CHAN, Box 66.

4. Rumor Control Center Daily Log, 28 May 1969, DOS, 1966–92, 1994, Box 18, Folder: Rumor Center (SPAS), 1969.

5. Jack Peltason, "Statement to the Board of Trustees," *Campus Report* 6 (1 February 1969): 2, EOP, Box 1, Folder: SEOP, Black Student Demands.

6. David Henry, "Statement to the Board of Trustees," 1, ibid.

7. J. W. Peltason to All New Undergraduate and Graduate Students, May 1969, Chancellor's Issuances, 1969–, Box 1, Folder: 1969.

8. It became Public Act 1583, 76th Cong., 2d sess. (26 September 1969).

9. It became Public Act 1582, 76th Cong., 2d sess. (26 September 1969).

10. It became Public Act 1580, 76th Cong., 2d sess. (26 September 1969).

11. David D. Henry to Richard B. Ogilvie, 8 August 1969, LCNS, Box 24, Folder: Student Demonstrations, 1969–73. A letter written by Chancellor Peltason and sent to all new students was partly a response to the state legislation making a policy on demonstrations mandatory (see Peltason to All New Undergraduate and Graduate Students).

12. *Department of Health, Education, and Welfare Appropriations Act of 1969,* Public Law 575, 90th Cong., 2d sess. (16 October 1968), 2361.

13. *Higher Education Amendments of 1968,* Public Law 557, 90th Cong., 2d sess. (11 October 1968), 1062.

14. Henry to Ogilvie, 8 August 1969.

15. The act permitting the revocation of state financial aid stood until 1973, when the Undergraduate Student Association filed a civil rights suit against Chancellor Peltason. The undergraduates charged that the definition of the level of disorderly conduct necessary to lose state-funded scholarships was imprecise and too broad. The case went before a three-judge panel in a district court, and

the act was declared unconstitutional. *Undergraduate Student Association et al. v. Peltason et al,* 367 Fsupp 1055 (ND IL 1973).

16. See Ron Hoffman to William Rice, 15 October 1970, LCNS, Box 24, Folder: Student Demonstrations, 1969–73; and Charles Percy, "An Open Letter to College and University Students, Faculty, and Administrators in Illinois," 14 September 1970, attached in Lloyd Berry to Deans, Directors, and Heads of Academic Units at Urbana-Champaign, 24 September 1970, Chancellor's Issuances, 1969–, Box 1, Folder: 1970.

17. Mitchell Ware to Dean of Students, 30 July 1970, LCNS, Box 24, Folder: Student Demonstrations, 1969–73.

18. Joseph E. Gonzalez Jr., "Legislative Response to Student Unrest and Campus Disorders," 21 July 1969, paper given at American College Public Relations Association Conference, New York, attached in Edwin M. Crawford (Director, Office of Institutional Research) to Heads of Member Institutions in NASULGC and AASCU, 14 August 1969, ibid.

19. National Commission on the Causes and Prevention of Violence, "Interim Statement on Campus Disorder," 9 June 1969, 1 (first quote), 2 (second quote), LASDS, Box 4, Folder: Student Demonstrations, 1969–73.

20. Ibid., 1.

21. Alexander Heard, "Statement by Alexander Heard on Completion of His Mission as Special Advisor to the President," 23 July 1970, 6 (first quote), 13 (second quote), LCNS, Box 2, Folder: Student Demonstrations, 1969–73.

22. Ibid., 3. President Nixon expressed his disappointment in the Heard statement. Rather than locate problems in the federal government, Nixon shifted blame to campus administrators and faculty ("President Says Blaming Government for Campus Unrest 'Short-Sighted,'" 2 August 1970, attached in University Counsel to Campus Council, 25 August 1970, ibid.).

23. The commission and Heard reports also were on target for white student protest at Illinois. In a 1970 telephone survey of students regarding the strike initiated by white students in May 1970, university investigators found that international issues dominated the minds of campus youth and precipitated protest. The top three concerns of students polled included American intervention in Cambodia, the police murders of students at Kent State, and continuing involvement in Vietnam (Frank L. Nasca, "Telephone Survey regarding the Student Strike, University of Illinois Urbana-Champaign Campus," 1970, OMBUD, Box 2, Folder: Demonstrations, 1969–70).

24. "Senate Council Resolutions Based on Meetings Held on 14, 15, 17, and 20 February 1969," 21 February 1969, presented at a special meeting of the Urbana-Champaign Senate, CHREO, Box 1.

25. The catalyst in the commission's formation is unclear. BSA maintained that its demands precipitated the formation of the commission, while the university maintained that faculty and administrators conceived the concept before BSA submitted its demands.

26. "CORE Touches Racial Issues," *Daily Illini,* 5 October 1966; "Plan Negro History Course," *Daily Illini,* 18 November 1966.

27. *School Code Amendments of 1967,* 75th General Assembly, 1st sess. (26 June 1967), 816.

28. College of Liberal Arts and Sciences, "Annual Report, 1967–1968," June 1968, LAS, Box 14, Folder: Annual Reports, 1963–70.

29. Robert Rogers, "A Proposal," 8 October 1968, RRP, Box 3.

30. Robert Waller to Billy Jackson, 20 September 1968, ibid.

31. Colón, "A Critical Review of Black Studies Programs," 17, citing Elias Blake Jr. and Henry Cobb, *Black Studies: Issues in Their Institutional Survival* (Washington, D.C.: Institute for Services to Education, 1976).

32. Attachment in Robert Eubanks to Herbert Carter, 19 March 1969, RRP, Box 3.

33. Faculty-Student Commission on Afro-American Studies, "Definition of Afro-American Studies," Spring 1969, ibid.

34. Robert Rogers to Walter Massey et al., 25 March 1969, ibid.

35. "Afro-American Commission Issues Report," *Campus Report* 3 (October 1969): 1, AACL, Box 1.

36. "Afro-American Commission Offers Aid to Departments in Changing Curricula," *Campus Report* 3 (November 1969): 1, VPAAC, Box 9, Folder: Equal Opportunity, Blacks, 1969–71. In his version of the development of the Afro-American Studies Program, Eubanks did not mention the BSA demands. Instead, he traced the beginning of the program to discussions he had with other faculty members interested in developing such a unit (Robert Eubanks, "A Brief Survey of the Afro-American Studies Program at the University of Illinois," 1971, DOS, Box 2, Folder: SEOP).

37. Billy Jackson and William Plater to Robert Waller, 2 July 1970, LAS, Box 14, Folder: Culture Lecture Program.

38. Robert Waller to H. E. Carter, 14 April 1969, RRP, Box 3.

39. "History 199: Afro-American Culture Questionnaire Summary," 1969, 4, AACL, Box 1. See also College of Liberal Arts and Sciences, "Annual Report, 1968–1969," LAS, Box 14, Folder: Annual Reports, 1963–70.

40. Students could choose from the following list of books: *Myth of the Negro Past* (Melville Herskovits), *Black Rage* (William Grier and Price Cobbs), a *Report of the National Advisory Committee on Civil Disorders*, *Nobody Knows My Name* (James Baldwin), *Soul on Ice* (Eldridge Cleaver), *Before the Mayflower* (Lerone Bennett), *Invisible Man* (Ralph Ellison), *Souls of Black Folk* (W. E. B. Du Bois), *Selected Poems* (Gwendolyn Brooks), and *Betrayal of the Negro* (R. W. Logan). See William Plater to G.O.D. Bookstore, 12 December 1969, AACL, Box 1.

41. R. K. Applebee to LAS Staff, 23 January 1970, "LAS 199: Black Awareness: A Spectrum," LAS, Box 17, Folder: SEOP.

42. College of Liberal Arts and Sciences, "LAS 199, Grade Distribution," 1969, AACL, Box 1. A separate report found similar results: 312 students completed the course, and the average grade was a 3.16 (see Robert Rogers to H. E. Carter, 17 July 1969, LAS, Box 17, Folder: SEOP).

43. Clarence Shelley to Robert Waller, 31 March 1969, AACL, Box 1.

44. Eubanks, "A Brief Survey of the Afro-American Studies Program at the University of Illinois," 3.

45. Ibid., 9–10. Eubanks's concerns regarding the consequences of hiring faculty without doctorates was shared by other scholars interested in the development of Black studies. The historian John Blassingame reflected on the implications of

the adjusted policy for hiring faculty and worried what it would mean for the status of the new programs. See John Blassingame, "Black Studies: An Intellectual Crisis," in *New Perspectives in Black Studies,* ed. John Blassingame, 149–66 (Urbana: University of Illinois Press, 1971).

46. Wermers, *Enrollment at the University of Illinois by Racial/Ethnic Categories: Fall Terms, 1967–1975,* 12.

47. Jackson and Plater to Waller, 2 July 1970.

48. Delano Cox, Billy Jackson, and Bill Plater to Persons Interested in Afro-American Studies, 9 October 1970, LAS, Box 14, Folder: Culture Lecture Program. These lectures also reached an audience outside the university. All lectures were audiotaped, and the tapes were then used in classrooms at nearby Parkland Community College and local high schools and were rebroadcast on two local radio stations (College of Liberal Arts and Sciences, "1971 Afro-American Culture Lecture Series," 1971, AACL, Box 1). For a listing of audiotapes at the University of Illinois at Urbana-Champaign Archives, see "The Black World: Perspectives. Sound Recordings in the University Archives," 15 October 1970, AACL, Box 1.

49. Eubanks, "A Brief Survey of the Afro-American Studies Program at the University of Illinois," 6.

50. According to a university press release, Gaines was a minister in Urbana who held a Doctor of the Ministry degree (Press Release, 21 January 1970, UPR, Box 6, Folder: A).

51. Ibid.; Eubanks, "A Brief Survey of the Afro-American Studies Program at the University of Illinois"; Press Release, 16 October 1970, UPR, Box 6, Folder: A.

52. BSA to Vice Chancellor, September 1970, Clipped Article File of James Anderson.

53. Press Release, 16 October 1970.

54. Ibid.

55. Colón, "A Critical Review of Black Studies Programs," 8, identifies these three purposes in his work.

56. "Proposal for an Afro-American Studies Program," [Spring 1970], 2 (first quote), 3 (second quote), RRP, Box 3.

57. Ibid; Walter Strong, "Afro-American Studies," October 1972, LASDS, Box 60, Folder: Afro-American Culture Lecture Series; John Stewart to Robert Rogers, 25 June 1974, ibid. The Afro-American studies minor became a reality in the 1973–74 academic year.

58. Jeffrey Roberts, "Interview with Walter Strong: Black Studies," *Irepodun,* 1972, n.p., BSAP. Another obstacle in establishing Black studies was locating financial resources. One indication of the financial picture for Black studies is a letter from William Plater, the Afro-American lecture series coordinator, to Robert Waller, dean of the College of Liberal Arts and Sciences. In his request for funding for the 1970 lecture series budget, Plater called the 1969 honorariums given to invited speakers inadequate and "ridiculously low." Also, the increased cost of advertising and staffing necessitated a larger budget for the 1970 series. He estimated the series budget to reach approximately $20,000. Dean Rogers forward the request to H. E. Carter, the vice chancellor for academic affairs. In his letter responding to the request, the vice chancellor stated that his office could offer only $10,000. The budget funds already had been allocated for the fiscal year

(William Plater to Robert Waller, June 1969, and H. E. Carter to Robert Rogers, 27 June 1969, AACL, Box 1).

59. Dan Perrino, interview with author, Champaign, Ill., 20 February 2001.

60. "Afro-American Commission Offers Aid to Departments in Changing Curricula," 1; Press Release, 12 September 1969, UPR, Box 6, Folder: A (quote).

61. Roberts interview.

62. Eubanks, "A Brief Survey of the Afro-American Studies Program at the University of Illinois," 5. Unfortunately, Val Gray Ward could not be contacted for an interview.

63. BSA to Vice Chancellor, September 1970, Clipped Article File of James Anderson.

64. Jeffrey Roberts, "Interview with Robert Ray: Black Cultural Program," *Irepodun,* 1972, n.p., BSAP.

65. Eubanks, "A Brief Survey of the Afro-American Studies Program at the University of Illinois"; "Petition to Force the Resignation of Robert Eubanks, FSCAALC Chair," 13 October 1970, Clipped Article File of Tony Zamora.

66. Eubanks, "A Brief Survey of the Afro-American Studies Program at the University of Illinois," 7.

67. Zamora, like Val Gray Ward, did not have a college diploma.

68. BSA Ad-Hoc Committee to Incoming Black Freshmen, 23 July 1970, BSAP (emphasis added).

69. Williams, "Report of the Hearing Panel on Black-White Relationships," 6. According to the report, in the first three weeks of September 1970, Illinois Street Residence Hall witnessed twenty-six racial incidents requiring intervention, ranging from false alarms to a shooting. Black nonstudents also were involved in the disturbances.

70. George Frampton, "Statement of Vice Chancellor George T. Frampton to the Williams Hearing Panel as the Campus Administration's First in a Series of Public Reports or Responses to the Panel's October 28, 1970 Recommendations," [December 1970], 3 (first quote), 2 (second quote), CHAN, Box 66.

71. "Petition to Force the Resignation of Robert Eubanks, FSCAALC Chair."

72. Dan Perrino discussed the development of the Black Chorus in his interview by the author.

73. "Afro-American Cultural Program: Purpose of the Center," 1970–71, Clipped Article File of Antonio Zamora.

74. Lerone Bennett Jr., *The Challenge of Blackness* (Atlanta: Institute of the Black World, 1970), 3.

75. Zamora interview.

76. Roberts, "Interview with Robert Ray."

77. Ibid.

78. Spencer, "University of Illinois Program for the Culturally Deprived."

Chapter 6: A Lasting Influence

1. For a discussion of the commission to hear Black student grievances, see "Senate Council Resolutions Based on Meetings Held on 14, 15, 17, and 20 February 1969." For a discussion of affirmative action in academic and nonacadem-

ic positions, see J. W. Briscoe (Vice Chancellor for Administrative Affairs) to Deans, Directors and Heads of Academic and Administrative Units at Urbana-Champaign, 18 December 1972, OMBUD, Box 1, Folder: Affirmative Action, 1970–77. For a discussion of outreach programs, see "Community Relations Planning and Development Program," attachment in R. E. Martin (Assistant Vice Chancellor for Academic Affairs) to J. M. Atkin et al., 7 April 1972, DOS, 1963–71, Box 2, Folder: Volunteer Projects.

2. For instance, the university was interested in the status of African American employment prior to the Black student demands, but the civil rights movement and the assassination of Dr. Martin Luther King Jr. made the issue more urgent. See Jack Peltason, "Chancellor Issues Statement concerning Employment Status of Negroes on Urbana Campus," *Campus Report* 1 (1 May 1968): 1, Clipped Article File of Joseph Smith.

3. For example, both the Black Panther Party and SNCC, two of the most important organizations spreading Black Power principles, were undermined by the federal government counter intelligence program, COINTELPRO. The murder of Black Panthers Fred Hampton and Mark Clark is an example of the violent repression Black Power advocates faced. See Carson, *In Struggle,* 8; and Wilkins and Clark, *Search and Destroy.*

4. Clayborne Carson charts the decline in the Black Power movement through a discussion of the demise of SNCC (Carson, *In Struggle,* chap. 18).

5. The reasons the Illinois Black student movement dissolved are not unique. Other authors have demonstrated similar reasons for decline at other campuses. For example, see Exum, *Paradoxes of Protest;* McCormick, *The Black Student Protest Movement at Rutgers;* and Donald Alexander Downs, *Cornell '69: Liberalism and the Crisis of the American University* (Ithaca, N.Y.: Cornell University Press, 1999).

6. Chris Benson, "Black Activism Deactivates," *Illio,* 1975, 26–29, Illini Publishing Company File.

7. All registered student organization information was gathered from Student Organization Constitutions and Registration Cards File, 1909–81, Box 4.

8. Bro. Woody, "Coalition of Afrikan People," *Irepodun,* Spring 1973, n.p., BSAP. The use of *k* in the spelling of *Afrikan* was significant. Black students at Illinois ascribed to notions advocated by Don L. Lee (Haki Madhubuti), who stated, "Most vernacular or traditional languages on the continent spell Afrika with a K; therefore the use of K is germain to us. Europeans . . . polluted our languages by substituting C whenever they saw K. . . . Therefore the K symbolizes our coming back together again" (Don L. Lee, *From Plan to Planet, Life Studies: The Need for Afrikan Minds and Institutions* [Chicago: Third World Press, 1973], 13).

9. Bro. Woody, "Coalition of Afrikan People," *Irepodun,* Spring 1973, n.p., BSAP.

10. Quoted in Benson, "Black Activism Deactivates," 28.

11. Holtz interview. Her husband's letter to the draft board is included in "Ex-Editor of *Drums* Indicted," *Plain Truth,* December 1968.

12. Stanback-Williams interview.

13. Woodtor interview.

14. "We Demand," *Black Rap,* 18 February 1969, BSAP.

15. They were somewhat successful in their demands. For articles on Latina/o student protest, see *Daily Illini,* March–May 1992.

16. For a discussion of such themes, see ibid., September 1989–December 1990.
17. Walter Strong, interview by author, Turlock, Calif., 3 May 2001.
18. Clarence Shelley, interview by author, Champaign, Ill., 21 February 2001.
19. Peltason interview.
20. Shelley interview, 29 August 1997.

INDEX

accommodationism, 13
ACT. *See* American College Test
activism. *See* campus activism
Addison, David, 39, 83, 92, 93, 106, 159n.79
Ad Hoc Committee of Students for Human Dignity and Social Peace, 61
Ad Hoc Senate Committee on University Disciplinary Authority and Procedures, 114
administration, university. *See* university administrators
admission requirements, 68, 69, 163n.46
affirmative action: Black enrollment affected by, 26, 55, 159n.3; Chalmers on, 59; federal initiatives and, 26, 56–57; Humphreys's criticism of, 102–3; Johnson on, 160n.13; racialization of, 60; University Committee on Human Relations and Equal Opportunity recommending, 59. *See also* Special Educational Opportunities Program
African American. *See under* Black
Afro-American Cultural Program, 127–33; activities of, 133; Black students' loss of role in, 137, 138; budget request for, 130–31; Champaign-Urbana residents' use of, 128, 132; Nesbitt as director of, 133; Ray as director of, 129, 132–33; staff of, 132; Ward as director of, 128–29, 131; workshops at, 128; Zamora as director of, 129, 131–32
Afro-American History Conference.

See Third Annual Conference on Afro-American History
Afro-American Studies and Research Program, 119–27; academic minor in, 176n.57; and Afro-American lecture series, 120, 122; Afro-American Studies Commission and, 125–26; becomes institutional reality, 126–27; Black students' loss of role in, 137–38; committee for choosing director of, 121; and Department of History, 120, 122–23; Faculty-Student Commission on Afro-American Life and Culture in formation of, 119–21, 125; financing of, 176n.58; and LAS 199, 123, 124–25, 175n.40; and LAS 291, 125, 176n.48; no formal major in, 127; shortage of qualified faculty for, 121, 124, 175n.45; structure of, 127
Afro-American Studies Commission, 125–26, 129, 131
Afro hairstyle, 52, 100, 101, 104
Alpha Chi (fraternity), 20
Alternative Teacher Education Program (ATEP), 77–78, 166n.89
American Association of University Professors, 22, 59, 70
American College Test (ACT), 63, 67, 68, 159n.3, 165n.77
American Council on Education, 169n.50
Asian American students, 140
Asian American studies program, 140
assimilation, 14, 32

JOY ANN WILLIAMSON received her doctorate from the University of Illinois at Urbana-Champaign. She is an assistant professor of education at Stanford University, where she conducts research on the intersection of social movements and higher education. She has published articles in the *Journal of Negro Education* and the *Journal of the Midwest History of Education Society* and has contributed to several edited collections.

The University of Illinois Press
is a founding member of the
Association of American University Presses.

Composed in 9.5/12.5 Trump Mediaeval
by Jim Proefrock
at the University of Illinois Press
Manufactured by Thomson-Shore, Inc.

University of Illinois Press
1325 South Oak Street
Champaign, IL 61820-6903
www.press.uillinois.edu